RATIONAL CHOICE
THEORY

KEY ISSUES IN SOCIOLOGICAL THEORY

Series Editors

JEFFREY C. ALEXANDER, *University of California, Los Angeles*
& JONATHAN H. TURNER, *University of California, Riverside*

This series of annual publications is designed to crystallize key issues in contemporary theoretical debate. Each year, the chair of the Theory Section of the American Sociological Association has the authority to organize a "conference within a conference" at the annual meeting. The intention is to provide a forum for intensive public discussion of an issue that has assumed overriding theoretical importance. After the miniconference, the chair assumes the role of volume editor and, subject to final approval by the series editors, prepares a volume based on the reworked conference papers.

We hope that this periodic focusing of theoretical energy will strengthen the "disciplinary matrix" upon which theoretical progress in every science depends. Theoretical consensus may be impossible, but disciplinary integration is not. Only if a solid infrastructure is provided can communication among different orientations be carried out in the kind of ongoing, continuous way that is so necessary for mutual understanding and scientifically constructive criticism.

Volumes in this series:

1. **Neofunctionalism**
   edited by *Jeffrey C. Alexander*

2. **The Marx-Weber Debate**
   edited by *Norbert Wiley*

3. **Theory Building in Sociology:**
   Assessing Theoretical Cumulation
   edited by *Jonathan H. Turner*

4. **Feminism and Sociological Theory**
   edited by *Ruth A. Wallace*

5. **Intellectuals and Politics:**
   Social Theory in a Changing World
   edited by *Charles C. Lemert*

6. **Metatheorizing**
   edited by *George Ritzer*

7. **Rational Choice Theory:**
   Advocacy and Critique
   edited by *James S. Coleman* and *Thomas J. Fararo*

RATIONAL CHOICE THEORY
Advocacy and Critique

Edited by

JAMES S. COLEMAN
THOMAS J. FARARO

7

KEY ISSUES IN
SOCIOLOGICAL THEORY

SAGE Publications
International Educational and Professional Publisher
Newbury Park   London   New Delhi

For information address:

 SAGE Publications, Inc.
2455 Teller Road
Newbury Park, California 91320

SAGE Publications Ltd.
6 Bonhill Street
London EC2A 4PU
United Kingdom

SAGE Publications India Pvt. Ltd.
M-32 Market
Greater Kailash I
New Delhi 110048 India

Printed in the United States of America

Library of Congress Cataloging-in-Publication Data

Rational choice theory: advocacy and critique/edited by James S.
  Coleman, Thomas J. Fararo.
      p. cm.—(Key issues in sociological theory ; 7)
   Includes bibliographical references.
   ISBN 0-8039-4761-5 (cl) — ISBN 0-8039-4762-3 (pb)
   1. Sociology—Methodology. 2. Social exchange. 3. Choice
(Psychology) 4. Rationalism. I. Coleman, James Samuel, 1926-
II. Fararo, Thomas J. III. Series.
HM24.R33   1992
301'.01—dc20   92-15932
                                                              CIP

92 93 94 95 96 10 9 8 7 6 5 4 3 2 1

Sage Production Editor: Judith L. Hunter

CONTENTS

PART II: CRITICAL PERSPECTIVES

PART III: METATHEORY: RATIONAL
CHOICE PRO AND CON

PREFACE

FOR A NUMBER OF YEARS, the Theoretical Sociology Section of the American Sociological Association has called on its elected Chair to organize a miniconference around a theme chosen by the Chair. The conference is held at the annual meetings of the association, and the papers are published by Sage Publications in the following year. For the 1991 meetings, held in Cincinnati, the Chair was James S. Coleman. Following on his choice of the theme of "Rational Choice Theory: Advocacy and Critique," Thomas J. Fararo joined him in organizing and moderating the two sessions devoted to the theme and also joined in the subsequent editing of the book. Following the usual section procedures, the papers were partly invited and partly self-initiated. The latter category turned out to be rather large, a situation to which we adapted in part by expanding the number of papers on the program.

To help stimulate ideas, the October 1990 issue of *Perspectives*, the section's newsletter, contained a "Message From the Chair" that announced and elaborated on the theme. That message is now part of our introduction to this volume.

We were pleased by the very large attendance at the sessions and by the efforts of our participants, which led to some exciting intellectual exchanges on what constitutes one of the more controversial areas of current theorizing in sociology.

JAMES S. COLEMAN
THOMAS J. FARARO
June 1992

INTRODUCTION

JAMES S. COLEMAN
THOMAS J. FARARO

WHAT IS RATIONAL CHOICE THEORY in sociology? A relatively straightforward way of gaining a sense of rational choice theory in sociology is to specify three kinds of criteria that many would agree should be met if sociological theory is to be wholly satisfactory:

1. The set of phenomena to be explained by the theory is the behavior of social systems (large or small), and not the behavior of individuals.
2. Explanation of the behavior of social systems requires explanation in terms of the behavior of actors in the system, thus implying
   a. a theory of transitions between the level of social system behavior and the level of behavior of individual actors, often expressed as the micro-macro problem; and
   b. a psychological theory or model of the springs of individual action.

No wholly satisfactory theory exists in sociology because no theory has been able to simultaneously meet these criteria. Different theoretical traditions can be characterized by the criterion or criteria they sacrifice or give short shrift to. These sacrifices constitute theoretical wagers that the element sacrificed is less important than those taken as problematic.

The class of theories that maintains the first criterion and sacrifices criteria 2a and 2b can be termed *holistic*. Functionalist theory is perhaps the prominent example but is by no means the sole member of this class. The version of structuralism in which agency plays no role is another specimen of this class of theory.

ix

The class of theories that maintains criteria 1 and 2b but ignores 2a is that class which explains system behavior in terms of like behavior or tendencies on the part of individuals. The micro-macro transition is assumed to occur through simple aggregation. This class is exemplified by theories of panic or crowd behavior that posit some emotional "tendency" at the individual level that gives rise to the behavior which, when aggregated, constitutes panic. Another example is a theory that tries to explain why revolutions are associated with improving conditions by positing increased frustration of expectations under such conditions. Such a theory then employs an expressive mechanism (an instance of criterion 2b), namely frustration is expressed in aggression. The step from the level of individual aggression to the systemic level of revolution is not treated, so by tacit implication it involves only simple aggregation of similar behavior tendencies in the population. Thus in such theories what is taken as problematic are the properties of individual psychology that lead to the tendencies to behave in observed ways, for example, some form of collective behavior (Coleman 1990, pp. 472-479).

Rational choice theory in sociology belongs to still another class of theories: Little attention is paid to criterion 2b, that is, the psychological model of the springs of individual action. It may seem odd to describe a theoretical approach named after its chief psychological assumption as giving short shrift to psychology. We believe this is accurate, however. What is problematized in rational choice theory is not individual psychology; it is the component of the theory labeled 2a above—the transitions between the micro level of individual action and the macro level of system behavior. In what is probably the most significant instantiation of this distinction, the macro level can be described as the institutional structure, and the micro level as the behavior of the actors within such a structure.

An example will illustrate the point about the minor role of psychological ideas in this approach: The *free rider* phenomenon is a mainstay of rational choice theory. But this phenomenon does not refer to some aspect of individual psychology. It refers to the structure of incentives, a structure that would lead a "normal" or "reasonable" or "rational" person to leave to others an action that benefits both self and others, if the action is costly. The free rider phenomenon is not a description about empirically observed behavior; it is a description of the structure of incentives confronting an individual. No matter that experiments with such structures nearly always show that some persons do not free-ride. Rational choice theory would argue that the problem is with the experimental design: Other incentives have been allowed to creep in, such as the ties of friendship or merely the desire to be thought well of by others. This is not to say that rational choice theory is always right in holding to the principle that persons act "rationally," even if the incentives are fully specified. It is, rather, to say that it constitutes one strategy for developing theory about the way institutional structures produce systemic behavior. It is a strategy that blinds itself to deviations from rationality, with the aim of getting on with a different task—the task of moving between micro and macro levels.

Rational choice theory contains one element that differentiates it from nearly all other theoretical approaches in sociology. This element can be summed up in a single word: *optimization*. The theory specifies that in acting rationally, an actor is engaging in some kind of optimization. This is sometimes expressed as maximizing utility, sometimes as minimizing cost, sometimes in other ways. But however expressed, it is this that gives rational choice theory its power: It compares actions according to their expected outcomes for the actor and postulates that the actor will choose the action with the best outcome. At its most explicit, it requires that benefits and costs of all courses of action be specified, then postulating that the actor takes the "optimal" action, the action that maximizes the differences between benefits and costs.

Without this postulate, most social theorists who have any recourse to the level of action would be characterized as using a rational choice approach, although post hoc: Most such theory is based on an account of actors' actions as "reasonable" or "understandable." What rational choice theory does in contrast is to impose the discipline of using optimization as a criterion at all points. Beyond that, its principal aim is not to understand how a particular action can be seen as reasonable by the actor but to show how actions that are reasonable or rational for actors can combine to produce social outcomes, sometimes intended by actors, sometimes unintended, sometimes socially optimal, sometimes non-optimal. It is in this last respect that rational choice theory differs most sharply from functionalist theory: Functionalist theory postulates optimization or efficiency or equilibrium at a systemic level, then shows how various institutions contribute to that social optimum.

In the remainder of this introduction, our aim is to highlight some significant intellectual developments and issues in social science as an orientation to the theme of this volume. We will conclude the introduction with a short characterization of the organization of the volume. It will not be part of our objective to summarize the chapters, although we will draw attention to one or another of them at various points. Our aim is more prefatory than comprehensive: The chapters themselves will reveal the range of controversy within sociology about rational choice theory.

INTELLECTUAL BACKGROUND

In the background of the ideas expressed in rational choice theory are a number of important developments both in sociology and in neighboring disciplines. What these developments share is a commitment to analytical theorizing featuring clear premises and arguments, seeking simplicity but also deductive fertility and explanatory power. Examples of such work follow.

Schelling's (1971) important neighborhood and related models demonstrated emergent macro effects from micro level rational but interdependent actions. In particular, Schelling showed that even with only very mild preferences for living close to those of "one's own kind," over time a totally segregated system can emerge. Bainbridge (1987) created a computer program that vividly demonstrates this and a large number of other emergent outcomes. By varying the preferences that govern the decision to move or to stay, as well as the constraints of available housing, a variety of systemic outcomes can be generated, corresponding to variations in given macrostructure and in actor preferences. A macro-to-micro effect may also exist, as a feedback from the combined actions. In such an effect, the emergent segregated

outcomes alter the preferences of actors in the upcoming generations that live in the more segregated circumstances, thereby
tending to freeze-in the emergent outcome, converting it into an
unalterable socially constructed reality for the actors.

Boudon (1981, 1987) has analyzed the classic ideas of Pareto, Weber, and
Durkheim to argue that they converge on methodological individualism as a presupposition. All three, he argues, share the idea
that sociology tries to explain phenomena that arise in a system
of interaction. Thus, as Lindenberg argues in this volume, they
analytically focus on the system or macro level. It is obvious that
Pareto and Weber are action theorists. Both argue for a generalized theory of action, in which action that appears irrational may
be subjectively rational from the point of view of the actor. The
case of Durkheim is undoubtedly less obvious. Durkheim's *sui
generis* social level of existence refers to the emergent features of
social association, including collective representations. But
Boudon argues that even Durkheim can be brought within the
scope of the postulate of methodological individualism if the
details of his arguments are considered carefully. Boudon himself
constructs theoretical models that exemplify the strategy he sets
out, relating it also to the use of game models to describe social
situations.

The methodological arguments of Wippler and Lindenberg (1987) and
other papers by the latter (e.g., Lindenberg 1985), as well as his
contribution to this volume, are important in making clear the
rationale for adopting a broadly rational choice standpoint in
developing social theory. In particular, a distinction is made
between the analytical focus of psychology and the analytical
focus of the social sciences. The former aims to explain individual
conduct, while the latter aims to explain social systemic phenomena. The argument is that these divergent aims justify a different
model of the individual actor in these disciplines: In psychology,
the model necessarily becomes more complex in its treatment of
cognitive and motivational aspects of action, while in the social
sciences, the model will be self-defeating in its instrumental function (to aid in the derivation of systemic outcomes) if it follows
the logic of psychological analysis.

Hechter's (1987) work on dependence and compliance with collective
obligations has attempted to show that rational choice theory can
be brought to bear on a core concern of classical sociology: the
nature and sources of solidarity. Solidarity, he argues, varies with
the product of the extent of obligations and the extent of compliance with those obligations. Developing the theory in detail, he

goes on to empirically test derived implications in such contexts as legislative roll-call voting and commune survival. In other work, Friedman and Hechter (1988) have produced generalized arguments in favor of a rational choice approach in sociology. Their chapter in this volume is a substantive illustration of their approach.

Abell's (1989) use of Margolis's (1982) dual-utility model for self and group components of utility is another attempt to show that rational choice theory in sociology need not remain within strict neoclassical boundaries. His chapter in this volume adopts the interesting perspective of theory choice as a problem in rational choice.

These and numerous other works in sociology embody the conception of purposive-rational action and also the construction of explicit models, often formal, that embody this conception. The basic ideas are explicated by Margaret Marini in her chapter in this volume.

When the rational action principle is made formal, what one gains from this work is a clear vision of the problematic character of social order: in particular, how collectively irrational outcomes arise out of the interaction of rational actors (especially the free rider type of problem mentioned earlier). Here is an analogy: We only see light as "bending" if we postulate it as traveling in straight lines and thereby define an explanatory problem, a departure calling for explanation. Similarly, the idea of seeing collective life as "irrationally bent"—as featuring collectively irrational outcomes—arises from the postulate of individual action as rational. It does not arise from the empirical generalization that all action is manifestly rational. Neither are all light emissions literally straight from A to B with no bending. As Toulmin (1953, 1961) puts it, a theoretical discipline is often founded on a principle of natural order: Light tends to go in a straight line, bodies tend to continue with the same velocity (speed and direction), and so forth.

When the principle of natural order for social action is that action is nonrational, the problems are inverted: Individual rationality becomes problematic and needs to be explained. This viewpoint is expressed by Etzioni (1988), for instance. Thus, quite apart from the focus on the economy, the latter's socioeconomics is a kind of theory-dual of rational choice theory. If the analogous situations in the history of science are any lesson (e.g., Galileo versus Aristotle on the natural tendency of motion), a tension exists between such competing principles that implies that eventually one of them will be selected and the other will not survive. We seem to be in the middle of a major presuppositional dispute (Alexander 1987) about the relative merits of these two principles, interpreted as principles of natural order in Toulmin's sense rather than as empirical generalizations. This volume may be interpreted as a discourse embedded in this metatheoretical situation. Although the debate may be expected to persist in the coming years, a possibility exists that one of these two principles will prove superior as a foundation for social science. Another possibility is some sort of "third way" that incorporates aspects of both principles into a more comprehensive and unified approach. We suspect that the outcome will be a matter of how well one or another such framework-defining principle functions in terms of implications at the level of theoretical models. In turn, the families of models that are enabled by such a principle will be evaluated in terms of how well they address the key problems of theoretical sociology with analytical power and empirical adequacy (Fararo 1989).

Two other sets of ideas are worth noting as part of the background—one set quite recent in origin, and the other of a more classic character:

> The iterated Prisoner's Dilemma work of Axelrod (1984) and others shows how cooperation and trust can emerge from self-interested interactions when the actors anticipate that they will interact again in the future. Moreover, the work shows the importance of much of postclassic sociological thinking about ties among actors and their consequences, especially in the social networks tradition. More recently, in a volume edited by Hechter (1990) devoted to the problem of analyzing institutions from a rational choice perspective, Ziegler (1990) shows how the famous Kula Ring arrangements can be explained in terms that draw on Axelrod's fundamental ideas. Ceremonial exchange systems are integrative in function, but that does not explain how such convenient structures arise. Ziegler asks us to notice that before the Ring existed,

the groups inhabiting the various islands had a history of conflict. Thus the problem is one of explaining how a solidarity-functional institution arises from a somewhat Hobbesian type of situation.

The generalized idea of profit, used by Homans ([1961] 1974) and Blau (1964) and numerous social psychologists, was an important antecedent to rational choice theory in sociology. This work showed that profit was in no way rigidly linked to the institutions of money and market, being framed at the level of general action, as Parsons (1977) called it, in fact agreeing with the exchange formulation underlying this idea (Parsons and Smelser 1956, p. 10, Footnote 2). But the Homans-Blau exchange formulations found it difficult to make the micro-to-macro transition. More analytically, we can say that they focused on the transition from the actor in a situation to the coupling of such actors to constitute a social network of interactions. This led them to deal in detail with social interaction. The present-day rational choice sociologists present us with a somewhat different version of the micro-to-macro transition, with a principal interest in the systemic outcomes, often the implied equilibria.

Why this difference between the older exchange theory and the present-day rational choice theory? One answer is that the older version both inspired and grew out of the small groups focus of much of scientific sociology in the 1950s. The micro-to-macro transition in that context was a matter of the temporal development of interactions among a small number of actors as observed, for instance, in Homans's (1950) generalizations about small groups. Today more of sociological analysis is directed to accounting for historical phenomena often large in scale. For such work, micro-to-macro transition mechanisms are required that can treat interdependence without attention to the moment-to-moment flow of interaction among concrete actors. This is a difficult problem, addressed in this volume, for instance, by Lindenberg in a manner that might draw critique even among those friendly to rational choice theory in sociology. Meanwhile, however, the older exchange theory tradition has evolved into an exchange-network paradigm (Cook and Emerson 1978; Markovsky, Willer, and Patton 1988; Willer and Anderson 1981) focused on differential power as a function of network position and its impact of exchanges. In this volume, Willer argues that the theory he and his colleagues are developing constitutes an approach that satisfies criteria 1, 2a, and 2b above.

Mention was made earlier of Talcott Parsons. It is worth noting that Parsons was trained as an economist and defined his project as one of *generalizing* analytical economics. His complex theoretical strategy combined elements of Pareto and Weber in its action theory foundations. Like Pareto, he accepted the rational action postulate for economic analysis but argued that sociology addressed a set of problems left open by economics that required attention to nonrational mechanisms. Eventually this led him to incorporate the personality system, treated in terms of Freudian ideas, into the theory of action, while analytically separating out the social system. Thus the motivational basis for social action was addressed quite directly in terms of the postulated nonrational aspects. These were conjectured to involve internalization of given cultural traditions involving cognitive, expressive, and moral standards. Hence actors were social products whose choices were parameterized by nonrational commitments to nation, ethnic group, family responsibilities, and the like.

In this volume, the contribution by Scheff is closest to Pareto in its focus on the significance of the nonrational in social life, the emotional side of human beings, and the importance of rationalization—giving post hoc reasons for conduct that is emotionally driven. Scheff, however, is far from the viewpoint taken by Parsons in attempting to create a general system of action.

In Parsons's evolving work, blended with the Paretan-Freudian nonrational foundation of action, was a Weberian focus on what we can call the sociology of rationality. Here concrete systems of action—such as firms and universities—are treated as embodying more or less rational procedures and standards. Under the rubric of the generalized pattern variable called *universalism*, for instance, Parsons was treating phenomena described not only by Weber but by Durkheim ([1893] 1964) when the latter discussed the increase in abstraction and generalization that occurred in the passage from the small communal society to the large complex system.

For all its ambitious rendering of the classic ideas on a formal basis, the Parsonian formalism proved unable to function in a deductively fertile way. Moreover the growing complexity of the theoretical system made it less and less understandable to other theorists. For these and other reasons, Parsonian action theory went into eclipse by the mid-1960s. In the 1980s, it was reborn as *neofunctionalism*, featuring the work of Alexander and others.

These authors critically revise the Parsonian scheme but agree with its fundamental approach. In particular, they distrust the rational choice approach as a revival of utilitarianism, with its inherent vulnerability to the critique stated by Parsons (1937) early in his career (see, for instance, Lechner 1990). In this volume, the chapters by Münch and Sciulli come out of his tradition. An important background element here is Alexander's (1987) way of classifying traditions within sociological theory: Two fundamental presuppositional problems exist in the history of social theory. One pertains to action and centers on the conceptual problem of purposive-rational action elements versus other action elements (e.g., emotions, interpretations, communications). The other pertains to order and centers on the conceptual problem of the individualist strategy as contrasted with the collectivist strategy. For the latter, because actors are social products, there cannot be any sensible general solution to the problem of social order on an individualist basis.

Because each problem (action, order) has a binary opposition associated with it, four tendencies in social theory are derived. For instance, Parsonian and Durkheimian theory are nonrational-collectivist, according to Alexander, while exchange and rational choice theories would be rational-individualist. Yet Alexander is not saying that we must choose among these four. Quite the contrary, he argues that some sort of "multidimensional" approach is required in order to properly incorporate both sides of each binary opposition in a comprehensive theoretical framework. It is likely that Münch, in particular, shares this ideal in his approach to the critique of rational choice theory, while Sciulli would add the normative-theoretical element that Alexander also thinks should be an explicit component of general social theory.

One of the chapters in our volume makes a case that provides a useful cautionary note on the criteria set out at the beginning of this introduction. Michael Hannan argues that experiences with population ecology models, as well as an interpretation of the historical case of biological theory, suggest that a kind of decoupling of the micro and macro levels might be desirable for macrosociology. The problems are two: First, if the levels are too tightly coupled, the problematic issues about the rationality of individual choice make the derived macrosocial outcomes less secure than if the latter are made theoretically independent of principles of action such as maximization of utility. Second, in systems involving three levels (such as persons, organizations, and wider systems of action involving organizations as actors), the micro-to-macro transformation from person to organization need not result in rational action on the part of the organization. Thus the postulate of rational action on the part of organizations as actors is flawed, Hannan argues.

As Hannan puts it, macrosociological theory should be "robust" in the sense that its predictions do not depend too strongly on the details of actor-level functioning. In one sense, the argument is close to that made by Lindenberg in his chapter, that the model of the actor should be kept simple for sociological purposes. But Hannan goes beyond this; he argues in effect that no theory of action should be introduced in accounting for macrosocial outcomes. This constitutes a sacrifice of criterion 2b (on the springs of action) in order to maximize attention to criterion 1 (systemic behavior) using a micro-macro linkage (criterion 2a) that involves a theory of selection rather than a theory of action.

ORGANIZATION OF THE BOOK

As our previous remarks should make obvious, sociologists are divided in their orientation to the role of rational choice theory in sociology. Our theme is "Advocacy and Critique." In organizing this book to reflect this theme, we almost certainly have done some violence to the specific arguments of each chapter by grouping and labeling them as we have. For example, some "advocates" are critical of some modes of rational choice thinking in the broader social science environment. Similarly, some "critics" recognize contributions from rational choice theory. Although we are aware of this simplification, we believe that the structure of the book, and even the labels, will help orient the reader who is interested in understanding the pros and cons of rational choice theory in sociology.

Part I presents what we have called "themes of advocacy." In the opening chapter, Siegwart Lindenberg argues that theory construction programs are time-extended enterprises that involve a gradual extension of scope. As he puts it, a method of decreasing abstraction exists through which significant advances in social theory can be made. The importance of rational choice theory is that, at its best, it exemplifies this method.

In her chapter, Margaret Mooney Marini presents a comprehensive statement about human purposive action in which rational choice is conceptually located. Perhaps one could think of her complex purposive action model as an entity to be approached through the method of decreasing abstraction, if the methodology recommended by Lindenberg is followed.

The third and fourth chapters in this first part are implicit arguments that not metatheoretical debate but the production of theoretical explanations will demonstrate the significance of rational choice thinking in sociology. David Willer shows that his approach to social exchange theory, which he calls *elemental theory*, satisfies the criteria set out at the start of this introduction. Willer's elemental theory aims to treat not only voluntary exchanges but also coercive elements in social relationships, building both on Weberian concepts and on the idea of rational choice as a principle. Together the Willer chapter and the Hechter et al. chapter make the claim that at least two important classes of social phenomena, relating to social integration and social exchange, can be treated in terms of theories utilizing a principle of rational choice at some point.

Michael Hechter and his collaborators treat the problem of social order in the context of heterogeneous modern societies. As is typical among advocates of rational choice reasoning in sociology, their advocacy is not unqualified. While they are dubious of the functionalist solution in terms of internalization, at least so far as this would apply to societies characterized by normative diversity, they also are critical of a Hobbesian-type solution in terms of the role of the state. Instead, drawing on Hechter's theory of group solidarity, they try to show that the global order in such societies is a by-product of local solidarities.

In Part II we turn from themes of advocacy to various critiques of rational choice theory in sociology. This part of the book opens with a microsociological critique by Thomas Scheff. He advances one of the key criticisms of rational choice theory: that it is devoid of treatment of the emotional element in human action and thereby cannot make the transition to the macro level without severe conceptual limitations. The second chapter in this part is a macrosociological critique framed by Michael Hannan. It is grounded in the idea, dis-

cussed above, that macrosociology should not be too closely artic-
ulated with disputable assumptions about motivation or about the
connections between micro and macro levels.

The chapter by Richard Münch presents a neofunctionalist critique
of rational choice theory. One point he makes is that social and
cultural systems of action have aspects that are truncated or missed
entirely in typical rational choice models. Münch regards the limitations of the theory as rooted in a conceptual structure derived from
neoclassical economics. In the final chapter in this part, David Sciulli
presents a critique of what he sees as the core ideas of rational choice
theory with a more explicit normative viewpoint than the other
critical analyses. According to him, key sociological works in the
rational choice tradition present a perspective on modern society that
cannot be defended on rational normative grounds.

Finally, in Part III, we present two metatheoretical positions that
sum up key issues about the use of rational choice theory in
sociology. The authors take principled stands on it that are essentially opposed. Peter Abell, well aware of philosophical and other
critiques of rational choice theory, concludes that in the current
state of sociological theory a good argument can be made that it
is reasonable for a theorist to choose to frame explanatory problems within that framework. By contrast, James Bohman tries to
show that this strategy cannot work because the theory is highly
scope restricted. Using an analytical philosophical approach, he
argues that within its restricted scope, rational choice theory is a
good theory. The danger, he maintains, lies in the attempt to
extend it to explanatory tasks for which it will lead to misleading
empirical claims.

REFERENCES

Abell, Peter. 1989. "Games in Networks: A Sociological Theory of Voluntary Asso-
    ciations." *Rationality and Society* 1:259-282.
Alexander, Jeffrey C. 1987. *Twenty Lectures: Sociological Theory Since World War II.*
    New York: Columbia University Press.
Axelrod, Robert. 1984. *The Evolution of Cooperation.* New York: Basic Books.
Bainbridge, William Sims. 1987. *Sociological Laboratory: Computer Simulations for
    Learning Sociology.* Section B: "RACE: Segregation in Schellingdale Neighbor-
    hoods." Belmont, CA: Wadsworth.
Blau, Peter M. 1964. *Exchange and Power in Social Life.* New York: John Wiley.

Boudon, Raymond. 1981. *The Logic of Social Action.* Boston: Routledge & Kegan Paul.

————. 1987. "The Individualistic Tradition in Sociology." Pp. 45-70 in *The Micro-Macro Link,* edited by J. Alexander, B. Geisen, R. Münch, and N. Smelser. Berkeley: University of California Press.

Coleman, James S. 1990. *Foundations of Social Theory.* Cambridge, MA: Harvard University Press.

Cook, Karen S. and Richard M. Emerson. 1978. "Power, Equity and Commitment in Exchange Networks." *American Sociological Review* 43:721-39.

Durkheim, Emile. [1893] 1964. *The Division of Labor in Society.* New York: Free Press.

Etzioni, Amitai. 1988. *The Moral Dimension: Toward a New Economics.* New York: Free Press.

Fararo, Thomas J. 1989. *The Meaning of General Theoretical Sociology.* (ASA Rose Monograph.) New York: Cambridge University Press.

Friedman, Debra and Michael Hechter. 1988. "The Contribution of Rational Choice Theory to Macrosociological Research." *Sociological Theory* 6:201-18.

Hechter, Michael. 1987. *Principles of Group Solidarity.* Berkeley: University of California Press.

Hechter, Michael, Karl-Dieter Opp, and Reinhard Wippler, eds. 1990. *Social Institutions: Their Emergence, Maintenance, and Effects.* Hawthorne, NY: Aldine.

Homans, George C. [1961] 1974. *Social Behavior: Its Elementary Forms.* rev. ed. New York: Harcourt Brace Jovanovich.

Lechner, Frank J. 1990. "The New Utilitarianism." *Current Perspectives in Social Theory* 10:93-111.

Lindenberg, Siegwart. 1985. "An Assessment of the New Political Economy." *Sociological Theory* 3:99-114.

Margolis, Howard. 1982. *Selfishness, Altruism and Rationality: A Theory of Social Choice.* Chicago: University of Chicago Press.

Markovsky, Barry, David Willer, and Travis Patton. 1988. "Power Relations in Networks." *American Sociological Review* 53:220-36.

Parsons, Talcott. 1937. *The Structure of Social Action.* New York: Free Press.

————. 1977. *Social Systems and the Evolution of Action Theory.* New York: Free Press.

Parsons, Talcott and Neil J. Smelser. 1956. *Economy and Society.* New York: Free Press.

Schelling, Thomas C. 1971. "Dynamic Models of Segregation." *Journal of Mathematical Sociology* 1:143-86.

Toulmin, Stephen. 1953. *The Philosophy of Science.* London: Hutchison.

————. 1961. *Foresight and Understanding.* New York: Harper.

Willer, David and Bo Anderson, eds. 1981. *Networks, Exchange and Coercion.* New York: Elsevier.

Wippler, Reinhard and Siegwart Lindenberg. 1987. "Collective Phenomena and Rational Choice." Pp. 135-52 in *The Micro-Macro Link,* edited by J. Alexander, B. Geisen, R. Münch, and N. Smelser. Berkeley: University of California Press.

Ziegler, Rolf. 1990. "The Kula: Social Order, Barter and Ceremonial Exchange." Pp. 141-68 in *Social Institutions,* edited by M. Hechter, K. D. Opp, and R. Wippler. Hawthorne, NY: Aldine.

PART I

Themes of Advocacy

Chapter 1

THE METHOD OF DECREASING ABSTRACTION

SIEGWART LINDENBERG
ICS, the University of Groningen

RATIONAL CHOICE SOCIOLOGY IS, among other things, an attempt to combine the advantages of theory-guided research, as found in economics, with the strong empirical tradition of sociology. In order to succeed in this endeavor where previous attempts did not, it is necessary to find new methodological tools. In order to find an adequate solution, it is first necessary to find out why a combination of these advantages did not succeed in the past. It is then necessary to bring to bear the methodological developments in the recent past, especially the following points: First, the disaggregation of utility theory into a fixed core of assumptions on human nature and a variable belt of bridge assumptions that can be subjected to the method of decreasing abstraction (or increasing closeness to reality); and second, the heuristics needed to reduce the uncertainty about appropriate bridge assumptions when using the method of decreasing abstraction. These heuristics include the theory of social production functions, the theory of framing, and the heuristic of a dual structure of explanation. With the aid of these tools, it is possible to work out models that are clearly theory-guided in their earlier versions, while their realism can be adapted in later versions. Insights from neoclassical economics and from traditional sociology are then essential in the entire process of model development.

INTRODUCTION

Recently the method of decreasing abstraction has been elaborated as a means to integrate economic, sociological, and psychological lines of research without losing the analytical power of the economic approach or the descriptive advantages of the sociological and psychological approaches. As it turns out, this method also allows a stronger integration of model building with empirical research in general. What does the method look like? In a variety of different papers (Lindenberg 1985, 1990), I have worked out this method, and in this overview its main points will be summarized.[1]

Theories are subject to conflicting claims. First, the more empirically accurate a theory in prediction and explanation, the better. Second, the more diverse the fields within which a theory can be applied, the greater the analytical power of the theory and the more theory-driven the analyses can be. In order to have theory-driven analyses, one has to simplify the description of phenomena severely; that is, one has to abstract from many features of reality. Thus the theory is rendered empirically less accurate. In order to make the theory empirically more accurate, one has to make it more complex and more tailored to the phenomena in question, thus losing analytical power (see also Coleman 1990, p. 19). For most economists since Adam Smith, analytical power has been the most important point about theorizing, and for many sociologists, the descriptive closeness to social reality has been the important goal, be it in the form of the Durkheimian causal analysis or in the form of the Weberian casuistic analysis. Economists thus generally are unwilling to forego their highly simplified (and therefore often very unrealistic) models in favor of more realistic but analytically less powerful models, and sociologists generally are unwilling to forego descriptive richness. As so often, the truth does not seem to lie in the middle, in doing a bit of both. Adding such "sociological" variables as norms and community to economic models is not a satisfactory solution because this addition does not integrate the presumed behavioral mechanisms involved in rational choice and norm-following behavior. The same holds true for sociological explanations enriched with such "economic" variables as cost and utility. For more than 100 years, another possibility to integrate both desiderata has been discussed: a method whereby one would begin with a very simple model and gradually make it more realistic. For example, Lange (1875) calls this the *method of successive approximation to the truth*. Later the term *method of decreasing abstraction* became more widely accepted. Still this method was not elaborated, and economists never got very far with it. To my knowledge, the most advanced attempt in the past to reconstruct this method is Haller's *Typus und Gezetz in der Nationalökonomie (Type and Law in Economics)* [1950]. Inspired by Weber and Sombart, Haller took the assumption of the ubiquity of rational action itself to be a simplification, and he introduced other behavioral principles (e.g., traditionalism) for certain groups (e.g., peasants) in order to make economic models more realistic. But there is a clear difference from Weber's ideal typical method: Haller uses the more "realistic" behavioral assumptions in the original model, coming to new predictions on the macro level. While this attempt was an advance on what had been done before, it ran aground by the fact that, by using different behavioral principles, Haller lost the ability to model the influence of constraints. For this reason, the models turned out to be driven by given behavioral tendencies rather than by social circumstances, a result that ran counter to the very intentions for using the method of decreasing abstraction in the first place. These intentions were after all focused on bringing to bear on economic models sociological insights on the importance of group structure and institutions.

After Haller, the method of decreasing abstraction was not taken up again for the integration of economics and sociology until very recently. Instead the sociologists and psychologists focused on the irreality of economics. For example, the sociologist Daniel Bell wrote that "economic theory is a convenient fiction . . . but it is not a model of reality. But even as a fictional ideal, it is inherently problematical" (Bell 1981, p. 70). The psychologists Kahneman and Tversky state that the theory of rational choice as used by economists is a normative theory and that "the deviations of actual behavior from the normative model . . . are too fundamental to be accommodated by relaxing the normative system" (Tversky and Kahneman 1987, p. 68). This discussion underlined the abstractness and irreality of economic models, but it completely ignored the issue of analytical power. Not surprisingly, economists were very reluctant to pick up the suggestions. In this chapter, I present the bare bones of a method of decreasing abstraction that will allow analytical power and descriptive accuracy. It thereby also pleads for a different understanding of model building. A model should be a collection of different versions, such that the highly simplified versions offer analytical power and the later versions offer more descriptive accuracy.

SOME CORE DISTINCTIONS

Model building has been linked mainly to the achievement of analytical power. The requirement is "keep it as simple as possible." In order to increase the model's empirical accuracy, one has to add the requirement "make it as complex as necessary." The method of decreasing abstraction (i.e., decreasing simplification) attempts to achieve theory-driven analyses and empirical accuracy by taking model building to be a sequence of versions of theory in which empirical accuracy is stepwise approached, while the early versions of the theory provide analytical power. In order to achieve this—that is, in order to avoid the pitfalls of earlier attempts—it is essential to observe some methodological distinctions that often have been ignored in the past.

Core Theory and Bridge Assumptions. A *core theory* consists of a number of guiding ideas that can be made more specific by auxiliary assumptions that bridge the gap between the core and a more or less simplified reality. These auxiliary assumptions therefore are called *bridge assumptions.* This distinction is to be contrasted with *bastard theories,* in which core and bridge assumptions are combined into one package. For example, if rational behavior is by definition meant to include gain maximization, then rationality (as a core theory) is inextricably intertwined with gain maximization into one bastard theory. Given such a package, it is not possible to make the assumption about gain maximization more complex (say, by stating the conditions under which it may or may not occur) without simultaneously letting go of the core theory of rationality. Because this is a very unattractive option for theory development, bastard theories should be avoided and bridge assumptions should be kept separate from the (quite empty) core.

Individual₂ Theories. The second important distinction pertains to differences in the goals of a discipline. Those goals profoundly affect the requirements concerning the individualistic theories used in an explanation (see Lindenberg 1985). The main task of sociology (and economics) is to analyze social systems. Coleman states this as follows: "The focus must be on the social system whose behavior is to be explained. This may be as small as a dyad or as large as a society or even a world system, but the essential requirement is that the explanatory focus be on the system as a unit, not on the individuals or other components which make it up" (Coleman 1990, p. 2) The *analytic* primacy thus lies at the aggregate level. Yet the explanation of social systems is based on explaining the mechanisms that go on in the system and that produce the system effects. In sociology, all such mechanisms involve purposive action of human beings. For this reason, the *theoretical* (or explanatory) primacy lies on the individual level. For easy identification, I have called this individualistic level *individual₂*. A different situation can be found for psychology. Here both the analytical and the theoretical primacies lie on the individual level; that is, psychologists are interested in analyzing phenomena of individuals, and for this purpose they use theories pertaining to the individual level.[2] The explanatory task of the individualistic theories in psychology (*individual₁*) is thus different from that of individualistic theories in economics and sociology (*individual₂*). Individual₂ theories are used to provide explanations for phenomena on the aggregate level, and individual₁ theories cannot be expected to do the job even though they often may be the more realistic theories.

Individual₂ theory must meet a variety of requirements, and I will mention here the three most important ones (see Lindenberg 1985).

1. The more a theory allows fruitful application without much information about each individual to whom it is applied, the better it can function in an individual₂ context. Individual₁ theories are mostly quite greedy with regard to information about each individual. For learning theories, it would be most appropriate to have the reinforcement schedules; for cognitive theories, it would be most appropriate to have information on schemas and biases; for psychodynamic theories, one would require information about individual traumas and so on.

2. The more a theory allows us to minimize the distance between the individual and the collective level, the better it can function in an individual$_2$ context. For example, if profit maximization is seen as a human motive (i.e., as pertaining to an individual$_1$ theory), then all the attention will be drawn toward questions concerning the development of a personality with this motive. The distance to the collective level is quite large. An individual$_2$ interpretation of profit maximization is an institutional one, in which the right to the residual creates an incentive for the holder of this right. Here the individual level is modeled very closely to the collective level.

3. The more a theory allows that its bridge assumptions are simplified and are made more complex, the better it can function in an individual$_2$ context. For example, the constitutive assumptions of Weber's ideal types of action cannot be simplified or made more complex. They are fixed with the construction of the type. This point is similar (but not identical) to the one about bastard theories.

HEURISTICS I: THE LOGIC OF THE SITUATION

A core theory that satisfies these three requirements for an individual$_2$ theory more than others is a model of man[3] that seems to emerge more and more as a common core of the social sciences (see Lindenberg 1990): RREEMM (an acronym for Restricted, Resourceful, Expecting, Evaluating, Maximizing Man). This core theory of action is as simple as the bridge assumptions that are made for each element. For example, with regard to "evaluating," a simple linear utility function may be assumed, and in a later version of the model a nonlinear function (say, with decreasing marginal utility) may replace the simple assumption of the first model. A still more complex (and possibly more realistic) assumption would be that utility depends on the way the situation is cognitively framed by the actor. Thus psychological assumptions can enter as bridge assumptions without replacing the individual$_2$ core theory. From this example, it can be seen also that the increasing complexity of bridge assumptions makes the model more realistic but also renders it analytically less powerful because it greatly increases the information that is needed per situation and per individual. For this very reason, the bridge assumptions should at first be as simple as possible and then be stepwise adapted to make the model as complex as necessary. Making bridge assumptions of a cognitive kind more realistic means that the action theory is moved more in the direction of an individual$_1$ theory. For this reason, a definite order of priority exists: Make the structural bridge assumptions more realistic first and only then withdraw the simplified cognitive assumptions, if necessary. Thus one should work first on making the *restrictions* more realistic and then the *goals* and only then the *expectations.*

Not every core theory allows this stepwise development as well as any other. For example, as we have seen in Haller's case, if one uses as a core theory the idea that people are either rational or traditional, then one cannot go very far with the development of bridge assumptions. By contrast, RREEMM offers an immediate guide to bridge assumptions: an analysis of the *action situation* (the "logic of the situation," as Popper would say[4]). Notice that the questions generated by this heuristic are constraint-driven. What are the restrictions? What are the goals? What are the expectations in the action situation? In order to make this heuristic work—that is, in order to be able to bring sociological insights into model building—two other heuristics are essential.

HEURISTICS II:
SOCIAL PRODUCTION FUNCTIONS AND FRAMING

Due to role-playing man, sociologists had approached preferences not from the standpoint of choice under constraints but from the standpoint of social control. Two sociological messages are involved in the traditional sociological treatment of preferences. One is the idea that because of socialization effects on internalization, one does not have to bother about choice. How is behavior socially determined? By *socializing* an individual in such a way that he or she will want to do what he or she is socially expected to do. Thus "wanting" was removed from choosing. The other message is that preferences are products of social processes. The trouble is that both messages are linked: If socialization is successful, the desired (preference) is socially engineered to coincide with the desirable (value) and the individual will act according to his or her preferences. Through this link, it has proven difficult to use the second message without endorsing the first. The first message, however, is incompatible with a constraint-driven heuristic (a logic of the situation). What is needed is a way to use the important sociological insight on the social origin of preferences without thereby throwing choice out of the analysis.

Recent developments do offer a likely solution. They center around a change in economics that has come about as a response to nonmarket applications and can be summarized by a shift from man the consumer to man the producer. What is so important about this shift is that it allows preferences to appear entirely in an instrumental context whereby they would have to be explained as part of the social structure and thus as part of the given constraints.

This feat is accomplished by the assumption of two kinds of preferences (see Stigler and Becker 1977): *universal* preferences (goals) that are identical for all human beings and therefore need no explanation, and *instrumental* preferences for the means that lead to the ultimate goals, which are in fact constraints and thus can be explained in a constraint-driven approach. Technically speaking, only one utility function exists for all humankind, but systematically different production functions exist for different kinds of people. Buying a particular good is now not an act of consumption but the purchase of a means of production, such as a compact disc for the production of music pleasure.

This approach fits nicely into the bridge-assumption methodology outlined above because the specification of production functions can be seen as providing bridge assumptions about instrumental preferences. So far so good. But without a specification of what the ultimate goals are, the old danger of ad hoc theorizing looms large and little has been gained. For this reason, Becker's approach was further developed into what may be called the *social production function approach* (see Lindenberg 1986, 1991). In the social sciences, two general human goals have emerged time and again. In economics, *physical well-being* has played an important role as general goal, making any form of effort costly, rendering an increase of leisure a benefit, and focusing attention on consumption of goods and services.[5] In sociology, *social approval* has always been considered to be a crucial general human goal. Thus status, behavioral confirmation, reputation, prestige, respect, deference, dignity, and so on are various forms of one general goal. Adam Smith had worked with these two goals already in the *Theory of Moral Sentiments,* and he included the craving to get approval from your own self, which observes your actions. These goals are central to anybody and everybody, and therefore the means people have to reach these goals are of utmost importance to them—so important that a systematic threat to these means may cause a revolution (see Lindenberg 1989a). These means vary with social position and are called *social production functions.* They work like standard operating procedures for the production of one or both of the general goals.[6] The more clearly role expectations are formulated and sanctioned, the clearer the social production functions are. When the positive and/or negative sanctions connected to the expected behavior decline, then the individual will look for alternative means of getting physical well-being or social approval. And because the individual is assumed to be resourceful, he or she will look actively for alternatives rather than follow the role expectations until somebody else tries to resocialize him or her.

Let us take an example (see Lindenberg 1991). In a traditional industrial social structure with segregated gender roles, the man has his job and his life-style as sources of social approval, and the woman has the making of a home and the raising of the children as sources of social approval. When making a home and raising children yield less and less social approval, women will seek to adapt their social production functions, for example by entering the labor market if they have not done so already for the sake of money (physical well-being). Here the difference between the old and the new situation is quite apparent. In sociology, it has been known for a long time that social approval is an important reward connected to holding a job (see for example Morse and Weiss 1955), but due to "role-playing man," this insight could not be theoretically worked into a theory of labor market participation until "the logic of the situation" replaced "automatic control of human action by internalization" as a guiding heuristic. Notice that effects of norms on behavior are entirely compatible with a social production function approach. Norms heavily influence social production functions.

The social origin of preferences was only one important stabilizer of the internalization heuristics in sociology. The other was the important insight that the definition of the situation matters. Again this insight was linked to the idea that the individual is steered automatically by internalized norms. Because men would be socialized into defining situations in the "appropriate" way, one could assume safely that they are steered automatically by norms. When one introduces choice under constraints, one has to find a way to incorporate the impact of the definition of the situation. Up to now, this has not been done satisfactorily. The introduction of subjective probabilities in the SEU (Subjectively Expected Utility) theory was a step in the right direction, but it did not incorporate the structuring of the situation, including the selection of alternatives. Various other suggestions (such as Simon 1957, and Kahneman and Tversky 1979) offered improvements, but they were individual[1] theories and therefore did not fit the distinction between core theory and bridge assumptions, a distinction that is crucial for the method of decreasing abstraction. Goffman wrote *Frame Analysis* (1974), which offers an elaborate analysis of framing in everyday life. Giving many examples, Goffman shows how vulnerable the organization of experience is (to joke, dream, accident, mistake, misunderstanding, deception, etc.) and how we use all sorts of stories and scenarios to stabilize the frames. While Goffman's work clearly shows the importance of social processes for framing, it does not offer a behavioral theory that combines rational choice and framing.

Learning from all three approaches, I elaborated a framing theory, called *discrimination model,* in the early 1980s. For reasons of space, it is not possible to present this model here in great detail (for a recent formulation, see Lindenberg 1989b).

The basic idea is that people have various competing potential goals in any action situation and that one goal wins out. It will then structure (i.e., "frame") the situation by providing the criteria for selecting and ordering the alternatives. The winning goal is the one that discriminates best; that is, the one that provides the most structure by creating the largest difference between the alternatives. This difference translates itself directly into choice probabilities with which the alternatives are chosen.

For example, you bought a theater ticket for $100 and, before you leave for the theater, it begins to rain heavily; you know that you will get quite wet even with an umbrella. Three obvious candidates for goals exist in this short scenario: the anticipated enjoyment of the show, the wish to avoid getting wet, and the wish to avoid throwing away $100 by not going. Due to a part of the theory on the motivating power of loss (not presented here), the prediction is that unless unusual circumstances arise about which we were not told (for example, you are meeting your childhood sweetheart at the show or you just won big in a lottery), loss avoidance will be the frame for this situation. One hundred dollars for a ticket is quite a lot, and if you stayed at home in order not to get wet, this amount of money would be lost without compensation. This loss would bother you so much that the utility difference between going and not going (in terms of loss) is larger (i.e., the choice probabilities of the alternatives are farther apart) than the difference between going and not going in terms of enjoyment of the show or of not getting wet.

Although one goal won out, the other two goals do not simply vanish from the situation. The effect of the given utility difference between alternatives on choice probabilities is enhanced or lowered with changes in the *salience* of the frame, that is, with changes in the other potential goals that influence this salience. In our case, the enjoyment of the show increases the salience of the loss frame because it favors going (as does the loss frame), and the prospect of getting wet will lower it because it favors staying. Background goals thus influence behavior by affecting the salience of the frame.

Frames can and will change. Frame switches allow seemingly irrational (inconsistent) behavior across situations. They also explain apparent preference changes without the assumption of unstable preference structures. For example, when the power of the present frame to discriminate between alternatives is reduced greatly (when the choice probabilities approach an even distribution over the alternatives), then the frame is likely to switch and the goal that potentially discriminates best between alternatives will become the new frame. Such a reduction in the ability to structure the situation can come about either through changes in the expected outcome of each alternative or through a reduction in salience. In the example, imagine that before you leave for the show your spouse hands you $90 of the $100 you had originally given to him or her to pick up the ticket for you; a mixup had occurred, and the ticket really cost only $10. In that case, the potential loss would be so small that the probability of "not going" approaches the probability of "going," which renders the situation virtually unstructured. As a result, a new frame will emerge from the background (in this case, probably the wish not to get wet). So hearing the news of the price of the ticket is likely to make you stay at home.

The important difference with the SEU theory is this: In the SEU theory, the weight of each outcome is independent of the structuring of the situation; in the framing theory, the weight of a goal (utility argument) does not depend just on the expected utility of the outcome but also on the *position* of this goal (either as frame or as background). Thus changes in outcomes that affect only the salience of the frame have a relatively much smaller effect on behavior than do changes in outcomes directly relating to the frame. For example, in light of the loss frame, hearing just before you leave for the theater that the show has gotten bad reviews will have only a relatively small effect, while hearing that the ticket was less expensive than you thought will have a relatively large effect. Had the frame been "enjoyment of the show," you would have been much more sensitive to hearing about bad reviews and much less sensitive to hearing news about the price of the ticket. In other words, if I can influence the way you structure the situation, I can thereby also influence your sensitivity to various factors.

The need to bring in this framing theory as a complex bridge assumption will not arise in every model. In early versions of model development, it is quite appropriate for the researcher to ignore the distinction between background and frame and to decide on the basis of knowledge of the action situation which of the utility arguments (goals) are operative. The researcher thereby abstracts from the fact that a situational influence exists on the weight of the utility arguments, just as he or she might abstract from the fact that the actor is not well informed. At this point, the need for the framing theory arises because we need to know how the simplifying assumptions can be made more concrete. The advantage of postponing the introduction of framing effects is that thereby the emphasis on structural constraints is stronger. Investigate social structural conditions before you introduce *indirect* social effects that are operative only via framing.[7] But when we have reached the point at which we want to introduce framing, we need a framing theory that allows us to expand the previous (structurally oriented) model rather than to replace it with a psychological one. This is only possible with an individual$_2$ framing theory. The other two alternatives are very unattractive: Either we follow Haller's procedure by working with behavioral "tendencies" (say, maximizing vs. satisficing), or we follow Kahneman and Tversky's suggestion of replacing the behavioral theory with a more complex cognitive theory. In the first case, we make it very difficult to introduce constraints. In the second case, we introduce a theory that does not satisfy the three crucial requirements for a behavioral theory geared toward explanation on the aggregate level: (a) fruitful *application* without much information about each individual to whom it is applied, (b) minimal distance between the individual and the collective level, and (c) explicit bridge assumptions that can vary in concreteness. Thus the important point is to be able to introduce cognitive complexity in such a way that we retain the ability for model building. The framing theory described above was designed for that purpose.

OTHER ASSUMPTIONS

The method of decreasing abstraction is not restricted to bridge assumptions. All assumptions that are made in model building are subject to the method. And thus a heuristic should exist for the other assumptions as well. What kind of assumptions are they?

The combination of the analytical primacy of society (or the collective level) with the theoretical (or explanatory) primacy of the individual necessitates a dual structure of explanation (see Lindenberg 1977). The first step explains individual effects in the social context; the second step explains how the individual effects are "transformed" into a collective effect. For this very reason, one also needs *actor assumptions* and *transformation assumptions*. And because the model has to be tested, one also needs *measurement assumptions*. Let me briefly take up each of these kinds of assumptions.

Before one can make bridge assumptions on restrictions, goals, and expectations for actors, one first has to decide on the kind and number of *actors* to be considered. Because of the requirement of model building to be "as simple as possible," one should begin with as few actors as possible. But because of the analytical primacy of the collective, the minimum number of actors should be two rather than one. Yet this seemingly simple requirement could introduce a high degree of complexity of strategic behavior even in the early stages of model development. In order to avoid dealing with strategic behavior at this stage, one can leave the actors implicit altogether by combining only variables on the aggregate level, such as "the tighter the labor market, the lower the rate of reemployment." The implicit actors are minimally the people looking for jobs and the employers, but because they are not made explicit, no bridge assumptions are to be made about them. And because it remains entirely on the collective level, no transformation assumptions are to be made. Only the measurement assumptions concerning both variables can be improved from "quick and dirty" measures to complex and detailed ones. When, in the next step, actors are explicitly introduced, one can begin with one central actor and introduce the other actor only via restrictions on this central actor. In the next step, one can model both actors as central actors, each restricting the other. Thus one should have specific reasons for beginning with strategic interaction (for instance in [undecomposed] game theoretic models).

The heuristics for assumptions for the transformation step are not well worked out. In contrast to bridge assumptions, the *transformation assumptions* are not guided by the heuristics of situational analysis. For this reason, I have suggested first the (partial) definition of the dependent variable in terms of interdependencies or aggregates. Second, I have suggested the use of background knowledge on the subject matter under investigation in order to locate relevant conditions for the transformation. In the simplest case, this will lead to a relative unproblematic aggregation; in a more complex stage, one will look for aspects that differentially influence the individual effects, that is, aspects that create interaction effects. Thereby a distribution of individual effects more complex than linear aggregation can be explained. Depending on the dependent variable, still other kinds of transformation are possible, but I will not discuss them here (see Lindenberg 1977).

The reason that *measurement assumptions* are also subject to the method of decreasing abstraction is that some inverse relationship exists between simplification and cost. This relationship can be quite imperfect and still exert an important influence on the method of decreasing abstraction. So far, no explicitly worked out heuristic exists for measurement assumptions, other than the maxim that the measurement assumptions should be made on the basis of substantive theory. Of course, here as for the other assumptions, the general maxim is: *Choose among the many possible assumptions the one that leaves least uncertainty about the further development of assumptions.* By including measurement assumptions explicitly in the method of decreasing abstraction, the modeling part of an analysis is also explicitly extended to the testing part. For example, important variables often are measured only by a rough proxy. Take "labor market opportunity" measured by the number of unfilled vacancies. This measure is very rough indeed because it ignores the fact that labor is heterogeneous, that local segments exist, and that labor supply (and thus competition) in a particular category may still be high even if many vacancies exist. When the empirical results are disappointing, then applying the method of decreasing abstraction at this point to the measurement assumptions would be preferable to applying it to bridge assumptions or to the actor assumptions.

Where to Stop. The last point about the method of decreasing abstraction is the question of where to stop. It is difficult to provide a definite criterion, but I suggest the pragmatic stance that if the added satisfaction of the last step of model development does not outweigh the extra trouble one has taken for this last step, one should not only stop but actually go back one step. In addition, I suggest that one attempt to find the threshold for different subgroups. For one group, the most complex version of the model may be needed, but for another group (for example, one that is much less restricted in its action), a far simpler version of the model can be used without much loss of (relative) descriptive and explanatory power.

SUMMARY

By way of summary, the major principles leading to the importance of the method are the following:

- Model building means that an explanation is as simple as possible and as complex as necessary.
- Highly simplified models often have the advantage of great analytical power; highly complex models often have the advantage of realistic descriptiveness.
- Theories should allow high analytical power and a high degree of realistic descriptiveness. In order to achieve this, they should be constructed according to the method of decreasing abstraction.

The major principles of the method are the following:

- Theories should be considered as sequences of models in which the first model is highly simplified and each subsequent model is more realistic.
- Most theories in sociology should explain phenomena on the collective level, and these explanations should be grounded in theories on the individual level.
- The theories on the individual level should not be psychological theories but combinations of a general model of man (the core theory) and bridge assumptions.
- The bridge assumptions should be developed in such a way that they are simple in the beginning models and more complex in the later models.
- Bridge assumptions should be made on the basis of an analysis of the action situation and on the basis of the heuristics of social production functions and of framing.
- Structural bridge assumptions should be made more realistic before one begins to do the same to cognitive bridge assumptions.
- Not just bridge assumptions, but also actor, transformation, and measurement assumptions should be subject to the method of decreasing abstraction.
- Aside from the possibility of beginning with an implicit actor model as a baseline model for later development, actor assumptions should be made in such a way that one begins with one central actor constrained by other actor(s). Strategic behavior should be introduced only in later versions of the theory, if at all.
- Transformation assumptions should begin with simple aggregation and move on to interdependencies, at first concentrating on interaction effects.

- Measurement assumptions should be made more complex on the basis of substantive theory.
- For all kinds of assumptions subject to the method of decreasing abstraction, the maxim holds: Choose among the many possible assumptions the one that leaves least uncertainty about the further development of assumptions.
- Stop the theory development when the additional complexity does not yield worthwhile results, and then go back one step for the final model.
- See which models of your theory can be applied to which subgroups of the population under investigation. No presumption exists that every subgroup should be explained with a model of equal complexity.

NOTES

1. A more elaborate paper is presently being prepared, with a more extensive overview of modeling preferences and difficulties in economics and the possibilities of improving this modeling through sociological insights without losing the advantages of modeling.

2. Sometimes psychologists even use theories below the level of individuals, such as physiological theories. But psychological theories of behavior refer by and large to the individual as the central unit.

3. *Man* refers to *humans* throughout the chapter.

4. See Popper 1960, pp. 147ff.

5. Frank (1990, p. 54) observed that economists are quick to defer to psychologists, sociologists, and philosophers when asked what people really care about. "As a practical matter, however, economists . . . are content to assume the consumer's overriding objective is the consumption of goods, services, and leisure—in short, the pursuit of material self-interest."

6. The general utility function is the one that links physical well-being and social approval to utility. All lower level goals are specified in production functions, which are not idiosyncratic but socially determined.

7. Coleman says that he prefers to keep the behavioral theory simple in order to be able to introduce complexity in the other parts of the model and still keep the model manageable. "I have chosen to trade off as much psychological complexity as possible in order to allow introduction of greater amounts of complexity in . . . the 'social organizational' components" (Coleman 1990, p. 19). This clearly indicates the emphasis on direct social constraints. Because Coleman does not distinguish between core theory and bridge assumptions, however, it is not quite clear when this trade-off takes place and whether he would consider varying the trade-off in different elaborations of a model.

REFERENCES

Bell, Daniel. 1981. "Models and Reality in Economic Discourse." Pp. 46-80 in *The Crisis in Economic Theory*, edited by D. Bell and I. Kristol. New York: Free Press.

Coleman, James S. 1990. *Foundations of Social Theory*. Cambridge, MA: Harvard University Press.

Frank, Robert H. 1990. "Rethinking Rational Choice." Pp. 53-87 in *Beyond the Marketplace*, edited by Roger Friedland and A. F. Robertson. New York: Aldine.

Goffman, Erving. 1984. *Frame Analysis. An Essay on the Organization of Experience*. Cambridge, MA: Harvard University Press.

Haller, H. 1950. *Typus und Gesetz in der Nationalökonomie. Versuch zur Klärung einiger Methodenfragen der Wirtschaftswissenschaften*. Stuttgart und Köln: Kohlhammer.

Kahneman, Daniel and Amos Tversky. 1979. "Prospect Theory: An Analysis of Decision Under Risk." *Econometrica* 47:263-91.

Lange, F. A. 1875. *Geschichte des Materialismus*. Leipzig: Baedeker.

Lindenberg, Siegwart. 1977. "Individuelle Effekte, kollektive Phönomene und das Problem der Transformation," Pp. 46-84 in *Probleme der Erklärung sozialen Verhaltens*, edited by K. Eichner and W. Habermehl. Meisenheim: Anton Hain.

———. 1985. "An Assessment of the New Political Economy: Its Potential for the Social Sciences and for Sociology in Particular." *Sociological Theory* 3(1):99-114.

———. 1986. "The Paradox of Privatization in Consumption." Pp. 297-310 in *Paradoxical Effects of Social Behavior, Essays in Honor of Anatol Rapoport*, edited by A. Diekmann and P. Mitter. Heidelberg/Wien: Physica-Verlag.

———. 1989a. "Social Production Functions, Deficits, and Social Revolutions: Pre-revolutionary France and Russia." *Rationality and Society* 1(1):51-77.

———. 1989b. "Choice and Culture: The Behavioral Basis of Cultural Impact on Transactions." Pp. 175-200 in *Social Structure and Culture*, edited by H. Haferkamp. Berlin: de Gruyter.

———. 1990. "Homo socio-economicus: The Emergence of a General Model of Man in the Social Sciences." *Journal of Institutional and Theoretical Economics* 146:727-48.

———. 1991. "Social Approval, Fertility and Female Labour Market Behavior." Pp. 33-58 in *Female Labour Market Behaviour and Fertility: A Rational Choice Approach*, edited by J. Siegers, J. de Jong-Gierveld, and E. van Imhoff. New York: Springer Verlag.

Morse, N. C. and R. C. Weiss. 1955. "The Function and Meaning of Work and the Job." *American Sociological Review* 20:191-98.

Popper, Karl. 1960. *The Poverty of Historicism*. London: Routledge & Kegan Paul.

Simon, Herbert. 1957. *Models of Man*. New York: John Wiley.

Stigler, George and Gary. S. Becker. 1977. "De gustibus non est disputandum." *The American Economic Review* 67:76-90.

Tversky, Amos and Daniel Kahneman. 1987. "Rational Choice and the Framing of Decisions." Pp. 67-94 in *Rational Choice*, edited by R. M. Hogarth and M. W. Reder. Chicago: University of Chicago Press, 1987.

Chapter 2

THE ROLE OF MODELS OF PURPOSIVE ACTION IN SOCIOLOGY

MARGARET MOONEY MARINI
University of Minnesota

IN THE TITLE OF THIS CHAPTER, I use the phrase *models of purposive action* rather than *rational choice model* or *rational choice theory* to emphasize that there is a broad class of fundamentally similar models in all of the social sciences. These models rest on the assumption that actors are purposive; that is, that they act in ways that tend to produce beneficial results. This assumption underlies theories of rational choice in economics, theories of exchange in sociology, and theories of judgment and decision making in psychology. Despite the prevalence of these models, their use in sociology is still relatively rare—confined primarily to the analysis of interpersonal relations and small groups. Only recently have attempts been made by sociologists to employ models of purposive action in understanding the functioning of larger social systems (for example, Coleman 1986, 1990; Hechter 1987). These attempts have been influenced heavily by theories of rational choice in economics, including their application to nonmarket decision making in the study of public choice. Because sociology is concerned primarily with the functioning of social systems, the usefulness of

AUTHOR'S NOTE: Work on this chapter was supported by Grants K04-AG00296 and R01-AG05715 from the National Institute on Aging, Grant R01-HD27598 from the National Institute of Child Health and Human Development, and funding from the College of Liberal Arts of the University of Minnesota.

models of purposive action in sociology hinges on the making of appropriate connections between the characteristics of social systems and the behavior of individual actors (the macro-micro connection), and between the behavior of individual actors and the systemic outcomes that emerge from the combined actions of multiple actors (the micro-macro connection).

In this chapter, I trace the development of models of purposive action in the social sciences and argue that these models are insufficient to explain human behavior because they do not take the origin of values and beliefs as problematic and do not consider the influence of emotions. Shared values and normative beliefs are part of the content of a society's culture. As the content of culture is learned via the process of socialization, social values and norms are internalized and become embedded in the cognitive structure of individuals. Influence on the thought patterns of individuals is particularly strong when social norms and values are tied to shared mental models that construct reality. The social structure of a society also affords a basis for the formation of descriptive beliefs about the nature of the world and the set of opportunities available.

In the first section of the chapter, I discuss the rational choice model, as axiomatized in expected utility theory, and the evidence that choice behavior does not always conform to its assumptions. I also discuss more recent attempts to provide a model that is more descriptively accurate. I point out that there is a broad class of models of purposive action within which the problematic assumptions of expected utility theory can be relaxed, including the assumption that preferences are unchanging and exogenous to the process of choice. I also point out that nothing is inherently egoistic about even the rational choice model because models of purposive action merely advance the postulate that human action is goal directed. They are theories about the way people, given their values and beliefs, make choices.

In the second section of the chapter, I argue that models of purposive action can be useful in explaining and predicting human behavior only when used in conjunction with knowledge or well-reasoned hypotheses about what people value and believe. Independent knowledge of values and beliefs must be brought to bear, and the origin of values and beliefs must be explained. Because the values and beliefs of individuals are shaped primarily by the socializing influences of society, especially as mediated through social relationships with "significant others," an understanding of the culture and structure of societies and of the positions of individuals within them is necessary.

MODELS OF PURPOSIVE ACTION

Although the models of purposive action that have emerged in various social science disciplines differ in the nature of the assumptions made about purposive action, they share the basic proposition that human beings are motivated to achieve pleasure and avoid pain and that this motivation leads them to act in ways that, at least within the limits of the information they possess and their ability to predict the future, can be expected to yield greater reward than cost. If reward and cost are defined subjectively and individuals are assumed to act in the service of subjective goals, this proposition links value to action. The rational choice paradigm developed in economics defines rational behavior not only as acting in the service of preferences to produce beneficial results but as maximizing net return.

The rational choice model received detailed formal treatment in *expected utility theory*, which is concerned with choice among alternatives in which probabilities can be attached to the consequences expected to ensue from the alternatives (see Schoemaker 1982 for a review). If we denote the consequences of alternatives by the vectors $\bar{x}_i$ (because an alternative may have multiple consequences) and the n associated probabilities by p_i such that $\Sigma_{i=1}^{n} p_i = 1$, expected utility theory prescribes that individuals maximize $\Sigma_{i=1}^{n} U(\bar{x}_i)p_i$. Rather than assume that people make choices on the basis of objective measures of expected value, or $\Sigma_{i=1}^{n} (\bar{x}_i)p_i$, people are assumed to choose on the basis of subjective measures of expected value, or utility. Because expected utility theory drops the property of linearity in the payoffs (the $\bar{x}_i$s), the model allows for the possibility that a gain of $400 may not be worth twice as much as a gain of $200 to the individual.

Von Neumann and Morgenstern (1944) founded expected utility theory on a set of axioms and showed that if a person's preferences conformed to the structure imposed by the axioms, the person was an expected utility maximizer. *Utility* was defined to represent preferences, and the structure of preferences imposed by the axioms was interpreted as a "rational" decision criterion. In their axiom system, probability values were given objectively. Subsequently in subjective expected utility theory as developed axiomatically by Savage (1954), *probabilities* were viewed as subjective degrees of belief. As models of choice under risk, the utility function in these models represents a compound mixture of (a) strength of preference for the consequences under certainty, and (b) attitudes toward risk (Schoemaker 1982).

As described by Tversky and Kahneman (1986), the axiomatic foundation of the theories of expected utility and subjective expected utility involves four substantive assumptions (in addition to the more technical assumptions of comparability and continuity). The four substantive assumptions, in order of increasing normative importance, are as follows: (a) *cancellation,* or elimination of any state that brings the same outcome regardless of one's choice; (b) *transitivity of preference,* which makes it possible to assign a value to each option that does not depend on the other options available; (c) *dominance,* whereby an option is chosen if it is better than another in one state and at least as good in all other states; and (d) *invariance,* whereby the preference between options is not affected by different representations, or descriptions, of the same choice problem. In recent years, mounting empirical evidence that choice behavior does not always conform to these assumptions has led psychologists and even some economists to view the expected utility model as descriptively invalid and to propose modifications that vary in the degree to which they adhere to its assumptions (Tversky and Kahneman 1986; Machina 1987; Simon 1987).

The most obvious problem with the axiomatization of utility and probability as a theory of the way people behave in choice situations is that it assumes that people have a high level of knowledge and computational ability with which to determine and evaluate a set of available alternatives. It assumes knowledge of all the alternatives available, as well as the consequences that will follow from each of the alternatives. It assumes certainty in the present and future evaluation of the consequences of alternatives and a holistic evaluation of alternatives in terms of a consistent measure of utility. It also assumes ability to calculate the probabilities of compound or conditional events and that probabilities and outcomes combine multiplicatively (under certain transformations).

Psychological research on human decision making and problem solving poses a challenge to these assumptions because it demonstrates a general human tendency to seek cognitive simplification. Although people may intend to be rational, they lack the mental capacity to behave as prescribed by expected utility theory. Research on human perception, recognition, and information storage and retrieval supports the "bounded rationality" view that limited information-processing capacity causes people to rely on a number of heuristic principles that reduce the complexity of even simple problems (Simon 1955). When a problem is presented in transparent form, choice behavior generally satisfies the axioms of expected utility theory (Plott 1986; Tversky and Kahneman 1986), but when a problem is presented in nontransparent form, the axioms often are violated (Simon 1979; Tversky and Kahneman 1986). Introducing uncertainty complicates the situation further.

In models in which utility maximization is assumed, the individual is seen as evaluating the outcomes of all possible alternatives before making a choice. As Simon (1955) has pointed out, in real decision-making situations, the individual often must consider alternatives sequentially and decide about them as they are presented. The individual then will choose the first alternative with an outcome at or above her or his level of aspiration, or the first satisfactory alternative. This "satisficing" model does not ensure a unique solution because the level of aspiration may change with the availability of information and the cost of search. As the number of alternatives perceived simultaneously increases, however, the satisficing model converges to a maximizing solution.

Work by psychologists on what is sometimes called *behavioral decision theory* has also sought to provide a more accurate description of the process of choice. Unlike expected utility theory, it distinguishes between the external world and an individual's perception of it and reasoning about it. It includes consideration of the processes that influence an individual's subjective representation of a decision problem and the computational strategies used in reasoning. By focusing on the processes by which aspects of reality are selectively noticed and taken as the basis for reasoning about action, behavioral decision theory examines what the actual representation, or frame, of the decision is, how that frame emerges from the decision situation, and how reasoning occurs within that frame. This consideration of the principles of perception and judgment that limit the rationality of choice, which is based on research in the laboratory and field at the micro level, provides a more accurate representation of human decision processes.

No single alternative theory explaining the observed violations of expected utility theory has yet emerged and been widely accepted in psychology or economics, but a number of simplifying rules and heuristics are recognized to produce framing effects that control the representation of options and give rise to nonlinearities of value and belief. In expected utility theory, alternatives are assumed to be evaluated in terms of their effect on final wealth levels. Mounting empirical evidence supports the alternative view that options are assessed in terms of gains and losses relative to some reference point, variously referred to as a *target* or *aspiration level* (Markowitz 1952; Simon 1955; Fishburn 1977; Kahneman and Tversky 1979; Payne et al. 1980, 1981; Holthausen 1981). A *return*, or *gain*, is defined in relation to "above target" probabilities and consequences and a loss in terms of "below target" probabilities and consequences. Assuming the existence of a reference point on the utility scale that plays a role in the nonlinear relationship between utility and objective value is consistent with empirical evidence that utility functions change significantly at a certain point, which is often (although not always) zero (Siegel 1957; Fishburn 1977; Payne et al. 1980, 1981; Holthausen 1981; Tversky and Kahneman 1986).

In Kahneman and Tversky's (1979) prospect theory, outcomes are expressed as positive or negative deviations (gains or losses) from a neutral reference outcome that is assigned a value of zero. An S-shaped value function is proposed, which is concave above the reference point and convex below it but less steep above than below. This function indicates that the effect of a marginal change decreases with the distance from the reference point in either direction but that the response to losses is more extreme than the response to gains. The asymmetry of the value function is in keeping with an empirically observed aversion to loss (Fishburn and Kochenberger 1979). In contrast to the assumption of uniformly concave (risk averse) utility functions in expected utility theory, risk-taking attitudes are different above versus below the reference point because perceived risk is primarily a function of the probability of loss or failure to achieve a target level of return (Fishburn 1977). Choices involving gains tend to be risk averse, whereas choices involving losses tend to be risk seeking—except when a small probability of winning or losing exists (Fishburn 1977; Tversky and Kahneman 1986). A ruinous loss may lead also to the screening out of an alternative from further consideration (Kahneman and Tversky 1979).

The reference point on an actor's utility scale, which defines whether an outcome is perceived as a gain or loss and therefore whether it brings satisfaction or dissatisfaction, is not static but changes with experience. People tend to raise their sights with success and to lower them with failure, and the stronger the success or failure, the greater the probability of a change in aspiration level (Child and Whiting 1954; Simon 1955; Starbuck 1963; also see Marrow 1969, pp. 44-5). Failure is particularly likely to lead to withdrawal by avoiding to set a level of aspiration (Child and Whiting 1954). The status quo (for example, current level of achievement) may be taken as an indicator of the reference point although the level of aspiration tends to be higher than the level of current achievement (Starbuck 1963). The level of aspiration is to a large degree socially determined. It is a "comparison level" influenced by the level of achievement of others whom the actor takes as referents.

In contrast to the holistic evaluation of alternatives assumed in expected utility theory, in which multidimensional alternatives are each assigned a separate utility level, decisions often appear to be made on a piecemeal basis by comparing alternatives one dimension at a time. Two approaches have been identified (Schoemaker 1982). In one, alternatives are compared according to a preset standard and are discarded if they do not meet that standard. A model is *conjunctive* if all attributes must meet minimum standards, and *disjunctive* if meeting the standard on at least one attribute is sufficient. In another approach, no preset standards are considered, but alternatives are compared directly in decomposed fashion. Tversky's (1972) theory of elimination by aspects describes *choice* as hierarchically structured, with selection made in stages on the basis of particular aspects on which objects of choice differ. The use of approaches of this type for initial screening is particularly likely when alternatives and dimensions are numerous.

In general, the decision strategy employed will vary with the complexity of the task.

In both economics and psychology, it has long been recognized that the utility, or value, function should be considered nonlinear. More recently, it also has been recognized that subjective probabilities relate nonlinearly to objective ones. Typically, low probabilities are overweighted, moderate and high probabilities are underweighted, and the latter effect is more pronounced than the former. A *certainty effect* also has been observed whereby outcomes obtained with certainty are given disproportionately more weight than those that are uncertain (Kahneman and Tversky 1979). Aspects of the decision situation influence assessments of probability. People tend to overestimate the probability of conjunctive events and to underestimate the probability of disjunctive events (Slovic 1969). Subjective probabilities also tend to be higher as outcomes become more desirable, reflecting a kind of wishful thinking and indicating that the level of reward, or payoff, can systematically affect assessments of probability. Prior experience of an event or information about its prior distribution will be taken into consideration although evidence exists that the representativeness of a current sample will be overweighted relative to prior information and that individuals overestimate the representativeness of small samples (Kahneman, Slovic, and Tversky 1982). Thus heuristics used in cognitive processing lead to systematic biases in the formation and manipulation of subjective probabilities.

Cognitive theories of decision making rest on models of bounded rationality rather than on utility maximization because psychological constraints are assumed to affect choice even if information is obtained easily. In many cases, discarding the assumption of utility maximization for the weaker assumption of procedural rationality does not affect the nontrivial conclusions that can be reached from models of purposive action (Simon 1987). In economics, however, utility maximization usually is assumed to occur in a competitive environment, where the actions of individuals are subject to feedback that forces them either to become effective or to withdraw from the market. Some history of learning and struggle for economic survival is assumed, and it is those who behave in accordance with rational choice principles who survive and keep the market efficient. Use of the optimization principle in this context is important for showing that a process has a unique optimum that is certain to be achieved. Economic theories of markets and ecological theories of competition are concerned with "efficient" processes that move rapidly to a unique solution, conditional on current environmental conditions. To the extent that equilibrium outcomes do not occur, the usefulness of the maximizing assumption in identifying a single optimum is questionable. Doubts about the validity of general equilibrium models have been raised by analyses showing that rational optimizing produces, at best, short-run partial solutions or solutions that are indeterminate or nonoptimal or, if determinate, impossible to achieve (Fusfield 1980; March and Olsen 1984).

In most applications of theories of purposive action, values (or preferences) are assumed to be not only exogenous to the choice process but stable, or unchanging (see, for example, Stigler and Becker 1977). In economics, the efficiency or Pareto optimality properties of general equilibrium models rest on the assumption of stable preferences. In the well-developed *revealed preference* version of the theory, assumptions about preferences are taken as axioms, and preferences are identified by a *revealed preference* function that satisfies the axioms and is consistent with choices made by the actor (Luce and Raiffa 1957). Preferences must be stable, and a consistent (and presumably perfect) relationship must exist between preferences and behavior for the theory to be testable because preferences are "revealed" by the actor's previous actions. Under the assumption that preferences are stable, previous choices can be taken as indicative of current and future preferences in settings presumed to be analogous. Change in the choices made by an actor then is attributed to relative price changes, and it is possible to predict future action from those price changes (Brennan 1990). Obvious problems with the revealed preference approach are that it fails to distinguish between attitudes (preferences) and behavior and to allow for the possibility of change in preferences or even a taste for variety. If people are assumed to choose what they value, and if what they value is revealed only by what they choose, a theory of purposive action is inherently tautological. It is a partial theory that cannot predict. The theory becomes useful only when motivational assumptions are made about what people value.

In some versions of the theory, preferences can change, but preference formation remains exogenous to choice and independent of the choice process. Choice itself does not generate a change in preferences. In applications in economics and political science, for example, the effects of information on changes in beliefs rather than changes in preferences are often considered. Variations in choice are attributed to change in access to information, with improved information increasing the "rationality" of choice. Experience provides information, which alters a person's knowledge of what he or she likes (for example, Cyert and DeGroot 1987). It is possible, however, that preferences themselves change and that this change can be endogenous to the choice process.

Models that allow for the possibility of endogenous change in preferences are of two basic types. One assumes that individuals know that their present choices will affect their future preferences (Strotz 1955-56). Actors are assumed to forecast long-term effects and discount returns on that basis. This approach raises the practical question of whether actors have the information, inclination, and cognitive ability to make such forward-looking calculations. It also raises technical problems about the consistency, existence, and stability of plans and choices over time (von Weizsäcker 1971; March 1978). For example, even if it is assumed that preferences to be held at every relevant future time are known and are consistent at any given time, allowing for change in preferences raises the problem of intertemporal comparison of preferences, which is technically similar to the problem of interpersonal comparison of utilities (March 1978; Cohen and Axelrod 1984). The same approaches developed to deal with interpersonal comparisons can be brought to bear, but these allow for a weaker solution than is possible under the assumption of a single, unchanging set of preferences. If it is assumed that the way in which actions taken now and the way in which the consequences of those actions will affect future preferences are known, actors can be seen as choosing their future preferences now and, if risk is involved, as choosing a probability distribution over future preferences. One attempt to make this problem tractable has been to assume some "super goal" and to evaluate alternative preferences in relation to it (March 1978).

Given the heroic assumptions about human capabilities required by this approach, an alternative *naive behavior* approach has emerged, which does not assume that the actor knows how current choices will influence future preferences. Experience resulting from current choices and from other environmental influences is assumed to provide information that affects future beliefs and preferences in an ongoing process of adaptation, or learning, that need not be conscious (von Weizsäcker 1971; Cohen and Axelrod 1984; Macy 1990). Positive reinforcement increases the preference for a behavior, whereas negative reinforcement decreases the preference although in some models it is the difference between expected and experienced utility to which the utility function adapts (for example, Cohen and Axelrod 1984). Decision is followed by feedback and course correction in a complex and uncertain environment that gives rise to a stochastic process in which the initial starting state and random events early in the process can have an important effect on long-term trajectories and produce multiple equilibria (Arthur et al. 1987; Arthur 1988). Because of the importance of small events and chance occurrences early in the process in determining long-term equilibrium behavior, which of a potentially large number of equilibria will emerge cannot be predicted in advance, and it cannot be assumed that the equilibrium actually reached is of maximum possible benefit.

Most applications of theories of purposive action have not only ignored the possibility of change in preferences but have tended to assume the existence of clear prior purpose as reflected in a complete and consistent set of preferences. Such terms as *preferences, tastes, values,* and *goals* are used interchangeably and are treated as reducible into a single ordering. It is likely, however, that some values, such as those internalized in childhood that become part of an individual's cognitive structure, are relatively stable (Glenn 1980; Sears 1983), whereas other preferences, lacking in symbolic or affective content, that are not tied to cognitive structure may be more open to change (Alwin Forthcoming). Distinguishing between internalized values and normative beliefs that are relatively unchanging and preferences that are more susceptible to ongoing revision in response to environmental influences requires a deeper understanding of what we refer to as *values, goals, preferences, wants,* and *desires.*

Despite evidence that the limited availability of information and the limited information-processing capacity of human beings render the expected utility models axiomatized by von Neumann and Morgenstern (1944) and Savage (1954) an inaccurate description of the process of decision making, it has been argued by economists and sociologists that the rational choice model remains useful for predicting aggregate level outcomes (Friedman 1953; Plott 1986; Coleman 1990; Cook and O'Brien 1990; Lindenberg 1990). In his famous essay on the methodology of "positive science," Friedman (1953) argued that a theory should be tested on the basis of its predictive ability and that the descriptive validity, or realism, of its assumptions was unimportant. As an economist, he believed that the correctness of the assumptions of expected utility theory could not be empirically tested in a direct way and that the only valid test was whether the assumptions led to tolerably correct predictions at the aggregate level. In this view, the important question is whether the magnitude of error in the predictions of aggregate phenomena is acceptable. If no concept of degree of acceptability is available, interest focuses on whether the model offers higher predictive accuracy than competing models. Most scientists agree with Friedman on the importance of prediction, but many give little weight to other aspects of his argument. The idea that the assumptions of expected utility theory cannot be tested directly would be true only if micro level behavior could not be observed directly, and an extensive body of research on the process of decision making by psychologists does just that. The idea that prediction is all that matters is also epistemologically unappealing because explanation is accorded a high priority in science. It is only by distinguishing genuine causes from noncausal associations—that is, by explaining the occurrence of events—that intervention for the production of desired effects is possible. Even if a misspecified model is demonstrated to have predictive power, one is interested to determine why.

Given the distribution of resources and interests among actors, the postulate that human action is purposive does not imply that aggregate level behavior patterns are affected only by the purposive actions of actors and therefore exist for a "rational" reason or represent a social optimum. Historical accident and randomness can play an important role in producing evolutionarily stable outcomes that are not optimal (Fusfield 1980; March and Olsen 1984; Arthur et al. 1987; Arthur 1988; Abbott 1990). The optimization principle has been popular in micro level theories of action in large part because it has been used to show that under certain conditions a process has a unique optimum that is guaranteed to be achieved. But as noted above, processes with multiple equilibria are easily specified and frequently observed. The functioning of a system at one time, including the effects of chance, influences the structure of the system and therefore its functioning at a later time. These intertemporal relationships produce a specific historical path because the chance fluctuations of history change the baselines on which the process operates at a later point in time. As Arthur and his colleagues (Arthur et al. 1987; Arthur 1988) have shown, path-dependent systems of the self-reinforcing type have multiple possible equilibria, and early random fluctuations determine which one of the multiple equilibria emerges. If one of several possible candidates for the emergence of a long-run stable pattern gets off to a good start by chance, its attractiveness and the probability that it will be chosen are increased, thereby reinforcing its early advantage and making it likely to become "locked in" as the long-run pattern. Examples of this are evident in the emergence of technological structure, during which several new technologies compete for shares of a market of potential adopters and small events early on become self-reinforcing, causing an inferior technology to win the market and become locked in. In a similar way, historical accident and chance events can cause aspects of social structure to become locked in. This possibility, of course, reminds us of the logical fallacy of a functionalist line of argument (Hempel 1965, Chap. 11). The fact that an existing social arrangement serves a function does not mean that it is the only social arrangement that could have emerged to serve that function. Similarly unless it can be proved that a process is not path-dependent—that is, that a process is not one in which events at one point in time condition events at a later time by producing changes in the baselines on which the process operates—it cannot be assumed that even behavior that conforms to the optimizing principle at the micro level will lead to the emergence of a social optimum over the long run.

THE SOCIAL ORIGIN
OF VALUES AND BELIEFS

Theories of purposive action do not in themselves specify the actual values and beliefs individuals hold, and they have nothing to say about the origin of those values and beliefs. They merely advance the postulate that human action is goal directed. They are theories about the way people, given their values and beliefs, make choices. To be capable of predicting action, the postulate of purposive action must be linked to a set of auxiliary assumptions about the values and beliefs of actors. These substantive assumptions, along with the postulate of purposive action, are necessary premises. To date, a major problem with the application of models of purposive action, particularly in such fields as economics and political science, in which the primary interest has been in aggregate level outcomes, is that the postulate of purposive action has been linked to arbitrary and narrow assumptions about what individuals value and believe. For example, it is commonly assumed that individuals seek to maximize their own self-interest (often operationalized as wealth). This assumption ignores the role of socialization in instilling values that promote action on behalf of others, as well as the role of emotions in prompting such action. The assumption that human behavior is narrowly self-interested and the use of the term *rationality* to refer to the efficient pursuit of economic ends have led to the incorrect assumption by many that theories of purposive action are inherently egoistic— that they regard individuals as calculating the expected benefit to themselves of alternative lines of action and acting accordingly. Correcting this problem requires an empirical basis for bringing independent knowledge of what individuals value and believe to bear, as well as knowledge of the way in which values and beliefs conjoin with environmental events to trigger emotions. Only when the postulate that human action is purposive is used in conjunction with knowledge or well-reasoned hypotheses about what people value and the alternatives they perceive to be available can an intentional explanation be useful in explaining and predicting human behavior. It is an important task of sociology to provide that knowledge and to account for the origin of values and beliefs through knowledge of the culture and structure of societies and the individual's cumulative knowledge and experience within society. The alternative actions among which actors choose derive from a socially structured set of opportunities. Choices among alternative actions are made on the basis of the outcomes expected to ensue from such action, to which the actor attaches some value and that the actor expects with some probability. Because rewards and costs are associated with each alternative, the finite resources of the actor constrain the possible choices. Action often results not from a conscious weighing of the expected future benefits of alternative lines of action but from a less deliberate response to values internalized through the socializing influences of society or experience in particular relationships (Emerson 1976, 1987; Macy 1990).

An extensive body of evidence indicates that human beings are capable not only occasionally but routinely of acting in ways that place the interests of particular others or the social group above their own self-interest (Staub 1978; Eisenberg 1986; Clary and Miller 1986). Virtually all explanations of such altruism assume that it is to a large degree a socialized behavior resulting from influences early in life that affect cognitive structure (see, for example, Scott 1971; Eisenberg 1986). To the extent that social norms and values, including those emphasizing not only the rights and interests of others but love and responsibility for others, become central elements of cognitive organization internalized early in life, they provide a guiding rubric that remains relatively stable (Bengston 1975; Jennings and Niemi 1981; Smith 1983; Clary and Miller 1986; Sears and Funk 1990).

Social norms and values promoting the well-being of others and the social collectivity are part of the content of culture transmitted from one generation to another. Via socialization, human beings become aware of and internalize social values and norms, which in turn become important determinants of the value attached to outcomes associated with alternative lines of action. A social norm is a collective evaluation of what behavior ought to be. It usually indicates what should or should not be done by particular types of actors in specific circumstances. When a social norm is known to have been violated, some type of formal or informal sanction will result. When the norm is embodied in a legal code or a set of rules to which penalties are explicitly attached, a formal sanction will result. When the norm is embodied in rules of etiquette or other nonlegal rules, an informal sanction, such as disapproval or social ostracism, will result. A social *value* is a collective standard of desirability that is more independent of specific situations. Because qualitatively different outcomes have relative value, values are arranged in a hierarchy of importance that implies a preference order. *Social* norms and values, in contrast to *personal,* or *internalized*, norms and values, are defined by the fact that they are collective, or shared. This collective property is demonstrated by a high level of consensus in a population or population subgroup. Because social norms and values cannot be defined by reference to a single individual, they are macro level characteristics.

Coleman (1990) has argued that demand for a social norm arises when an action has externalities, or consequences, for actors who do not control the action. Although he has focused on the emergence of informal norms, which he distinguishes from legal norms in an effort to explain why norms emerge and govern behavior in situations in which obedience to the law is not a motivation, demand for both informal and legal norms can be seen as arising when an action has externalities for actors who do not control the action. The externalities arise from the interdependence of actions in the social structure, and in the case of a "disjoint" norm, in which targets and beneficiaries of the norm differ, the distribution of rights and resources determines who can impose a norm because it is actors with more power who are able to impose a disjoint norm on the actions of those with less power.

Some social values are highly general and display considerable stability across societies both historically and at the present time (Schwartz and Bilsky 1987, 1990; Campbell 1988). For example, it is the essential function of the world's religions to promote the development of human potential and happiness through the experience of oneness and harmony with other individuals and the universe. This is accomplished through the conquering of egoistic desires and entry into a higher plane of being where one experiences connection to others and the physical world. To enter this higher plane, one must take the interests of others and the social group as one's own. Although this religious message often is obscured by the myths used to communicate it and can be perverted by the social and political agendas of religious organizations, it is the primary social value that undergirds religious teaching and moral philosophy.

Internalization of Social Norms and Values

Human beings internalize social norms and values to varying degrees. An individual's personal norms and values reflect the social norms and values of the society and the various subgroups within that society to which the individual is exposed, particularly (although not exclusively) during the early stages of the life course. Once social norms and values are internalized, they can direct the behavior of individuals irrespective of external influences. Internalized norms and values are a source of self-expectations that help determine the neutral point, or "comparison level," for the individual on the scale of pleasure and pain, satisfaction and dissatisfaction, associated with an outcome. They therefore become bases of self-evaluation, with the reward or sanction ensuing from an outcome being tied to the self-concept (Schwartz 1977). Adherence to self-expectations enhances self-esteem, producing a sense of pride and other favorable self-evaluations. Violation of self-expectations, or even its anticipation, reduces self-esteem, producing guilt, self-deprecation, and other negative self-evaluations. To preserve a sense of self-worth and to avoid negative self-evaluations, individuals seek to behave in ways consistent with their internalized norms and values. Internalized norms take on the role of what we colloquially call *conscience*, or what Freud ([1923] 1950) called the *superego*.

Decisions that involve consideration of internalized norms and values are irrational in the sense that they do not optimize external reinforcements for action (Schwartz 1977). In fact, it is the tendency of sociologists to see internalized norms and values as an important influence on human behavior that makes them see the social norms and values of society as governing, or constraining, the choices individuals make. Because individuals behave purposefully when they behave in accordance with their internalized norms and values, they may take action to promote the welfare of others at what appears to be considerable cost to themselves. At the time of its occurrence, this altruism need not be based on an attachment to those being helped, as discussed by Becker (1981), but may be to the benefit of strangers and derive from the individual's values and beliefs. For example, values and norms that are internalized early in life and that shape perceptions of what is in the public interest not only compete with but often overwhelm self-interest (direct personal benefit) as a determinant of policy preferences and voting (Lau et al. 1978; Sears et al. 1980; Cataldo and Holm 1983; Sears and Lau 1983). Although modern economists have tended to eschew consideration of such internal motivating

factors, Adam Smith ([1759] 1976), today regarded by most as the
founder of economics, saw internalized norms and values as play-
ing an important role in the determination of human behavior:

> It is not the soft power of humanity, it is not the feeble spark of benevolence
> which Nature has lighted up in the human heart, that is thus capable of
> counteracting the strongest impulses of self-love. . . . It is a stronger love, a
> more powerful affection, which generally takes place upon such occasions;
> the love of what is honorable and noble, of the grandeur, and dignity, and
> superiority of our own characters. (pp. 234-35)

> Nature . . . has not . . . abandoned us entirely to the delusions of self-love. Our
> continual observations upon the conduct of others insensibly lead us to form
> to ourselves certain general rules concerning what is fit and proper either to
> be done or to be avoided. . . . The regard to those general rules of conduct is
> what is properly called a sense of duty, a principle of the greatest conse-
> quence in human life, and the only principle by which the bulk of mankind
> are capable of directing their actions. (pp. 263-64, 269)

This view is maintained by most sociologists and psychologists,
who regard human action as attributable at least in part to internalized norms and values.

Norms and values are internalized through both observational
learning by an actor and direct attempts to teach and bring about
internalization by other actors. *Observational learning* occurs when
an actor observes the behavior of others and uses them as models for
behavior. Those likely to be adopted as models are other actors in
close proximity who are perceived to be attractive. One of the
factors affecting the attractiveness of another actor as a model is
the other actor's power relative to the actor, or the actor's dependence on the other actor. Thus children are particularly likely to
adopt their parents as models, and prisoners often internalize the
views of their captors.

Direct attempts by others to influence an actor play an important role in the internalization of social norms and values
(Maccoby and Martin 1983). Because the preservation of society
depends on both physical and social reproduction, it is in the
interest of the collectivity to transmit social norms and values that
preserve order and promote economic viability. Social norms and
values that encourage investment in parenting therefore tend to
be among those transmitted from generation to generation. These
norms and values bring parents social status for the inputs they

make to the parenting process (observation by others that they are caring for their children properly and well) and for the success of their children (e.g., see Nock and Rossi 1979 for evidence of the effect of children's success on the status of parents in the United States). Thus parents are motivated to invest in the internalization of norms and values in children by both the internal reward they receive from behaving in accordance with their own internalized norms and values and the external reward they receive from others who have internalized the same norms and values.

In the absence of direct personal benefit to the individual, benefit to the collectivity is unlikely to be sufficient to generate and maintain social norms and values that promote responsible parenting. Other benefits to parents are likely to be necessary. Prior to industrialization, the bearing and rearing of children was advantageous to parents because of the labor children provided for the family unit. However, direct reliance on the labor of children declined after industrialization, and even the importance of economic transfers from children to parents has been reduced by old-age security programs. In advanced industrial societies, it is the nonmaterial benefits of children to parents that are likely to motivate investment in parenting. These nonmaterial benefits include love, respect, companionship, stimulation, and the sense of meaning and fulfillment that comes vicariously through the achievements of children and the link they provide to posterity. All of these nonmaterial benefits are enhanced when social norms and values are internalized in children. Internalization of norms and values in children also has the short-term benefit of making life easier for parents because children who become increasingly self-regulating in a way that is approved of by parents require less parental control.

Investment in the internalization of norms and values in children is likely to be affected by a number of factors. One is the amount of external control that parents and other adults have over a child's future. The less the external control, or authority, that adults have over such things as the choice of a spouse, the inheritance of land, and the access to specific occupations, the more important internalization of norms and values becomes to directing the child's future. It is likely to be particularly important to parents of higher social status because it is the primary means by which they can transmit their advantaged position in society to their children.

A second factor affecting parental investment in the internalization of norms and values in children is the extent to which the social environment facilitates or impedes parental socialization. Parental investment is more important when children receive varied socializing inputs from the environment. The more heterogeneous the society and the lower the degree of normative and value consensus, the more likely that socializing influences outside the family will not be congruent with the messages communicated by parents. Similarly the less time parents spend with children relative to the time children spend with other socializing agents, the more diverse the socializing messages that children receive are likely to be. To the degree that social networks are unstable or lack closure, parents will be less able to rely on other adults to monitor their children's behavior. Thus the social environment in which children are raised influences the importance of parental efforts at the internalization of social norms and values for bringing about child outcomes in the interest of parents.

A third factor influencing the extent to which parents will invest in the internalization of norms and values in children is the extent to which children are the primary or only source of material and nonmaterial support for parents—that is, the degree to which parents are dependent on their children for survival and comfort. If parents have other sources of support and satisfaction that compete with children for their interest and time, parents will be less dependent on child outcomes for the satisfaction of their own needs and will therefore invest less to secure child outcomes that serve their interests.

A fourth factor influencing parental investment in the internalization of norms and values in children is the extent to which the parent expects return on the investment. If a parent is distant from the child as a result of divorce or other factors that interfere with a close relationship, there will be little incentive to invest in the child because the outcome is of little consequence to the parent. In fact, to the extent that such investment is seen as benefitting an estranged spouse, there will be a disincentive to invest in the socialization of that spouse's children.

All norms and values are not the object of attempts at internalization. These attempts are directed primarily at long-term, general norms and values and those that are specific to major social roles. They are unlikely to be directed at norms that emerge only in specific situations at specific times. Long-term, general norms are likely to be legal norms or norms imbued with moral significance although they also may be norms indicating what is proper. The influence of long-term, general norms and values on behavior therefore occurs via both internalization and external social pressure, whereas situation-specific norms and values emerging at specific times influence behavior primarily via external pressure.

Other factors influence the likelihood that attempts to bring about the internalization of norms and values will be successful. Once such factor is the developmental age of the individual being socialized, because evidence indicates that the internalization of at least some types of norms proceeds by developmental stages early in the life course. These internalized norms become part of the individual's enduring cognitive structure. Internalization occurs when effective efforts are made to bring it about and the child has the capacity to absorb the input.

Success at the internalization of norms and values is affected also by parental knowledge of effective methods of childrearing. Setting clear and sometimes stringent requirements for mature behavior and enforcing those demands are effective strategies when accompanied by parental affection, responsiveness to the child's needs, and open communication (Maccoby and Martin 1983). Knowledge and skill at effective parenting therefore have an important effect on the success of efforts to internalize social norms and values.

External Pressure to Comply
With Social Norms and Values

Social norms and values influence the choices human beings make not only because they are internalized and affect the value attached to outcomes associated with alternative actions but also because social norms and values are internalized by "significant others" and thereby affect the actor's perception of others' expectations. To the extent that actors are motivated to comply with what they perceive the views of others to be, social norms and values may become a source of external pressure exerting an independent influence on the utility expected to be derived from an action. As described by Fishbein and Ajzen (1975), external *normative pressures* are a function of (a) the actor's perception that specific referent individuals or groups think the actor should or should not perform the behavior in question and (b) the actor's motivation to comply with those expectations. These investigators suggest weighting the perceived expectations of each reference group or individual by the actor's motivation to comply with that group or individual. Thus for each action, A_i,

$$A_i = \sum_{k=1}^{K} b_{ik} m_{ik},$$

where b_{ik} is the actor's belief that reference group or individual k thinks he or she should or should not perform action A_i, m_{ik} is the motivation to comply with referent k, and K is the number of relevant referents. The actor's motivation to comply with any referent can be affected by characteristics of the referent, the relationship of the referent to the actor, and personality characteristics of the actor.

Normative Implications

Economists have argued that the rational choice model is useful as a "normative" theory, or a prescriptive theory providing guidelines for action. Just as rational choice theory is incapable of predicting action unless the postulate of purposive action is linked to a set of auxiliary assumptions about what actors value and believe, the rational choice model is incapable of performing as a normative theory of action unless an auxiliary basis exists for assuming that the ends being pursued "rationally" are good. Rational choice theory focuses on calculative mechanisms and can be at most a prescriptive theory of *calculation*. Because behaving in accordance with the axioms of rational choice theory is "good" in a larger sense only if the ends being pursued rationally are good, rational choice theory is not itself a prescriptive theory of *action* (Brennan 1990).

CONCLUSIONS

Models of purposive action in the social sciences have evolved considerably since the axiomatization of expected utility theory led to adoption of the rational choice paradigm in economics. Now considerable evidence exists that choice behavior does not always conform to the assumptions of the expected utility model, leading psychologists and even some economists to propose alternative models of purposive action. In real decision-making situations, the individual often must consider alternatives sequentially and decide about them as they are presented. In such situations, the individual will satisfice (choose the first satisfactory alternative) rather than maximize, and it is only as the number of alternatives perceived simultaneously increases that the satisficing model converges to a maximizing solution. Even if information is obtained easily, evidence that psychological constraints affect choice has caused psychologists to abandon the assumption of utility maximization in favor of a model of bounded rationality.

In many cases, discarding the assumption of utility maximization for the weaker assumption of procedural rationality does not affect the usefulness of models of purposive action. The rational choice paradigm has been used often as a heuristic device that requires the investigator to take the position of the actor and to consider the alternative courses of action available. Rewards and costs are associated with each alternative, and the finite resources of the actor constrain the choices possible. In focusing attention on explanatory mechanisms and providing a basis for reasoning that is internally consistent and avoids possible logical inconsistencies, this paradigm has been useful. Now a broad class of models of purposive action exists within which the problematic assumptions of expected utility theory can be relaxed.

Of particular importance to sociology is the fact that theories of purposive action do not in themselves specify the actual values and beliefs held by actors and have nothing to say about the origin of those values and beliefs. They merely advance the postulate that human action is goal directed. They are theories about the way people, given their values and beliefs, make choices. Without additional information about what individuals value and believe (which in many applications has been provided only by assumption), it is impossible for models of purposive action to predict, let alone explain, behavior. An important task of sociology is to provide empirical evidence about individual values and beliefs and to account for the origin of values and beliefs through knowledge of the culture and structure of societies and the individual's cumulative knowledge and experience within society.

Within sociology, models of purposive action are best viewed as part of a larger whole. They permit direct connections to be made between the characteristics of social systems and the behavior of individual actors (the macro-micro connection) and between the behavior of individual actors and systemic outcomes that emerge from the combined actions of multiple actors (the micro-macro connection). Except in rare circumstances, however, a single model of purposive action cannot simultaneously bridge more than two levels of social organization. Although a model of purposive action can be used at any level because the actors can be corporate bodies rather than individual persons, the outcomes predicted usually will bridge the elementary units in the model to only one higher level of social organization. As a result, many macro level phenomena, particularly those occurring at the organizational, national, and international levels, cannot be predicted by models of purposive action in which the elementary units are individual persons. Moreover, some macro level phenomena can be understood only at the macro level, with individuals entering the explanation as members of populations with certain characteristics. It would be a mistake to assume that all aggregate level behavior patterns arise through the purposive actions of actors and therefore exist for a reason or represent a social optimum, given the distribution of resources and interests among actors, because historical accident and randomness can play an important role in producing evolutionarily stable outcomes that are not optimal.

REFERENCES

Abbott, Andrew. 1990. "Comment: Stinchcombe's 'Reason and Rationality'. " Pp. 317-23 in *The Limits of Rationality*, edited by C. S. Cook and M. Levi. Chicago: University of Chicago Press.

Alwin, Duane F. Forthcoming. "Aging, Personality, and Social Change." In *Life-Span Development and Behavior*. Vol. 12, edited by D. L. Featherman, R. M. Lerner, and M. Perlmutter. Hillsdale, NJ: Lawrence Erlbaum.

Arthur, W. Brian. 1988. "Self-Reinforcing Mechanisms in Economics." Pp. 9-31 in *The Economy as an Evolving Complex System*, edited by P. W. Anderson, K. J. Arrow, and D. Pines. Reading, MA: Addison-Wesley.

Arthur, W. Brian, Yu. M. Ermoliev, and Yu. M. Kaniovski. 1987. "Path-Dependent Processes and the Emergence of Macro-Structure." *European Journal of Operational Research* 30:294-303.

Becker, Gary S. 1981. *A Treatise on the Family*. Cambridge, MA: Harvard University Press.

Bengston, Vern L. 1975. "Generation and Family Effects in Value Socialization." *American Sociological Review* 40:358-71.

Brennan, Geoffrey. 1990. "Comment: What Might Rationality Fail to Do?" Pp. 51-9 in *The Limits of Rationality*, edited by K. S. Cook and M. Levi. Chicago: University of Chicago Press.

Campbell, Joseph with Bill Moyers. 1988. *The Power of Myth*, edited by B. S. Flowers. New York: Doubleday.

Cataldo, Everett F. and John D. Holm. 1983. "Voting on School Finances: A Test of Competing Theories." *Western Political Quarterly* 36:617-31.

Child, I. L. and J. W. M. Whiting. 1954. "Determinants of Level of Aspiration: Evidence From Everyday Life." Pp. 495-508 in *The Study of Personality*, edited by H. Brand. New York: John Wiley.

Clary, E. Gil and Jude Miller. 1986. "Socialization and Situational Influences on Sustained Altruism." *Child Development* 57:1358-69.

Cohen, Michael D. and Robert Axelrod. 1984. "Coping With Complexity: The Adaptive Value of Changing Utility." *American Economic Review* 74:30-42.

Coleman, James S. 1986. "Social Theory, Research, and the Theory of Action." *American Journal of Sociology* 91:1309-35.

———. 1990. *Foundations of Social Theory*. Cambridge, MA: Harvard University Press.

Cook, Karen S. and Jodi A. O'Brien. 1990. "Individual Decision Making Versus Market-Level Predictions: The Applicability of Rational Choice Theory." Pp. 175-88 in *The Limits of Rationality*, edited by K. S. Cook and M. Levi. Chicago: University of Chicago Press.

Cyert, Richard M. and Morris H. DeGroot. 1987. *Bayesian Analysis and Uncertainty in Economic Theory*. Totowa, NJ: Rowman and Littlefield.

Eisenberg, Nancy. 1986. *Altruistic Emotion, Cognition, and Behavior*. Hillsdale, NJ: Lawrence Erlbaum.

Emerson, Richard M. 1976. "Social Exchange Theory." *Annual Review of Sociology* 2:335-62.

———. 1987. "Toward a Theory of Value in Social Exchange." Pp. 11-45 in *Social Exchange Theory*, edited by K. S. Cook. Newbury Park, CA: Sage.

Fishbein, Martin and Icek Ajzen. 1975. *Belief, Attitude, Intention and Behavior: An Introduction to Theory and Research*. Reading, MA: Addison-Wesley.

Fishburn, Peter C. 1977. "Mean-Risk Analysis With Risk Associated With Below-Target Returns." *American Economic Review* 67:116-26.

Fishburn, Peter C. and Gary A. Kochenberger. 1979. "Two-Piece Von Neumann-Morgenstern Utility Functions." *Decision Sciences* 10:503-18.

Freud, Sigmund. [1923] 1950. *The Ego and the Id.* London: Hogarth.

Friedman, Milton. 1953. *Essays in Positive Economics.* Chicago: University of Chicago Press.

Fusfield, Daniel R. 1980. "The Conceptual Framework of Modern Economics." *Journal of Economic Issues* 14:1-52.

Glenn, Norval D. 1980. "Values, Attitudes and Beliefs." Pp. 596-640 in *Constancy and Change in Human Development,* edited by O. G. Brim, Jr., and Jerome Kagan. Cambridge, MA: Harvard University Press.

Hechter, Michael. 1987. *Principles of Group Solidarity.* Berkeley: University of California Press.

Hempel, Carl G. 1965. *Aspects of Scientific Explanation.* New York: Free Press.

Holthausen, Duncan M. 1981. "A Risk-Return Model With Risk and Return Measured as Deviations From a Target Return." *American Economic Review* 71:182-88.

Jennings, M. Kent and Richard G. Niemi. 1981. *Generations and Politics.* Princeton, NJ: Princeton University Press.

Kahneman, Daniel, Paul Slovic, and Amos Tversky. 1982. *Judgement Under Uncertainty: Heuristics and Biases.* Cambridge, UK: Cambridge University Press.

Kahneman, Daniel and Amos Tversky. 1979. "Prospect Theory: An Analysis of Decision Under Risk." *Econometrica* 47:263-91.

Lau, Richard R., Thad A. Brown, and David O. Sears. 1978. "Self-Interest and Citizens' Attitudes Toward the Vietnam War." *Public Opinion Quarterly* 42:467-83.

Lindenberg, Siegwart. 1990. "*Homo socio-economicus:* The Emergence of a General Model of Man in the Social Sciences." *Journal of Institutional and Theoretical Economics* 146:727-48.

Luce, R. Duncan and Howard Raiffa. 1957. *Games and Decisions.* New York: John Wiley.

Maccoby, Eleanor E. and John A. Martin. 1983. "Socialization in the Context of the Family: Parent-Child Interaction." Pp. 1-101 in *Handbook of Child Psychology,* edited by P. H. Mussen, Volume IV edited by E. M. Hetherington. New York: John Wiley.

Machina, Mark J. 1987. "Choice Under Uncertainty: Problems Solved and Unsolved." *Journal of Economic Perspectives* 1:121-54.

Macy, Michael W. 1990. "Learning Theory and the Logic of Critical Mass." *American Sociological Review* 55:809-26.

March, James G. 1978. "Bounded Rationality, Ambiguity, and the Engineering of Choice." *Bell Journal of Economics* 9:587-608.

March, James G. and Johan P. Olsen. 1984. "The New Institutionalism: Organizational Factors in Political Life." *American Political Science Review* 78:734-49.

Markowitz, Harry M. 1952. "The Utility of Wealth." *Journal of Political Economy* 60:151-58.

Marrow, A. J. 1969. *The Practical Theorist: The Life and Work of Kurt Lewin.* New York: Basic Books.

Nock, Steven L. and Peter H. Rossi. 1979. "Household Types and Social Standing." *Social Forces* 57:1325-45.

Payne, John W., Dan J. Laughhunn, and Roy Chum. 1980. "Translation of Gambles and Aspiration Level Effects in Risky Choice Behavior." *Management Science* 26:1039-60.

―――. 1981. "Further Tests of Aspiration Level Effects in Risky Choice Behavior." *Management Science* 27:953-58.

Plott, Charles R. 1986. "Rational Choice in Experimental Markets." *Journal of Business* 59:301-27.

Savage, Leonard J. 1954. *The Foundations of Statistics.* New York: John Wiley.

Schoemaker, Paul J. H. 1982. "The Expected Utility Model: Its Variants, Purposes, Evidence and Limitations." *Journal of Economic Literature* 10:529-63.

Schwartz, Shalom H. 1977. "Normative Influences on Altruism." Pp. 221-79 in *Advances in Experimental Social Psychology,* edited by L. Berkowitz. New York: Academic Press.

Schwartz, Shalom H. and Wolfgang Bilsky. 1987. "Toward a Universal Psychological Structure of Human Values." *Journal of Personality and Social Psychology* 53:550-62.

―――. 1990. "Toward a Theory of the Universal Content and Structure of Values: Extensions and Cross-Cultural Replications." *Journal of Personality and Social Psychology* 58:878-91.

Scott, John Finley. 1971. *Internalization of Norms: A Sociological Theory of Moral Commitment.* Englewood Cliffs, NJ: Prentice-Hall.

Sears, David O. 1983. "The Persistence of Early Political Predispositions: The Role of Attitude Object and Life Stage." Pp. 79-116 in *Review of Personality and Social Psychology.* Vol. 4, edited by L. Wheeler. Beverly Hills, CA: Sage.

Sears, David O. and Carolyn L. Funk. 1990. "The Persistence and Crystallization of Political Attitudes Over the Life-Span: The Terman Gifted Children Panel." Unpublished manuscript.

Sears, David O. and Richard R. Lau. 1983. "Inducing Apparently Self-Interested Political Preferences." *American Journal of Political Science* 27:223-52.

Sears, David O., Richard R. Lau, Tom R. Tyler, and Harris M. Allen, Jr. 1980. "Self-Interest vs. Symbolic Politics in Policy Attitudes and Presidential Voting." *American Political Science Review* 74:670-84.

Siegel, Sidney. 1957. "Level of Aspiration and Decision Making." *Psychological Review* 64:253-62.

Simon, Herbert A. 1955. "A Behavioral Model of Rational Choice." *Quarterly Journal of Economics* 69:99-118.

―――. 1979. "Rational Decision Making in Business Organizations." *American Economic Review* 69:493-513.

―――. 1987. "Rationality in Psychology and Economics." Pp. 25-40 in *Rational Choice: The Contrast Between Economics and Psychology,* edited by R. M. Hogarth and M. W. Reder. Chicago: University of Chicago Press.

Slovic, Paul. 1969. "Differential Effects of Real Versus Hypothetical Payoffs on Choices Among Gambles." *Journal of Experimental Psychology* 80:434-37.

Smith, Adam. [1759] 1976. *The Theory of Moral Sentiments.* Indianapolis: Liberty Classics.

Smith, Thomas Ewin. 1983. "Parental Influence: A Review of the Evidence of Influence and a Theoretical Model of the Parental Influence Process." Pp.

13-45 in *Research in Sociology of Education and Socialization*. Vol. 4, edited by A. Kerckhoff. Greenwich, CT: JAI.

Starbuck, William H. 1963. "Level of Aspiration Theory and Economic Behavior." *Behavioral Science* 8:128-36.

Staub, Ervin. 1978. *Positive Social Behavior and Morality*. Vol. 1, *Social and Personal Influences*. New York: Academic Press.

Stigler, George J. and Gary S. Becker. 1977. "De Gustibus Non Est Disputandum." *American Economic Review* 67:76-90.

Strotz, Robert H. 1955-56. "Myopia and Inconsistency in Dynamic Utility Maximization." *Review of Economic Studies* 23:165-80.

Tversky, Amos. 1972. "Choice by Elimination." *Journal of Mathematical Psychology* 9:341-67.

Tversky, Amos and Daniel Kahneman. 1981. "The Framing of Decisions and the Psychology of Choice." *Science* 211:453-58.

———. 1986. "Rational Choice and the Framing of Decisions." *Journal of Business* 59:251-78.

von Neumann, John and Osker Morgenstern. 1944. *Theory of Games and Economic Behavior*. Princeton, NJ: Princeton University Press.

von Weizsäcker, Carl Christian. 1971. "Notes on Endogenous Change of Tastes." *Journal of Economic Theory* 3:345-72.

Chapter 3

THE PRINCIPLE OF RATIONAL CHOICE AND THE PROBLEM OF A SATISFACTORY THEORY

DAVID WILLER
University of South Carolina

INTRODUCTION

I WILL CLAIM IN THIS CHAPTER that *elementary theory* is a satisfactory rational choice theory. It is satisfactory in that it does what Coleman suggests that such a theory must do; that is, it explains social system behavior in terms of actors' behavior, connecting the two theoretically while modeling the sources of individual action (Coleman 1990a). It also makes predictions and has been experimentally tested. I will get to those issues later.

Something should be said about elementary theory for those previously unacquainted with it. The term *elementary* refers first to Einstein's famous maxim that theories should be composed of elements as simple and few in number as possible ([1934] 1954, p. 272) and second to the ease with which the theory is used. The elementary theory (ET) has three components: principles, laws, and a procedure for modeling social phenomena. In fact, physical theories have these same three components (Toulmin 1953). Elsewhere the three have been presented and applied to a variety of

AUTHOR'S NOTE: Grant #-SES 9010888 from the National Science Foundation supported research and development of the elementary theory. Thanks to James S. Coleman for helpful suggestions.

problems. (cf. Willer and Anderson 1981; Willer 1984, 1985, 1987; Markovsky et al. 1988; Willer and Markovsky 1991.) I introduce the three components and some of their uses in a number of applications below.

Rather paradoxically, if ET is a satisfactory rational choice theory, it is so to the extent that it avoids assumptions often made by rational choice theorists. Perhaps more accurately, it avoids the assumptions of the economic approach. According to Becker, those assumptions are "maximizing behavior, market equilibrium and stable preferences" (1976, p. 5). The first assumption postulates rationality as explanatory of behavior. I discuss this under the *rationality question*. The second assumption treats all social structures as if they were markets at or near equilibrium. I discuss this under the *structure issue*. The third assumption treats all people everywhere as having the same stable preference structure. I treat this under the *value problem*.

Those acquainted with Olson (1965) or Buchanan and Tollison (1972, 1984) recognize that much of value can be done under Becker's assumptions. I will not attempt to show that the economic approach precludes a fully satisfactory rational choice theory; that is, I will not attempt to show that Becker cannot satisfy Coleman. Instead I will show that none of the three assumptions are needed because the more flexible approach of ET is at least as rigorous. I will show also that none of the three are wanted because ET's more flexible approach offers the opportunity of broader scope—an opportunity already fulfilled to some degree. These amount to showing that a sociological rational choice theory is quite distinct from the economic approach.

THE RATIONALITY QUESTION

The Problem

The purpose of this section is to show that rationality performs two very different functions in theory. Over a very narrow range of conditions, rationality operates like a law producing predictions and explanations. Elsewhere rationality operates like a theoretical principle whose function is to pose problems in theory. Once rationality poses problems, other procedures are evoked to produce explanations and predictions. Because it poses problems systematically, rendering them tractable, rationality performs a very important function.

Rationality explains activity for certain narrow conditions. If alternatives form an ordered set and if the actor's choice alone determines action, the alternative chosen by a single maximizing actor and its realization in action are determined. For example, Elster's (1979) studies in rationality and irrationality focus on acts that people can do alone. Call these the *narrower conditions of rationality*. I mean to include in these conditions all games in which one strategy strictly dominates all others and in which payoffs are awarded automatically. It is within the narrower conditions that rationality functions as a law.

In Elster's terms, the narrower conditions of rationality include parametric decisions and exclude strategic decisions. "In a parametric decision the agent faces external constraints that are in some sense given or parametric. . . . A strategic situation is characterized by interdependence of decisions" (Elster 1986, p. 7). The case in which one strategy strictly dominates is included in the narrower conditions because, though technically strategic, each actor can take as given the choice of the other.

An example within the narrower conditions is the famous "voting paradox," which concerns an individual's choice and action under known value conditions. The benefits gained from voting are infinitesimal, while the costs of voting, though small, are finite. Thus rationality predicts that people do not vote while recognizing, paradoxically, that many, often most, do vote. Note that the act of voting is treated as wholly dependent on the choice of each actor considered alone. Thus once valuations of the two alternatives are given, a simple maximization assumption explains both choice and action.

Outside the narrower conditions, rationality does not have an explanatory role. Instead, as Fararo explains (person communication), its role is that of a theoretic principle. Principles are used to pose problems in theory. For example, the principle of rectilinear propagation of light asserts that light travels in straight lines. That principle allows ray diagrams to be drawn that pose problems of, for example, focal length. Applying Snell's law, a solution is derived (Toulmin 1953). In social theory, the principle of rationality functions similarly. It is used to pose problems that other parts of theory are evoked to solve. For sociology, the most important examples in which rationality operates as a principle are social relationships. These are most important because the core of our concern is action in relations—especially action in structures that are composed of relationships. I intend to show that social relationships and structures fall outside the narrower conditions of rationality.

Social Relationships

I take as given that the central concern of sociology is social relationships. ET is a theory of social action but considers action only in social relationships. In ET, structures are composed of connected relationships; that is, relationships are used in theory as building blocks to develop formulations for structures. To the extent sociology is concerned with social structures, from ET's point of view it is action in social relationships that will be its central concern.

Relationships are always outside the narrower conditions of rationality for one reason and frequently also for a second. First, payoffs are not automatic; that is, the payoffs in social relationships are the resources that actors bring to them. Whether payoffs occur depends on whether resources are transmitted and received, which in turn is always determined by the decisions of two or more actors. For example, in exchange both actors must agree on a rate for exchanging to occur. Because payoffs occur when the actors transmit resources to each other, they are not automatic, and exchanges, like all relationships, are always outside the narrower conditions.

Unless a strictly dominant strategy exists, relationships also will fall outside the narrower conditions for a second reason; and only in unusual and limiting conditions will social relationships have a strictly dominant strategy. For example, for a bilateral monopoly a strictly dominant strategy exists only when one price is possible. Then actors either prefer to exchange at that price and exchanging occurs, or they do not and exchanging does not occur. By contrast, when a range of rates can be negotiated, no strictly dominant strategy exists. (See below.) Occasionally structural conditions produce a dominant strategy allowing us to treat decisions as if they are parametric. For example, though the decisions that move a market toward equilibrium are strategic, once equilibrium is reached, market prices can be treated as parametric.

It is useful to consider the consequences of some of these issues for theory. In this section, I show (a) that rationality alone does not predict action in isolated social relationships, (b) but nevertheless the principle of rationality poses problems in a systematic way, which (c) leads to evoking further procedures resulting in predictions and explanations. Given its focus on relationships, rationality is explicitly used as a principle in ET. Principle 1 states:

ALL SOCIAL ACTORS ACT TO MAXIMIZE THEIR EXPECTED PREFER-ENCE STATE ALTERATION.

In ET there are two types of acts: positive sanctions, which increase the preference state of the other, and negative sanctions, which decrease the preference state of the other. Composing social relations out of two acts, as in Figure 3.1, creates three types of social relationships: exchange, conflict, and coercion. Subtypes also occur. In Figure 3.2 are given two subtypes of exchange. I will focus here on economic exchange.

When building theoretic formulations, ET moves from simpler to more complex, with the more complex being composed out of simpler parts. Thus the single economic exchange relation—the bilateral monopoly—is dealt with before more complex structures, such as markets. This is exactly the opposite from the historical development of economics, in which markets were solved first and then attention turned to simpler structures, such as the bilateral monopoly. In fact, economists have known since Edgeworth (1881) that the rationality principle alone does not solve the dyad.

Sanction signs indicate actors' interests. In Figure 3.2a, for each actor a transmission is a loss, while a reception is a gain. Let at least one of the two sanctions vary quantitatively such that an array of rates of exchange has positive payoffs for both actors. Applying principle 1, A makes the offer to B, which minimizes the A-B flow and/or maximizes the B-A flow because that is the offer maximizing A's preference alteration—that is, A's payoff from exchanging. Similarly B makes the offer that minimizes the B-A flow and/or maximizes the A-B flow because that offer maximizes B's payoff from exchanging. These two offers at the opposite

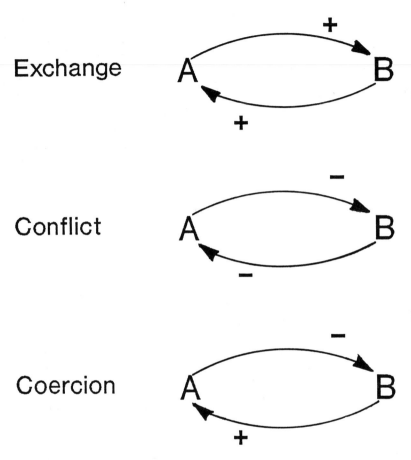

Figure 3.1. The Three Pure Types of Social Relationships

extremes of the negotiation set are the only acts predicted by the principle of rationality.

That is, evoking the principle of rationality asserts that A and B each make their best offer to the other and assert no more. Because the rates are at the opposed extremes of the negotiation set, no agreement exists and no rate is predicted. In fact, no exchange is predicted; that is, maximizing actors do not exchange. That they do not poses a problem because we know people under the cited conditions will exchange. This problem is not unlike the voting

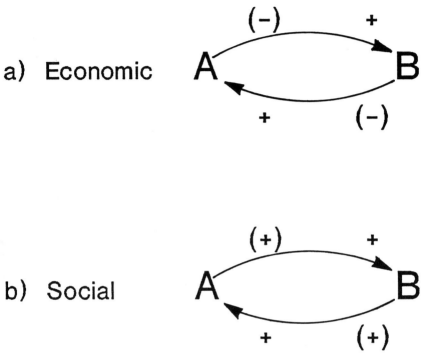

Figure 3.2. Subtypes of Exchange

paradox and, following Edgeworth, could be left as the *Paradox of Exchange*. A better direction for theory in sociology is to recognize that the paradox indicates the limits of rationality as a principle. In that case, the paradox is a problem and the purpose of theory to solve it.

In terms introduced above, exchange under the cited conditions falls outside the narrower conditions of rationality. Thus application of the principle of rationality produces not a prediction but a problem. To solve that problem, ET introduces a second spring of action.

Think of maximizing as an interest pursued by actors. In Coleman's terms, it is a *spring of action*. The solution to the problem posed by the maximizing interest is the postulation of a second interest, a second spring of action which impels both actors toward compromise. Here we formulate a second principle, subordinate to the first:

ALL SOCIAL ACTORS ACT TO AVOID MINIMIZING THEIR EXPECTED
PREFERENCE STATE ALTERATION.

ET's social actors act on both principles in the following way. First, they act on principle 1 alone. Then, on encountering another ET actor in a social relationship, both act on the two principles together. To predict the result of joint action within relations, the two are used to form a law called *resistance* (Willer 1981, 1984; Heckathorn 1984). When Pi is i's payoff, Pi_{max} i's maximum payoff, and Pi_{con} i's payoff at disagreement (*con*frontation), then i's resistance

$$Ri = \frac{Pi_{max} - Pi}{Pi - Pi_{con}}$$

Another principle of the theory asserts that compromise occurs at equiresistance. For example, for the A-B exchange relation, at A's best offer $P_A = P_{Amax}$ and R_A is minimal at zero, while R_B is maximal because P_B is just noticeably different from zero. Conversely at B's best offer, R_B is minimal at zero and R_A is maximal. The predicted compromise point then is

$$R_A = \frac{P_{Amax} - P_A}{P_A - P_{Acon}} = \frac{P_{Bmax} - P_B}{P_B - P_{Bcon}} = R_B$$

Note that each numerator is the size of the interest in maximization and one over the denominator the size of the interest in avoiding minimizing. Because they are ratios, utilities can be substituted for payoffs. For exchange frequently, $P_{con} = 0$ because no sanctions flow.

In many cases, resistance gives the same rate as Nash's axiomatic solution, but to reach this conclusion requires direct comparison of utilities. Nash's solution predicts exchange when the product of the two actors' utility vectors, $u_A \times u_B$ is maximal. If the two are inverse linear functions of each other, when $u_A = u_B$, the product is maximal *and* $R_A = R_B$.

Beyond its use in theory for predicting compromise in exchange, *resistance* can be used to explain an array of substantive issues. For example, in modern societies, coercion is by no means unknown. For example, Weber's definition of the *state* as that organization that monopolizes the means of violence over a given geographical area means in ET terms that the state stands in potential coercive relations with all actors within it. Furthermore, coercive laws are used to produce property rights that are essential to modern exchange structures (Willer 1985) (see below); that is, coercion is used to regulate exchange. Yet coercion is not normally mixed with exchange.

Resistance explains why coercion is not mixed with exchange. Figure 3.3 displays a mixed exchange-coercive relationship. In that relationship, A can transmit costlessly the negative sanction to B, which will reduce the size of P_{Bcon} below zero. By threatening transmission of its negative, A reduces B's resistance to any offer; that is, the threat shifts the equiresistance price to one more favorable to A. As P_{Bcon} becomes smaller, the rate of exchange shifts in A's favor until $P_A = P_{Amax}$ and A gains something for nothing. A pays no price. More generally, mixing coercion with exchange renders prices impossible, thereby eliminating the interest in producing for exchange. Thus coercion regulates exchange but is not mixed with exchange.

The Rationality Principle

In this section, I have shown that rationality performs two functions in theory, the most important of which is to act as a principle in posing problems. It is a great strength of rational choice theory that the principle of rationality poses problems systematically and in a form tractable to solution. At times, however, the economic approach leaves these problems unsolved, calling them *paradoxes.* The approach that I propose does not stop at so-called paradoxes but instead recognizes them as problems that call for solutions in theory.

Whereas the analysis of social relationships is now almost wholly missing in mainstream sociological research, the great contribution of rational choice theory in sociology should be to offer a systematic

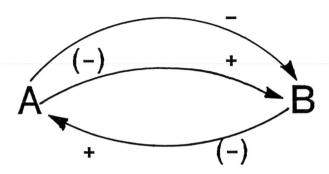

Figure 3.3. A Mixed Relationship

theoretic treatment for social relations and the structures that they compose. ET offers the first steps toward such a theory of relations in structures. It uses *rationality* as a principle and *resistance* as a law to predict rates of sanction flow in relationships. Structures are built out of connected relationships. This mode of construction is intended to allow seamless movement, in theory, from actions in relations to structural dynamics—that is, from micro to macro level. Issues of structure are central to the chapter. Before they can be more fully considered, however, the value problem must be addressed.

THE VALUE PROBLEM

The Problem

The economic approach to rational choice assumes that all actors everywhere have the same stable preference structure. For Becker, this means that a utilitarian value system is postulated. Then rationality implies not merely that the actor makes choices or that the preference system on which choice is predicated is well ordered, but that the items of the preference system are a set of well-ordered utilities common to all actors.

Rational choice theory does not demand that a single value system be packed into all actors. According to Elster, a rational choice explanation of human action must satisfy only three requirements: "The action is the best way for the agent to satisfy his desire, given his belief; the belief is the best he could form, given the evidence; the amount of evidence collected is itself optimal, given his desire" (Elster 1986, p. 16).

Because all actors have one value system that applies at all times and places, as is assumed by the economic approach, then that value system will have a great number of elements, only some of which apply in a given choice situation. Selection from the larger set is called by Elster a process of filtering (1979) and its result the "feasible set" of alternatives (1986). "To act rationally, then, simply means to choose the highest-ranked element in the feasible set" (Elster 1986, p. 4).

I find no fault with the rigor of the economic approach's explanation of action. Because the actor's set of values is universally given, it is not values that need to be measured but objective conditions of the action situation, for it is the latter that filter the feasible set. After determining the feasible set, prediction of action follows immediately from its top element—at least when the narrower conditions of rationality are satisfied. In rigor, the economic approach stands in the greatest possible contrast to ad hoc explanations of action so commonly offered in sociology.

The fault I find here with the economic approach is its highly restricted scope. For many analyses, the content of values cannot be restricted to utilities. Furthermore, there are organizational and historical conditions important to a sociological treatment of values and beliefs in which systems of values cannot be treated as ordered utilities. Through these points I hope to show that ET's treatment of values (and beliefs) is more general in scope than the economic approach.

The Issue of the Content

There is a fundamental difference in the source of values in the economic approach and in ET. Whereas ET infers values from structures, following Elster, rational choice assumes that utilities given in the actor are "filtered" such that a subset is selected that is feasible. That is to say, the filtered subset consists only of utilities. This view could be fully adequate only if all choices in the world were parametric.

In this section, I point out, however, that the economic approach has drawn the content of values too narrowly. Quite independent from where values originate, when decisions are strategic, the feasible set can include not just utilities but also strategies and structures. This is because the interaction between values and structure can be more complex than suggested by Elster, an interaction that is obvious when values are reflected from structure. For example, a corporation attempting to maximize profit will search among markets, taking into account its varying market power in each case (Prechel 1990). The result of that search might be summarized as an ordering of profits. The ordering of profits, however, is a result of an ordering of market structures and strategies within them.

To show that strategies and structures can enter into value systems even when structural conditions are very simple, an example is drawn from a paradigm frequently used in network exchange theory. As shown in Figure 3.4, positions are connected by pools of profit points, typically 24, and exchange is simulated by division. Equal division indicates equal power, while unequal divisions indicate power exercised by the position favored in the division. Experimental study has shown that A will be high in power in the Figure 3.4 structure if and only if at least one B is routinely excluded from exchanging.

The discussion focuses on the network in Figure 3.5, which though quite simple contains strategic structural dynamics. That is to say, the structure changes over time, the changes favor some actors over others, and the changes of the structure are strategically selected. In dyadic exchange, actors' decisions are strategic within the relationship. In 3.5a, however, actors' decisions are strategic both within relationships and across structures.

The subscripts of the 3.5a branch indicate the maximum number of profit point pools that each position may divide for a given time period; the superscripts give the GPI values for each position (Willer and Markovsky 1991). In general, the higher the GPI value, the greater the power of the position (see below). When GPI > 1, the position is high power, and when GPI = 0, the position is low power, while pairs with GPI = 1 exchange at equipower. Thus C with a zero value is powerless, A with a 3/2 value is most powerful, and B with a 1/2 value is more powerful than C but less than A. In fact, B's value of 1/2 is a composite of GPI = 1 and GPI = 0, suggesting that B exchanges sometimes at low power like C and sometimes at equal power.

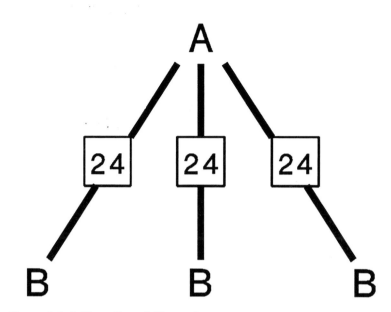

Figure 3.4. A Three-Branch Network

Figure 3.5b indicates dynamics of the structure as they are produced by the direction of A's first exchange. If A exchanges with B first, the resulting structure is the B-A-C branch, in which A is high in power and can expect to receive 23 profit points in each division. If A exchanges first with C, however, the resulting structure is the A-B dyad where A can expect to receive only 12. Preferring 23 to 12 profit points, A prefers the branch to the dyad and thus prefers exchanging with B first. Conversely preferring 12 to 1 profit point B prefers the dyad to the branch and prefers that A exchange with C first. In all cases, C is low in power and is indifferent insofar as structural dynamics are concerned.

As a consequence of these considerations, both A's and B's "feasible set" now includes not simply utilities but also substructures (the dyad vs. the branch), within which more or fewer utilities can be realized, as well as the strategies that lead to the more or less favored structure. But this discussion has oversimplified strategic elements of the network. To emphasize structural dynamics, it simply was assumed that, as structure varied, all actors would

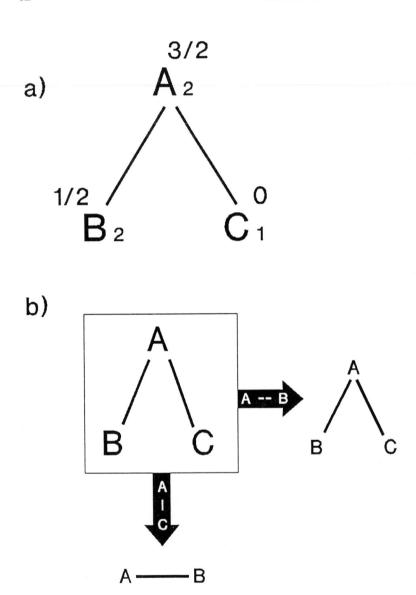

Figure 3.5. A Simple Problem in Strategic Action

always receive a given payoff. This treats strategic outcomes within relationships as if they were parametric.

In fact, actors in equal power relations do not automatically receive 12/12 divisions, but each must bargain to gain the best concessions possible. Similarly positions high in power do not automatically receive 23 profit points but must pursue the best offer they can gain from those low in power. Therefore the structure is *both* strategic within relationships and structurally strategic in its movement to either dyad or branch.

Because C is low power in all structural configurations, structures are not part of C's feasible set; but because the strategies pursued by others affect C's payoffs, others' strategies may be part of C's preference system. A's best strategy is to play B and C off against each other, to exchange first with B, and to repeat the process in the resulting branch. This strategy is best because its potential payoff to A is optimal at $23 \times 2 = 46$ profit points. B's optimal strategy, however, is to never exchange with A first. In that case, the structure always becomes the A-B dyad in which B hopes to receive 12, which is preferred to the $1 \times 2 = 2$ expected when B exchanges twice at low power. B's optimal strategy affects C because, if B refuses to exchange first, A and C exchange dyadically and C can hope to gain an equipower 12/12 division. Therefore B's strategies should be part of C's feasible set.

Though quite simple, the example illustrates how social system behavior is related to actors' behavior, how the two are linked theoretically, and the source of individual action; that is, it illustrates what rational choice theory must do according to Coleman. In addition, it points to the very important interaction between values and structure in strategic situations. As a consequence of this interaction, any actor's feasible set may include utilities, structures, strategies for self, and even the strategies selected and pursued by others. Though it is obvious that something more than a simple ordering of these diverse elements is needed, I will not pursue here how this complex might be organized.

The Issue of Scope

The economic approach to rational choice treats values as ordered utilities because it generalizes from neoclassical microeconomic theory. While there is no doubt neoclassical theory is the most systematic and powerful of all social theories, its scope of application is quite narrow. For example, neoclassical microeconomics has few applications in the statistical world of macroeconomics. It tells us little about how to structure economic organizations. It offers limited insight into state policies intended to stabilize the economy. Perhaps most striking is its inapplicability to precapitalist economies.

Even brief consideration of ancient society, such as Rome of the late Republic and early Empire, suggests that it is inappropriate to treat the values of historical actors as ordered utilities. It was not a world that had utilities in the modern sense, and the assumption of ordered utilities for ancient actors does not aid, but only blocks, an understanding.

The ancient world is a world alien to the concepts of modern economics, including terms normally employed in the economic approach to rational choice. For example, the ancients had no term for *economy*. Of course, the term *economics* stems from the Greek term *oikonomiai*. But to the Greeks, and later to the Romans, its reference was to the household, not to an array of markets. In fact, no term for economics existed until it was coined by the French political economists around 1750. Commenting on the absence of the term in antiquity, Finley asserts that it was not developed "because ancient society did not have an economic system which was an enormous conglomeration of interdependent markets" (1974, p. 22). In the absence of those markets, it is doubtful that any law of microeconomics applies.

More to the point for this chapter is what rationality means when even the idea of an economy in which rational economic action could be pursued is absent. One thing that *rationality* cannot mean is that ancient actors calculated like modern ones. Two conditions limited calculability. First, the Roman numeral system, while effective for simple addition and subtraction, was highly ineffective for multiplication and division. Only very few people could calculate rates, such as rates of interest and rates of profit. Because double entry bookkeeping was unknown, there is no question of ancient economic actors calculating investments with the precision that moderns normally do. Second, the general tendency of the ancient economy was to swallow up markets into the large households of the highest classes (Childe 1954). Though this normally was seen as an "economizing" move, it was not a result of cost calculations. Instead the aim was to reduce money spent by the family. Needless to say, as markets were swallowed, the opportunities to calculate diminished—quite apart from the frequency in which those opportunities were pursued or the competence of the actors in the pursuit.

Addressing the question of why capitalism did not develop in antiquity allowed Weber ([1918] 1968) to uncover many conditions that stood in contrast to modern society. Some of Weber's answer was that capitalism did develop, but in its political, not its industrial, form. For Rome, an important form of political capitalism was tax farming in which the right to tax a part of the Empire was purchased by a private individual. Because no limits typically were placed on the amounts of tax extracted, tax farming held the possibility of great profit. It also offered the advantage to the central government of a fixed and regular income (derived from the fee paid by the tax farmer), which was needed to support the bureaucracy.

Because wealth was very highly concentrated in the patrician class, the question of ancient capitalism comes down to why patricians were not industrial or financial capitalists and why their wealth was concentrated in land. The concentration of wealth in land freed the patrician class to pursue politics, and there is reason to suppose that the pursuit of politics was necessary to protect their property. This was because the right of exclusion was not as fully developed in antiquity.

In its fully developed form, the *right of exclusion* assures the owner of a thing that the state will intervene to support the owner in excluding others from the use of the private good. In the ancient economy, however, the state was as willing to expropriate property as to defend it. Whether a person's property was defended or expropriated depended on that person's political influence (Weber [1918] 1968); that is, property was private and safely so if and only if it was backed by political power.

The ongoing dependence of property on political influence explains two salient and apparently contradictory facts of the ancient economy—that the wealthy were city dwellers whose source of wealth was in the countryside. First, all wealthy classes were always city dwellers because only city life allowed ongoing political activity. Second, nevertheless their wealth was in the countryside because only rural land could be counted on to reproduce itself and a surplus *without direction*. Wealthy classes could not direct their "enterprises" for their time was absorbed in politics (see Jones 1966).

Though lacking an economy of related markets, it is entirely reasonable to treat actors in the ancient world as rational insofar as choice is concerned. Because their values could not have been ordered utilities, however, they were not "rational" in the sense normally assumed by the economic approach. Of course, ordered utilities could be attributed to historical actors for wholly theoretic purposes. But that attribution seems counterproductive for it would obscure and not uncover the immediate relations between what we see today as political and economic action.

In fact, the historians referenced above routinely assume that ancients had values that reflected their social structures and made rational choices accordingly; that is, they treated values not as they are treated in the economic approach but as they are treated in ET.

Scope Extension
Without Theory Extension

When rational choice was extended beyond economics, all actors were given the same values, values that are only appropriate to actors in modern markets. Because actors' choices are parametric for markets in equilibrium, their preferences can be limited to utilities. As we have seen, however, even when strategic action is quite simple, other units, such as structures and strategies, must find a place in preference systems. That actors of the economic approach cannot be applied to ancient European society strongly suggests that they do not apply to a wide variety of important cases. In general, stretching economic content beyond modern economies has attenuated explanatory and predictive power. (Also see Udehn In press).

For a market full of utilities, economics quite appropriately postulates an actor whose values reflect those utilities. At issue is how to extend this approach outside markets. The appropriate extension is not to postulate that all actors have marketlike values. Instead the more general extension is to postulate actors whose values, like the values of actors in markets, reflect their structural conditions. The more general extension is the one employed by ET.

While treating actors' values and beliefs reflectively would be an important advance for rational choice theory, reflection should be treated as a simplifying assumption. A fully general rational choice theory cannot ignore Weber's idea of value rationality. To cover value rationality, we need to see that actors' values and beliefs can reflect structures other than those immediately present. This means that a fully general rational choice theory cannot avoid developing a structurally governed cognitive component.

THE STRUCTURE ISSUE

The Problem

In outlining the economic approach to rational choice, Becker does not assert that all social structures are actually markets. Instead he first explains that "the economic approach assumes the existence of markets that with varying degrees of efficiency coordinate the actions of different participants" (1976, p. 5). He then goes on to assert that "these market instruments perform most, if not all, of the functions assigned to 'structure' in sociological theories" (1976, p. 5). In other words, social structures, though not actually markets, are treated as if they were markets.

The obvious defense of Becker's position is that the concept of *structure* has long been so empty in sociology that the treatment of all structures as markets will have to accomplish little to do better. The counter to that defense is rigorous concepts for structure such as those used in ET. Space will not allow me to demonstrate here the full scope and rigor of structural formulations of ET, which have been presented in detail elsewhere. (See references throughout the chapter.)

The section begins by noting that market structures require enforcement of private property rights. Must the enforcement of these rights be coercive? If so, fundamental questions arise concerning the treatment of all organizations as markets. Then the discussion turns to the consequences that follow from treating all structures as if they were markets. It is shown that that treatment results in bias-driven pseudo-explanations, biases that are avoided by the more flexible approach of ET.

Property Rights

Coleman's *Foundations of Social Theory* (1990b) brings to our attention the very important phenomenon of *rights*. Among the most important recent works on property rights in economics is Alchian and Demsetz's "The Property Right Paradigm" (1973). In that article, they point out that "What is owned are *rights* to *use* resources" (p. 17). Whereas the right of use is the only one they specify, in separate articles Gilham (1981) and I (Willer 1985) indicate that the right of use is only one of four rights needed to define *private property*. The Alchian and Demsetz paradigm does not indicate how rights are enforced, nor does it offer an adequate treatment of rights in any property condition, including private.

Here I will indicate briefly and nontechnically the four rights needed to define *private property*. Selecting one of those rights, I will demonstrate that its enforcement must be coercive. This demonstration strongly suggests that no adequate theory can treat all structures as markets. I will then show how the four rights can be used to derive two other historical property systems. This derivation highlights the one-sidedness of the Alchian and Demsetz paradigm, a one-sidedness due to its incompleteness. Finally I will suggest that their one-sidedness and incompleteness produce biases that are not strangers to the economic approach to rational choice.

As presented elsewhere, private property rights consist of the following:

> Exclusion is the right of an actor to exclude others from use of a thing. The thing in question may be a valued object or an event. In the market objects are called goods and events, services. Alienation is the right to pass over to another a valued object or event. Call this passing over a sanction transmission and note that it is the right of exclusion, and not necessarily the thing itself, which is being transmitted. Similarly, appropriation is the right to receive an exclusive right. Finally, market relationships are characterized by an enforceable right of reciprocity which is a contractual right to enforce mutual agreements concerning the mutual alienation of exclusive rights to the thing. (Willer 1985, p. 128)

Exclusivity allows property to be private, while the three other rights allow private property to move from actor to actor as in markets.

In ongoing bilateral monopolies, actors can themselves enforce at least the right of reciprocity. For example, let two actors be engaged in ongoing exchanges that are known by both to be their best alternative. Then if either does not reciprocate, the other will find a new partner and the first has lost the benefit of all future exchanges. Recognition of that possible loss produces reciprocity.

By contrast, all market relations are transitory. Because actors are continually switching to new partners, no right can be enforced by a cheated actor's unwillingness to exchange further with any other. If enforcement is needed, only an outside agent with sanctioning powers over all can enforce rights. In modern societies, the only agent with that capability is the state. Granted that actors cannot themselves enforce rights. Now at issue is whether enforcement is needed and, if so, whether it must be coercive.

Does, for example, the right of reciprocity need to be enforced? Figure 3.6 divides an economic exchange into two time periods for two rational actors. At t_1, A transmits the good or service to B, and later at t_2 B reciprocates. But for B, reciprocation is a pure loss. Therefore B prefers t_2' where no good or service is reciprocated; that is, when engaged in a single (not a repeated) exchange, no rational actor will reciprocate. Knowing that no rational actor will reciprocate, transmitting first is a pure loss. Thus no rational actor will transmit first. *Therefore exchange is impossible for rational actors unless the reciprocity right is enforced.*

Can the state enforce the right by offering actors inducements? Assume that the state's inducement to B is smaller in value than the good or service owed to A. Then as a rational actor, B will reject the state's offer and will not reciprocate. More generally, B will prefer not to reciprocate for any offer from the state lower in value than the good owed to A. To ensure reciprocity with inducements, the state must pay B at least the value owed to A. But that transforms B into an intermediary who merely passes on to A the state's payment; that is, the state buys B the good. More generally, enforcing the right of reciprocity by inducements implies that the state buys all actors all goods. Therefore any proposal to enforce the right by inducements is faulty by reductio ad absurdum, and the right must be enforced coercively.

It follows that the treatment by the economic approach of all structures as if they were markets is unacceptable even as a theoretical simplification. Because a market of rational actors cannot exist without the coercive enforcement of rights, markets presuppose another structure that is not at all like any market. In fact, the structure is the state that Weber defined as that organization which

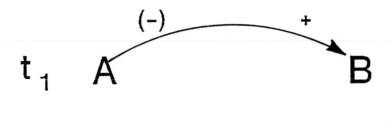

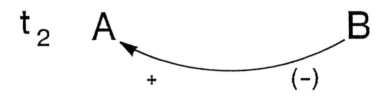

Figure 3.6. The Issue of Reciprocity

seeks to monopolize the means of violence over a given geographical area ([1918] 1968); that is, the state is that organization that stands, not in exchange, but in coercive relations with all other actors.

Because Alchian and Demsetz's property rights paradigm does not explain how any right is enforced, it does not recognize that markets cannot exist without the state. The state is not a market, and to treat it as if it were a market, as Becker does, is not a simplification. It is a misunderstanding, for it completely misses not only the state's function for markets but also the state's mode of financing and the way the state produces civil order. It is difficult to imagine a more fundamental misunderstanding not simply of the state but of modern society.

Other errors that follow from treating all structures as markets are seen when the four property rights are used to define economies in which no markets exist. For example, a system of exclusionary rights in which the right of alienation is negated is a feudal system. Under feudal property, no markets can exist. It is difficult to imagine how our understanding of marketless feudal structures is furthered by treating them as if they were markets. A system in which all four rights are negated is a *communal property system*. In a communal property system, no actor has the exclusive right to anything, none can alienate an exclusive right, and none can appropriate it. Because no passage of private property takes place, no reciprocity takes place.

By contrast, Alchian and Demsetz treat communal property not as a distinct system of rights but as a flawed variant on private property; that is,

> We shall use the phrase "communal rights" to describe a bundle of rights which includes the right to use a scarce resource but fails to include the right of an "absentee owner" to exclude others using the resource. Operationally this means that the use of the scarce resource is determined on a first-come, first-served basis. (Alchian and Demsetz 1973, p. 19)

The definition smuggles in the concept of *economic good* by use of the phrase "scarce resource." Yet is it obvious that, while things can be scarce, no goods are in any communal property system. Having smuggled in goods on the one hand and having defined *communal rights* by the absence of exclusion on the other, their definition contains the conditions for a Hobbesian war of all against all. The conditions for that war, however, are not necessarily in communal property but are only in their definition of *communal property*. Therefore their conclusion that "Persons who own communal rights will tend to exercise these rights in ways that ignore the full consequences of their acts" (p. 19) bears not on the world but only on their premises.

From even the most scant acquaintance with prehistory, it must be obvious that humans have lived in communal property systems for most of the time they have been human. It necessarily follows that communal property has stable forms and that any conception of communal property that asserts its unconditional instability is prima facie faulty. In fact, communal property rights, like private property rights, are stable only with coercive governance. How that stability is achieved is discussed elsewhere (Willer 1985).

The property rights paradigm contains a most unfortunate bias. The paradigm is not simply incomplete. The form that its incompleteness takes produces its conclusions, and those conclusions favor the private property form obviously preferred by the authors. The fault here is not that the paradigm fails to be value free. Theories are not value free, and values are not theory free. The fault is that the value biases that are built into the paradigm produce its conclusions.

Markets Versus the Structural View

Markets are neither logically nor historically prior to other relations, and nothing could be farther from the truth than a treatment that assumes either. As seen above, all exchange relations of the market type are inconceivable without the coercive enforcement of rights. Just as markets are impossible in theory without states, they did not occur historically before states. As Gilham has shown (1981), modern market development went hand in hand with the development of the modern state and its coercive enforcement of property rights.

Becker's assumption that all structures can be treated as markets contains a powerful bias: If one treats all structures as markets, only structures that actually are markets are good structures, while others, being more or less imperfect, are flawed. Thus a bias for market structures is incorporated into the economic approach, and the way that it is incorporated can produce conclusions that are no more than expressions of the bias. I see no way of avoiding bias of this kind but by dropping the market assumption. It is far better to use a flexible procedure to model structures as is done in ET.

It is as easy to construct antimarket pseudo-explanations as promarket ones. For instance, the development of the modern state is best described as an increasing centralization of all coer-

cive power (see Weber [1918] 1968). When all coercion is central-
ized, only exchange relations remain for those subject to the state.
Therefore state centralization directly produced markets. Because
capitalism requires markets, state centralization produced capitalism. To pursue this view further, however, would be to pursue an
argument as biased as any found in the economic approach.

Niskanen's view of public bureaucracy serves as an example of
how treating all structures as markets produces not explanation
but promarket bias. According to Niskanen:

> Among the several variables that may enter the bureaucrat's utility function
> are the following: salary, perquisites of the office, public reputation, power,
> patronage, output of the bureau, ease of making changes and ease of manag-
> ing. All of these variables except the last two, I contend, are a positive
> monotonic function of the total *budget* of the bureau. (1971, p. 38)

He then concludes that bureaucrats maximize budgets (1971, p.
42). His conclusion follows, however, only if budget selection is
parametric; that is, his conclusion assumes the narrower conditions of rationality.

It is obvious, however, that budget selections are rarely if ever
parametric; that is, bureaucrats do not simply get the budgets they
most prefer. Budgets are negotiated, and frequently none of the
officials engaged in negotiating them are bureaucrats. For example,
in publicly funded universities, budgets are formulated under presidents who are not bureaucrats but political appointees. Presidents
negotiate with boards, the members of which are notables, not
bureaucrats. In turn, boards report to legislators, who also are not
bureaucrats. Bureaucrats also do not select their most preferred
budgets in private corporations. To the contrary, budgets are
formulated for and must pass a board of directors whose function
is to represent stockholders. In general, I know of no case in which
budgets are selected unilaterally by bureaucrats.

Furthermore Niskanen commits the fallacy of composition. Transforming his argument, by analogy, to markets highlights the fallacy. What do actors in markets maximize? Each has an income,
each has perquisites of the position in the market, and so on. All
of these are positive functions of the rate of circulation of money.
Thus all actors in markets want to maximize money circulation.
Therefore money circulation in all markets is maximized. But we

know that conclusion is wrong because rational actors in markets want to maximize their own incomes. The appropriate conclusion for bureaucracies is analogous to the one just drawn for markets. Contrary to Niskanen, each bureaucrat attempts to maximize income and perquisites from his or her position in the hierarchy; that is, all bureaucrats seek upward mobility.

It is not an historical accident but the result of organization design that bureaucrats seek upward mobility. Weber's broad historical studies ([1918] 1968) indicate that a necessary condition of power centralization in organizations is that officials not appropriate their offices. Lack of office appropriation is a necessary condition for mobility in the hierarchy. Quite apart from whether they are public or private, contemporary or ancient, all bureaucracies have hierarchies that allow officials to be mobile. As I have shown in experiments reported elsewhere, hierarchy with mobility produces domination and obedience (Willer 1987). If hierarchy/ mobility is intended to produce domination and obedience, budget inflation may occur as claimed by Niskanen. But that inflation is an unintended consequence of an organization design intended to produce domination.

This discussion illustrates the bias incorporated in the economic approach. Because all structures are understood as if they were markets, bureaucracies must be imperfect markets. In fact, they are so imperfect that their budgets increase. ET does not take any structure as universal. Instead it focuses inquiry on structural dynamics in light of structural formulations. In the case of bureaucracy, experiments show that hierarchy and mobility produce domination and obedience. That test, together with historical evidence, leads to an understanding of bureaucracy on its own terms. That is to say, we understand its structural dynamics in light of the springs of individual action within it—an understanding that appears to satisfy Coleman's conditions.

CONCLUDING REMARKS

This chapter has examined the claim that elementary theory is a satisfactory rational choice theory under Coleman's criteria. ET locates the springs of actors' behavior in the relationships and structures in which actors are modeled. Actors' behavior in a system of social relations produces the behavior of the social system. Coleman's criteria suggest that a special theory is needed to resolve transitions between micro and macro levels. ET does not contain a distinct theory to resolve micro-macro transitions. Instead it uses one vocabulary of primitive and derived terms to model structures, relationships, values, and beliefs. Because this integrated approach does not divide the two levels, no special theory is needed to resolve them.

Problems were posed that contrasted the economic approach to the sociological approach of ET. The three assumptions of the economic approach do not lead in fruitful directions. Maximizing actors are appropriate only for parametric conditions. As a result, strategic conditions are either ignored or are reduced to parametric ones. Among the strategic conditions ignored are social relationships. Yet social relationships must form the core of any sociological approach.

The economic approach treats social structures as filtering out actors' feasible sets of utilities from the larger set common to all actors. This is not a fully satisfactory procedure. Because social structures are strategic, the content of actors' values cannot be limited to utilities but also will include parts of the structure itself and even others' strategies. ET avoids the limitations of the economic approach by modeling relationships in structures and inferring the content of actors' values from them.

Also raised was the issue of scope. Economic historians have shown that the concept of *economy* was unknown in ancient society. Because economy was unknown, no utilities existed as they currently are understood. Thus actors in ancient society could not have had value systems that were ordered utilities. Instead the content of their values must have reflected conditions then structurally present. In fact, ET models the values of those historical actors as reflecting their structural conditions.

The discussion of structural issues opened by showing that rational actors cannot exchange. More precisely, it was shown that rational actors will not exchange in markets unless private property rights are enforced. Markets presuppose a structure that enforces rights and, because it also is shown that rights cannot be enforced through inducements, the structure presupposed by markets cannot be like markets. Niskanen's view of bureaucracies as markets in which bureaucrats maximize budgets illustrates further why no theory that treats all structures as if they were markets can be fully adequate. In fact, Niskanen's view commits the fallacy of composition. Avoiding that fallacy, ET understands hierarchy and mobility as producing domination and obedience in bureaucracy.

Not rational choice, but the assumptions of the economic approach all too often lead to pseudo-explanations that are expressions of its bias, a bias that expresses promarket conservatism. But the fault that I find in the economic approach is not that it has a bias. To the contrary, I believe that no theory can hope to be value free—at least initially. The best hope is that theory can correct its biases. Yet all too often the economic approach has not been self-correcting. It has not been self-correcting because its bias directly produces its conclusions so that its correspondence to the world is not tested. To the extent that its conclusions simply restate its assumptions, the economic approach is not an adequate rational choice theory, nor will it become such.

The issue of bias suggests that to Coleman's criteria for adequate rational choice theory two more should be added: (a) Rational choice theory should be subject to ongoing tests, and (b) it should be structured to induce growth (Wagner and Berger 1985). Whereas neither of the two criteria has been satisfied by the economic approach, both have been satisfied by elementary theory. Applications of ET have been subjected to experimental test for more than 10 years (cf. Willer and Anderson 1981; Willer 1984; Willer 1987; Willer and Markovsky 1991). The general procedures for modeling structures allow inferences from smaller models tested in the laboratory to larger structures found in the field.

I have no doubt that a fully satisfactory theory of society will be a rational choice theory under Coleman's criteria. It also must satisfy the criteria of growth and testability. Such a theory will have a wide variety of implications for the behavior of social systems—implications that are much broader than those current to elementary theory. Though satisfying given criteria, elementary theory is now largely limited to power. As a theory of power, its scope is quite broad, but the phenomena explained by a fully satisfactory theory will be much broader.

REFERENCES

Alchian, Armen and Harold Demsetz. 1973. "The Property Right Paradigm." *Journal of Economic History* 33:16-27.

Becker, Gary. 1976. *The Economic Approach to Human Behavior*. Chicago: University of Chicago Press.

Buchanan, J. M. and R. D. Tollison, eds. 1972. *The Theory of Public Choice: Political Applications of Economics*. Ann Arbor: University of Michigan Press.

———. 1984. *The Theory of Public Choice II*. Ann Arbor: University of Michigan Press.

Childe, Gordon. 1954. *What Happened in History*. Harmondsworth, UK: Penguin.

Coleman, James S. 1990a. "Message From the Chair." *Perspectives* 13:1-2.

———. 1990b. *Foundations of Social Theory*. Cambridge, MA: Harvard University Press.

Edgeworth, Frederik Y. 1881. *Mathematical Psychics*. London: Kegan Paul.

Einstein, Albert. [1934] 1954. "On the Method of Theoretical Physics." In Albert Einstein. *Ideas and Opinions*. New York: Crown.

Elster, Jon. 1979. *Ulysses and the Sirens: Studies in Rationality and Irrationality*. Cambridge, UK: Cambridge University Press.

———, ed. 1986. *Rational Choice*. New York: New York University Press.

Finley, M. I. 1974. *The Ancient Economy*. Berkeley: University of California Press.

Gilham, Steven A. 1981. "State, Law and Modern Economic Exchange." Pp. 129-52 in *Networks, Exchange and Coercion*, edited by David Willer and Bo Anderson. New York: Elsevier/Greenwood.

Heckathorn, Douglas. 1984. "A Formal Theory of Social Exchange." *Current Perspectives in Social Theory* 5:145-80.

Jones, A. H. M. 1966. *The Decline of the Ancient World*. London: Longman.

Markovsky, Barry, David Willer, and Travis Patton. 1988. "Power Relations in Exchange Networks." *American Sociological Review* 53:220-36.

Niskanen, W. A. 1971. *Bureaucracy and Representative Government*. Chicago: Aldine-Atherton.

Olson, Mancur. 1965. *The Logic of Collective Action*. Cambridge, MA: Harvard University Press.

Prechel, Harland. 1990. "Steel and the State: Industry Politics and Business Policy Formation." *American Sociological Review* 55:648-69.

Toulmin, Stephen. 1953. *The Philosophy of Science*. New York: Harper & Row.

Udehn, Lars. In press. "The Limits of Economic Imperialism." In *Interfaces in Economic and Social Analysis*, edited by Ulf Himmelstrand. London: Routledge.

Wagner, David and Joseph Berger. 1985. "Do Sociological Theories Grow?" *American Journal of Sociology* 90:697-728.

Weber, Max. [1918] 1968. *Economy and Society*. Berkeley: University of California Press.

Willer, David. 1981. "Quantity and Network Structure." Pp. 109-28 in *Networks, Exchange and Coercion*, edited by David Willer and Bo Anderson. New York: Elsevier/Greenwood.

————. 1984. "Analysis and Composition as Theoretic Procedures." *Journal of Mathematical Sociology* 10:241-70.

————. 1985. "Property and Social Exchange." Pp. 123-42 in *Advances in Group Processes*. Vol. 2, edited by Edward J. Lawler. Greenwich, CT: JAI.

————. 1987. *Theory and Experimental Investigation of Social Structures*. New York: Gordon and Breach.

Willer, David and Bo Anderson, eds. 1981. *Networks, Exchange and Coercion*. New York: Elsevier/Greenwood.

Willer, David and Barry Markovsky. In press. "The Theory of Elementary Relations: Its Development and Research Program." In *Theoretical Research Programs: Studies in Theory Growth*, edited by Joseph Berger and Morris Zelditch. Stanford, CA: Stanford University Press.

Willer, David, Barry Markovsky, and Travis Patton. 1989. "The Experimental Investigation of Social Structures." Pp. 313-53 in *Sociological Theories in Progress*. Vol. 3, edited by Joseph Berger, Morris Zelditch, and Bo Anderson. Newbury Park, CA: Sage.

Chapter 4

THE ATTAINMENT OF GLOBAL
ORDER
IN HETEROGENEOUS SOCIETIES

MICHAEL HECHTER
DEBRA FRIEDMAN
SATOSHI KANAZAWA
Department of Sociology, University of Arizona

TWO QUITE DIFFERENT THEORETICAL TRADITIONS have emerged to account for social order. The first tradition, which is most popular among rational choice theorists, emanates from Hobbes. Its central idea is that order results from a large number of independent decisions to transfer individual rights and liberties to a coercive state in return for its guarantee of security for persons and their property, as well as its establishment of mechanisms to resolve disputes. The transfer of these various individual rights and liberties to the state does not in and of itself produce order, however, because individuals still have an incentive to disrupt order when they can profit by doing so. No state has sufficient resources to maintain order solely via policing; this is why Weber invoked the famous concept of *legitimacy*.

The second tradition, which is most popular among sociologists, emanates from Aristotle and is echoed by Rousseau, Durkheim, Parsons, and their contemporary followers. It views the ultimate source of social order as residing not in external controls but in a concordance of specific values and norms that individuals somehow have managed to internalize. In this tradition, the attainment of order generally is not considered problematic in socially and culturally homogeneous societies, for in these settings the internalized values and norms will tend to be common to all. Now this contention is controversial (for a critique, see Hechter and Kanazawa Forthcoming), but even if it is granted, how then is it possible to account for order in heterogeneous societies—those that encompass a variety of different normative orientations? In such settings, internalization is likely to sow the seeds of conflict rather than order.

In this chapter, we briefly outline the problematic nature of social order in heterogeneous societies and propose that the attainment of local order helps provide a solution. Because order is more easily explained in small homogeneous groups than in large heterogeneous ones, much is to be gained theoretically by reducing the global problem to a local one. Our argument is that the members of social groups can be expected to produce local order to satisfy their own private ends, and once produced, this local order, regardless of its normative content, often contributes to the production of global order. One counterintuitive implication of this argument is that *the more deviant the normative content of the local order, the greater its relative contribution to global order.*

In tacit recognition that global order rests, at least in part, on the local order produced in deviant social groups, we expect the state to tolerate the existence and parochial activities of social groups of any normative orientation unless they threaten the state as an autonomous and ultimate power broker or impose negative externalities on people who have sufficient resources to persuade the authorities to protect them. The argument is illustrated by discussions of the divergent fates of a number of cults and urban street gangs and by some evidence of the state's tolerance of vice.

THE PROBLEM OF SOCIAL ORDER
IN HETEROGENEOUS SOCIETIES

To understand variations in social order among homogeneous societies requires an appreciation of factors that permit one society to exercise social control more efficaciously than another (Hechter and Kanazawa Forthcoming). Although social control mechanisms remain operative in heterogeneous societies, one major difference makes the attainment of social order somewhat more difficult to capture analytically in these societies. The principal threat to social order in homogeneous societies emanates from individuals alone (because all groups in such societies will tend to share common norms and values), but in heterogeneous societies, threats to social order may emanate from groups, as well as from individuals.

The array of normative orientations in a homogeneous society is centered around a single mean, with a relatively small variance. Two quite different types of heterogeneous societies exist, however. One type is distinguished from homogeneous societies only in degree: Whereas still only a single mean exists, the distribution is much wider around that mean. A second type of heterogeneous society is characterized by its polymodal character. Whereas the second type of heterogeneity is qualitatively different from homogeneity, the first type is distinguished from it only by degree. The first type characterizes societies of immigration, such as the United States. The second type characterizes societies of amalgamation, such as the Soviet Union. In this chapter, we shall be concerned solely with the dynamics underlying social order in the first (unimodal) type of heterogeneous society.

All groups, even deviant ones, must produce social order locally to benefit their own group's solidarity. The production of local order creates a largely unintended by-product for large societies: social order on a global scale. States free-ride on the production of local order, particularly that produced by deviant groups. Local order always will contribute to global order, regardless of the norms of local groups, as long as the production of order or the failure to produce it does not consume state resources.

The deviance of a group turns out to be a rather poor predictor of whether it contributes to global order. Groups whose normative orientation diverges from that of the center but whose members do not engage in activities that create threats or externalities contribute more to global order than those whose normative orientation is closer to that of the center.

Regardless of their normative orientation, groups contribute to global order by regulating the behavior of their members. In order to provide themselves with jointly produced goods that provide the rationale for group formation and maintenance, members establish production and allocation norms and enforce them through monitoring and sanctioning mechanisms (Hechter 1987). Participation in groups regulates the behavior of members by demanding their compliance with group norms. Members of every group thus have a private interest in contributing to that group's solidarity and are willing to expend control resources to attain that solidarity. The mere regulation of behavior, for whatever end, represents a contribution to global order (given the exceptions noted above) even though this contribution is a by-product.

Consider, for instance, the Hare Krishna, a group that attracts and serves those who tend to be peripheral members of the society: individuals who are not in school, gainfully employed, or in traditional family arrangements. It is not the aim of the leadership of the Hare Krishna to get their members to finish school, take a job, or form traditional family units. Nonetheless, members are far from free to do as they wish: The obligations required of them are considerable (see the description of their rigorous daily schedule in Daner [1976, pp. 39-44] and Rochford [1985, pp. 13-8]). Members are consumed by the demands of the group, and although the group explicitly intends to provide an alternative to mainstream norms, that their members are compelled to satisfy corporate obligations limits their ability to engage in other, potentially antisocial, activities.

Yet groups that mobilize members who occupy the margins of society provide an even greater—albeit an unintended—service to the larger society. Individuals who are able to negotiate the social mainstream have the greatest opportunity to affiliate with multiple groups and therefore to establish the ties that regulate their behavior. The farther from the mainstream people are, the less their opportunity to join groups; *hermits* by definition are individuals who face the fewest social constraints on their behavior.

It follows, therefore, that Presbyterian church congregations—made up of people who work, people who have children, and the elderly—make a less important contribution to global order than do the congregations of the Nation of Islam, who draw their members disproportionately from African-Americans, the poor, the young, and the dispossessed. Were these two congregations disbanded simultaneously, threats to global order would be less likely to come from the Presbyterian congregations than from the Islamic ones, not because of a difference in norms but because of a difference in the number of ties that bind.

Groups cannot be classified, then, as either deviant or not for the purposes of understanding when they will contribute to global order. Yet the practice of classifying groups by their norms persists. This is because global order, like its local counterpart, is produced by monitoring and sanctioning mechanisms. *Monitoring* entails the collection and analysis of information, and *norms* often are regarded as a signalling device that economize on information: Threats to social order are thought to come less often from mainstream groups than from deviant ones.

Although it may well be the case that groups equally distant from the modal normative orientation of a society are subject to similar levels of monitoring, we will argue that they are not subject to similar levels of sanctioning. Were normative orientation the only concern for agencies of social control, we should expect no differences in sanctioning. Yet as we will demonstrate, sanctioning varies widely among comparably deviant groups. Sanctioning is reserved for groups whose members threaten the state as an autonomous and ultimate power broker or impose negative externalities on people with sufficient resources to persuade the authorities to protect them.

Like de Tocqueville ([1848] 1945, p. 119), we see global order as the product of group solidarities at lower levels of aggregation. Because global order is a collective good, however, no group can be expected to contribute directly to its provision. Our argument avers that global order is achieved as an unintended by-product of the efforts that members of social groups make in getting one another to comply with group-specific obligations through their social control efforts.[1]

Our argument extends beyond this. Whereas previous discussions regard social order as the product of the solidarities of groups that share many norms and values in common, such uniformity is not necessary to produce order at the global level. To illustrate this, we turn to a comparison of two normatively similar deviant groups—Hare Krishna and Rajneesh—and ask under what conditions the apparatus of state control will be brought to bear on their activities.

DETERMINANTS OF STATE INTERVENTION: THE CASES OF HARE KRISHNA AND RAJNEESH

Both Hare Krishna and Rajneesh were direct imports from India that belonged to the "neo-Hindu" tradition. Both movements are well outside of the Judeo-Christian tradition, and their normative status in the American society is marginal, at best. Both were led and brought into the United States by a charismatic leader, and both count mostly peripheral (although from white, middle-class background [Rochford 1985, pp. 46-57]) members of American society among their devoted followers. Despite these many similarities, these groups have had completely different fates in the United States, and the two factors identified above (threats to state autonomy and the imposition of negative externalities on resourceful others) hint at the reason why.

Hare Krishna emerged in the United States after the arrival of Swami Bhaktivedanta in New York in 1966 (Poling and Kenney 1986, p. 7); he established the International Society for Krishna Consciousness (ISKCON) and began to attract followers at his first temple on Second Avenue. In four years (1966-70), ISKCON grew from 1 temple with 16 initiated disciples to 30 temples, 35 initiated disciples, and 347 ministerial students (*Krsna Consciousness Handbook* 1970, pp. 98-105).[2]

While the Rajneesh movement in central Oregon had origins similar to Hare Krishna, its short history in the United States provides a notable contrast. Like Hare Krishna, Rajneesh began in 1981 following the arrival in the United States of its leader, Bhagwan Shree Rajneesh, but the movement came to its demise in 1985 with his deportation from the country. What accounts for its quick demise?

First, unlike Hare Krishna, the Rajneesh movement presented a threat to the autonomy of the state. It first took over political control of the small village of Antelope, Oregon, near their commune, and changed its name to Rajneesh (Carter 1990, p. xv). Then it successfully petitioned to incorporate the commune as another city, Rajneeshpuram (Price 1985, p. 19). Now two municipalities were under complete political control of this religious movement, in violation of the separation of church and state. Rajneeshees maintained their own police force ("Peace Force") whose leaders were trained by the Oregon Police Academy (Carter 1990, p. 92). They built their own airport, with three DC-3 planes in their Air Rajneesh fleet (Price 1985, pp. 25-6), and their free public transportation system was second in size only to Portland's in the state of Oregon (Androes 1986, p. 52). They also constructed and maintained a municipal water system conservatively estimated as capable of serving a population of 50,000 (Androes 1986, p. 53). The

Rajneeshees increasingly took on and over usual governmental functions, and the public services they provided were often better and more efficient than those provided by other municipalities in Oregon.[3]

Of course, no state (neither the state of Oregon nor the government of the United States) could tolerate any large social group, whatever its normative orientation, that threatened to become a sovereign state within its borders (cf. Arrington 1958 on the conflict between the Mormons of Utah, who had a similar aspiration, and the United States government in an earlier era).

Second, in its attempt to gain sovereignty, the Rajneesh movement and its activities imposed a host of negative externalities on its neighbors, who felt "intimidated, threatened, and slandered" (Carter 1990, p. xvii). At the outset, the movement had different effects on different people:

> Many locals appear to have reacted primarily to Rajneesh dominance and control moves, while other opponents were clearly offended by what they saw as immorality and the challenge to their religious traditions. The environmentalist group pursued the threat to its traditional "preservationist" goals as well as gains in regional popularity accruing from its opposition to an unpopular group. (Carter 1990, p. 130)

Some people were adversely affected by the movement's aggressive expansion to adjacent communities. Those who owned land across the river from the commune thus were among the strongest opponents (Carter 1990, pp. 133-4). When the followers eventually took over the nearby small village of Antelope, 32 of the original 49 inhabitants were forced to relocate, and those who stayed were continually harassed by the "Peace Force" (Carter 1990, p. 93). With the political takeover of the Antelope village government, the Rajneeshees also made some changes in the local public school system (Carter 1990, pp. 181-2). These changes forced the local school children to be bussed 50 miles to Madras, Oregon. The quiet way of life to which the prior residents had been accustomed was suddenly disrupted by intruders.

Religious fundamentalists in Oregon were alarmed when a "meditation center" established in Antelope suddenly changed its name to Rajneesh International Foundation and was officially categorized as a church (Carter 1990, p. 140). Furthermore, 1000

Friends of Oregon, a regional environmentalist group, was concerned with the Rajneesh's violation of county land-use plans when the followers began building non-farm-related buildings outside of the designated Urban Growth Boundaries (Carter 1990, pp. 139-40).

Eventually all these groups in the local communities united in their opposition to Rajneesh. As the opposition became increasingly organized, the Rajneeshees took a more militant stance and made further moves to alienate and threaten the local residents. One of these counterproductive moves was to treat Antelope as a "hostage town":

> Over the course of the year, the Rajneesh council of Antelope raised taxes and fees, hired security services from the Rajneeshpuram "Peace Force," and took control of the Antelope school. The increased taxes imposed some burden on retirees (most of whom left); the Peace Force instituted intimidating surveillance of locals; and the public school controversy broadened the base of public opposition. At one point, Rajneesh leaders offered to "trade" Antelope for a bill officially recognizing Rajneeshpuram. They would withdraw from Antelope to the ranch if the legislature would sanction their incorporated city. (Carter 1990, p. 167)[4]

The confrontation with locals escalated over time:

> Additional housing was acquired [in Antelope] and a campaign was begun to discomfit remaining locals. Milne [a Rajneeshee who was later excommunicated for ideological differences] reports instructions to sannyasin to hold loud, all-night parties near the residences of others and to offend locals with public displays of affection. . . . Milne reports several confrontations with locals when he took pictures of their homes in Antelope and dwellings in other parts of the state to document the part-time nature of their residency in Antelope. He also notes that his film "documentation" was intended to intimidate and harass these residents. (Carter 1990, p. 150)

The Rajneesh Peace Force stopped and occasionally searched non-Rajneeshees traveling on county roads in and around newly incorporated Rajneeshpuram. All access to the city was tightly controlled by these armed security guards (Carter 1990, pp. 182-3).

Toward the end of the conflict, the Rajneeshees resorted to criminal tactics (for which some of their leaders were later convicted). They set fire to the field of a rancher near Antelope who refused to sell land to the group. And they poisoned Jefferson

County District Attorney Michael Sullivan when he became alienated from the movement despite his earlier extended attempt to negotiate accommodation between the Rajneeshees and the locals (Carter 1990, pp. 198-200).

Local residents responded with equally strong, if legal, measures; they filed numerous lawsuits against the commune leaders and members. The assault on the Rajneesh movement eventually involved the federal government. In December 1982, the INS denied Bhagwan's application for permanent residency (Carter 1990, p. 163), and ultimately he was deported from the United States after pleading guilty to two counts of making false statements to federal INS officials. He was charged with 1 count of conspiracy and 34 counts of making false statements to a federal official. Under a plea bargain, Bhagwan was fined $400,000, given a 10-year suspended sentence, "allowed" to depart the country "voluntarily," and placed on probation for 5 years. Other leaders of the movement were charged similarly and pleaded guilty for such felonies as attempted murder and first-degree arson (Carter 1990, pp. 235-40).

The divergent histories of Hare Krishna and Rajneesh illustrate our earlier contention that the state tolerates the activities of deviant social groups as long as they do not threaten its exclusive exercise of power and do not impose negative externalities on others with collective action potential.

True, Hare Krishna devotees often accost people at airports and other public places (Rochford 1985, Chap. 7). The negative externalities the Hare Krishna impose on such people, however, are different from those the Rajneeshees imposed on Oregonians in two crucial respects. The occasional harassment of people at an airport hardly compares in magnitude or seriousness to the political takeover of an entire municipality or attempted murder. More important, victims of Hare Krishna harassment at an airport do not know one another (and thus have no social closure [Coleman 1988, 1990]); hence they have little potential to engage in collective action. In contrast, the Rajneesh movement adversely affected long-term residents of Antelope and other central Oregon communities who knew each other very well; these victims could pool their resources to combat their intruders collectively, and this is what they did.

Had Rajneesh not so obviously challenged the state and imposed negative externalities on resourceful actors, it might have survived to enjoy the same kind of parasitic relationship with the state that Hare Krishna seems to enjoy. Such relationships between the state and alternative social groups are parasitic because these groups enjoy the tolerance and even implicit support of the state for their deviant activities (as with the HUD grant to ISKCON), and in turn the state can farm out some of its responsibilities to produce and maintain global order to its constituent groups. (The mayors of New York and San Francisco once commended ISKCON for its total ban on drugs among its members [Daner 1976, p. 60].) Because most Americans regard both Hare Krishna and Rajneesh as deviant cult organizations, and most of the internal values, norms, and practices of both are equally incongruent with the values and norms of American society at large, their deviance alone explains nothing of the state's differential treatment of these two groups.

Nonetheless it may be argued that although the followers of Rajneesh were clearly marginal members of society, even if they were deprived of membership in this kind of group, they would be unlikely to engage in activities that would threaten global order. It is even the case, perhaps, that they were more likely to do so as members of Rajneesh than if they were left to their own devices. It would seem plausible that groups whose members are wont to engage in illegal behavior when left on their own are even more likely to do so when organized into a collectivity.[5] Urban street gangs appear to be the prime example; made up of disadvantaged youth with little to lose, they seem to be the principal threat to social order in the contemporary United States.

Gangs allow us to distinguish among groups on the edge. Because our proposition is that the state enjoys as a by-product the control mechanisms that social groups institute for their own purposes, those whose control mechanisms impose net negative externalities on society will not be tolerated, for they produce social *dis*order. No state countenances groups that challenge its monopoly of the means of violence and its role as ultimate power broker in civil society. Instances of social disorder will be acknowledged, however, let alone redressed, only if they affect individuals who have the capacity to engage in collective action on their own behalf.

These criteria should be important in explaining differential police harassment of deviant groups. Because the state always has extremely limited control capacity, it can only enforce the legal code selectively. The police are more likely to turn a blind eye to illegal activities of groups that contribute to global order (like gambling parlors in New York's Chinatown) than those that threaten it (like crack-dealing gangs in Watts).[6] Several excellent studies of urban gangs shed light on these issues.

SAINTS, ROUGHNECKS, GUARDIAN ANGELS, AND 37 URBAN STREET GANGS: AN ALTERNATIVE INTERPRETATION

In a classic study, Chambliss (1973) observed two youth gangs in Hanibal High School over the course of 2 years. The Saints were an upper-middle-class gang, while the members of the Rough-necks came from lower-class families. Despite the fact that both gangs engaged in delinquent activities, the community, the school, and the police consistently regarded the Saints as "good, upstanding, nondelinquent youths with bright futures" but the Roughnecks as "tough, young criminals who were headed for trouble" (Chambliss 1973, p. 28). Over the course of the study, none of the eight Saints even so much as received a traffic ticket. In contrast, each of the six Roughnecks was arrested at least once; several of them were arrested a number of times and spent at least one night in jail. If the Saints and Roughnecks were equally delinquent, what accounts for the differential police treatment of the two gangs?

Chambliss's answer was a typical interactionist one. The influential upper-middle-class parents of the Saints (and others like them) were able to exert subtle pressure on the police to disregard their children's delinquent acts as harmless pranks and the occasional sowing of wild oats, while the powerless lower-class parents of the Roughnecks (and others like them) were unable to do so. Further, the rich Saints had access to their own cars, which allowed them to travel to nearby Big City to commit their delinquent acts, an option that the poor Roughnecks, who owned no cars, did not have. The Saints' upper-middle-class appearance and demeanor also biased the police's perception of their behaviors in their favor. Chambliss argues that the local Hanibal residents perceived the seriousness of the delinquent acts committed by the Saints and the Roughnecks quite differently because of their different class backgrounds, and this distorted perception led to the unequal treatment of the two youth gangs by the police.

Our argument suggests a different interpretation. Differential police treatment may have been a result of the amount of negative externalities imposed by these two youth gangs and of the kinds of people who were adversely affected. Despite the fact that "in sheer number of illegal acts, the Saints were the more delinquent" (Chambliss 1973, p. 29), their delinquent acts created very few negative externalities for local community members.

> [The Saints] simply viewed themselves as having a little fun and who, they would ask, was really hurt by it? The answer had to be no one, although this fact remains one of the most difficult things to explain about the gang's behavior. Unlikely though it seems, in two years of drinking, driving, carousing and vandalism no one was seriously injured as a result of the Saints' activities. (Chambliss 1973, p. 26)

"The Saints were more continuously engaged in delinquency but their acts were not for the most part costly to property" (Chambliss 1973, p. 29); in contrast, the Roughnecks' delinquent acts were. They frequently stole from local stores and other students at school. "The thefts ranged from very small things like paperback books, comics and ballpoint pens to expensive items like watches" (Chambliss 1973, p. 27). Apart from occasional theft of gasoline, the only things the Saints stole were wooden barricades and lanterns from construction sites and road repair areas, which belonged to no private citizens. The Saints abandoned most of these stolen items, and these could thus later be recovered (Chambliss 1973, p. 29).

The Saints and the Roughnecks also had differential propensities toward violence. "The Roughnecks were more prone to physical violence" while "the Saints never fought" (Chambliss 1973, p. 29). The Roughnecks' fighting activities were frequent and often involved other members of the local community. It appears that the Roughnecks imposed more negative externalities on others both in their property crimes and violent crimes.

Moreover, on those rare occasions when the Saints' delinquent acts did impose some negative externalities, they hardly ever affected the local Hanibal residents, who knew the boys well, but instead were directed against the residents of Big City, who did not know them. In contrast, all of the Roughnecks' delinquent acts took place in Hanibal because they did not have access to cars. So while the Big City driver who drove into a hole in the road deliberately left unmarked by the Saints did not know who the pranksters were (Chambliss 1973, p. 25), the teacher whom one of the Roughnecks threatened to beat up and who had to hide under the desk in order to escape him had no illusion about the identity of the delinquent boy (Chambliss 1973, p. 28). Because the Saints' pranks affected the anonymous people of metropolitan Big City, who knew neither the boys' identities nor each other, they could not pool their resources to deal with the Saints' delinquency. In contrast, the Roughnecks' victims were mostly the local residents, who knew both the boys and each other very well. They were thus able to band together and deal with the Roughnecks' delinquency collectively.

No doubt the Saints were able to commit their pranks on strangers in Big City because they had cars, which their upper-middle-class status afforded; in that sense, their class position, which Chambliss emphasizes, is an important factor in this story. The unequal treatment of the two gangs by the police, however, may have happened *independent* of their class position *if* their respective delinquent acts affected, as they did, different segments of the society. With their nice cars, influential parents, and polite demeanor, the Saints may have been arrested anyway had some of their pranks actually resulted in some injuries and/or affected members of the local community, who could act collectively.

Our interpretation is reinforced by a new ethnographic study of 37 urban street gangs in New York, Los Angeles, and Boston. Noting that street gangs have been a feature of the American urban landscape for at least a century, Jankowski (1991) attributes their persistence to interdependence between gangs and their local communities (see also Suttles 1968, pp. 6-9, 189-229). The principal benefits that gangs provide their communities are two. The first is welfare: Through their participation in the underground economy (dealing drugs, running prostitution, and so forth), gangs produce wealth for their members, and this wealth also is available to meet some community needs. The second is security: Gangs are a local militia that protects neighborhood residents and small businesses from external predators far more effectively than the police. In return for these goods, members of the community provide the gang with social approval, a license to recruit their children, and—most important—a safe haven from the authorities. Most of the violence committed by gangs is strategic—designed to capture new territory—and is hardly ever directed against community members.[7] The most successful gangs (those with what Jankowski terms *vertical/hierarchical* organization) regulate their members' behavior by punishing those who engage in random violence that is unsanctioned by the leadership. Gangs who fail to keep their members from preying on the community are denied the community's safe haven and soon unravel.

Yet another variation on this theme is provided by a close examination of the Guardian Angels, who fit the standard definition of a gang but who are openly tolerated by the police. Despite their status as modern vigilantes (Kenney 1987) and their well-known propensity toward violence and extralegal activities (Reinccke 1982; Pileggi 1980; Cordts 1981), no chapter has come under concerted police control (Kenney 1987). One answer might be their sense of themselves as upholding the law, and their ability to communicate that to the general public. Yet these claims would be unlikely to convince police in the face of behavioral evidence to the contrary.

Instead state tolerance may be due to the inefficacy of the Guardian Angels: They do surprisingly little that affects others either positively or negatively. For instance, the Guardian Angels actually interrupted crimes and made arrests in only 258 instances in the entire nation after 3 years of active operation (Newport 1982, p. 10). It seems that the negative externalities that they impose on others are limited enough to account for police inattention despite their obvious similarity to other urban gangs.

STATE TOLERANCE OF VICE

If the state tacitly recognizes the positive contributions of deviant social groups toward global order and tolerates their existence as long as they do not challenge its authority or impose negative externalities on resourceful others, it follows that the formal legal status of social groups in and of itself does not affect how the state treats these groups. In particular, the police should be especially tolerant of groups that explicitly engage in "victimless crimes" (such as prostitution, gambling, drug use) unless these groups challenge the state's monopoly on violence and/or impose negative externalities on resourceful actors.

James Q. Wilson (1968) underscores these points in a study of police behavior in eight United States communities. Wilson argues that the primary function of patrol officers on the beat is the maintenance of public order rather than strict enforcement of the letter of the law. The police operate to emphasize public order over law enforcement and tolerate some vice in order to maintain order mostly because city officials, to whom the police chief is responsible, recognize, as we do, the important role that some deviant groups perform in the overall production of social order.

> The city administration [of Albany, NY] has changed its policy on vice slowly but in accordance with what it thinks public opinion expects. The Gut [the red-light district in Albany] was once defended by officials who felt that it kept the "riff-raff" in one place; no decent citizen would be offended unless he went there looking for action, in which case he could hardly complain. Toward the end, however, it was receiving too much unfavorable publicity. Most of the honky-tonks and brothels torn down by the governor did not reopen. (Wilson 1968, p. 240)

A Democratic leader in Albany tells one of Wilson's interviewers:

> There was gambling in the Stone Age, there's gambling today, there will be gambling when your grandchildren are as old as I am. I can't see enforcing a law against nature. Anyway, there's never been any gang murders or stuff like goes on in New York as a result of gambling and prostitution. The gamblers up here are nice people, otherwise; they're businessmen. (Wilson 1968, p. 245)

The implication in this politician's comment is that if "gang murders or stuff like goes on in New York as a result of gambling and prostitution" were to occur, then the government would act swiftly to close down these operations.

Further, some city officials seem to recognize that deviant groups are especially likely to regulate the behavior of marginal individuals:

> A high city official told an interviewer that "Nobody wants to eliminate all of the gambling and prostitution, *especially among the Negroes.* We feel that some of it has to go on, but it should be kept down and under control." After the charges made by the Negro minister at the February 1967 council meeting, the city announced that gambling and prostitution had been shut down. Some arrests were made, in fact, but privately a high city official told an interviewer afterwards that the city was not "closed tight"; he explained that "We couldn't close the place down totally *with the minority group that we have here* [emphasis added]—we have to allow some safety valve." (Wilson 1968, pp. 245-6)

Incidentally a wave of burglaries and the murder of a business-man in the area led to both the charges by the minister and the city's action ostensibly to crack down on gambling and prostitution—serious negative externalities as a result of otherwise tolerated vice operations (Wilson 1968, p. 244).

Wilson's research indicates that, at least in some American cities in the 1960s, the police treated some forms of "victimless crimes" in accordance with the argument in this chapter. Further, the police attitude toward vice operations seems to reflect the opinions of the municipal officials that these operations have important implications for the production of order, especially for peripheral members of the society (such as African-Americans in the context of the mid-1960s United States).

IMPLICATIONS

Order in heterogeneous national societies is enhanced by the existence of large numbers of relatively small groups that are unable to command control over resources that threaten the unique position of the state. Competition among groups for resources and members is likely to be advantageous from the standpoint of the production of global order.

The normative orientation of these groups matters not: The greater the number of groups that attract the membership of those on the margin of society, the better.

Still a question remains: Instead of fostering association among peripheral individuals, why not try to buy their loyalty through transfers and state entitlements? In a relatively heterogeneous society, this solution would be both politically infeasible and prohibitively expensive. Yet for a more important theoretical reason this kind of state co-optation is unlikely to be effective. Entitlements tend to decrease global order when they come from the state, because then citizens become dependent on an entity—the state—that necessarily has relatively weak control capacity. Entitlements increase global order only when they come from social groups—as they do, for example, in Japan—because then people are dependent on entities that have relatively great control capacity.

Global order therefore is enhanced by freedom of association, especially at the margins of society. The most efficacious way to produce global order is to strengthen the conditions for the production of local solidarity.

NOTES

1. This conclusion is the exact inverse of that averred by theorists of mass society (such as Arendt 1958, Part 3), who argued that the stability of states increased as the solidarity of their constituent social groups waned.

2. Although the Hare Krishna movement experienced a major crisis after the death of Swami in 1977 (Rochford 1985, Chap. 9), it has not faced any external intervention by the state. On occasion, outside deprogrammers hired by the parents of ISKCON members have kidnapped and deprogrammed some members in order to return them to their parents. In such cases, however, ISKCON has successfully prosecuted the deprogrammers and parents in criminal court for kidnapping and other First Amendment violations by claiming that it represents a genuine religious tradition (Poling and Kenney 1986, p. 10). State tolerance for ISKCON exists to such a high extent that, in Gainsville, Florida, ISKCON operated a Food For Life program that provided 2,400 meals a month for the urban poor, *with a HUD grant of $20,000*. As its own financial measure, ISKCON sold the official T-shirt of the Hare Krishna Food For Life Program for $7.75.

3. The purpose of this seemed to emanate from Bhagwan's aspirations, formulated at an earlier time in India, to create a self-sufficient "new society" that was independent of the host culture and thus fell outside of its political jurisdiction. With all of its institutions in place, the Oregon commune seemed very close to fulfillment of his dream. "The term 'new society' had become more than a metaphor for sannyasin [Rajneeshees] by 1982. The ranch provided sufficient isolation for members to see themselves as independent of outside institutions, effectively *a sovereign state*. The illusion of total autonomy developed quite naturally from the

increasing completeness of their institutions (agriculture, finance, medical services) and the separation from outside definitions of reality (an internal press, video and audio productions, limited and controlled outside contact)" (Carter 1990, p. 158 [emphasis added]).

4. Elsewhere the Rajneeshees also employed this tactic of raising the cost of living to drive people out. When they purchased the Martha Washington women's hotel in Portland for $1.5 million, they immediately raised the rent from $285 per month to $750 per month, effectively dislodging prior residents. The hotel then was used almost exclusively by devotees in transit to Rajneeshpuram (Carter 1990, p. 170).

5. LeBon (1899) was the first to suggest that members of a crowd are less restrained by social conventions and therefore more likely to engage in antisocial behavior than nonmembers.

6. Yet since successful prosecution of criminal behavior usually requires evidence held by community members, if such evidence is collectively withheld, the police will be powerless to act on their intentions (Jankowski 1991).

7. This is why the local order that is invariably produced by urban street gangs usually does not contribute to global order. Because a gang's ability to produce local order ultimately rests on territorial expansion, this leads to a high risk of violent conflict with the gangs that control the coveted territory. As this violence often imposes negative externalities on resourceful actors, it tends to attract police attention and to consume public resources.

REFERENCES

Androes, Louis C. 1986. "Cultures in Collision: The Rajneesh Search for Community." *Communities* 71-72:49-54.

Arendt, Hannah. 1958. *The Origins of Totalitarianism.* New York: World.

Arrington, Leonard. 1958. *Great Basin Kingdom: An Economic History of the Latter-Day Saints.* Cambridge, MA: Harvard University Press.

Carter, Lewis F. 1990. *Charisma and Control in Rajneeshpuram: The Role of Shared Values in the Creation of a Community.* Cambridge, UK: Cambridge University Press.

Chambliss, William J. 1973. "The Saints and Roughnecks." *Transaction: Social Science and Modern Society* 11:24-31.

Coleman, James S. 1988. "Social Capital in the Creation of Human Capital." *American Journal of Sociology* 94:S95-S120.

———. 1990. *Foundations of Social Theory.* Cambridge, MA: Harvard University Press.

Cordts, Michael. 1981. "I Was a Guardian Angel." *Chicago Sun Times,* November 8.

Daner, Francine Jeanne. 1976. *The American Children of Krsna: A Study of the Hare Krsna Movement.* New York: Holt, Rinehart and Winston.

Hechter, Michael. 1987. *Principles of Group Solidarity.* Berkeley: University of California Press.

Hechter, Michael and Satoshi Kanazawa. Forthcoming. "The Production of Social Order, with Special Reference to Contemporary Japan." In *Social Theory and*

Social Practice: Essays in Honor of James S. Coleman, edited by Aage Sorensen and Seymour Spilerman. New York: Praeger.

Jankowski, Martín Sánchez. 1991. *Islands in the Street: Gangs and American Urban Society.* Berkeley: University of California Press.

Kenney, Dennis Jay. 1987. *Crime, Fear, and the New York City Subways: The Role of Citizen Action.* New York: Praeger.

Krsna Consciousness Handbook: For the Year 484, Caitanya Era. 1970. Boston: ISKCON Press.

Le Bon, Gustave. 1899. *The Crowd.* London: Unwin.

Newport, John Paul, Jr. 1982. "Opinion on Angels: A Devil of a Division." *Fort Worth Star Telegram,* March 21, pp. 1-10a.

Pileggi, Nicholas. 1980. "The Guardian Angels: Help—or Hype?" *New York.* 24(November):14-9.

Poling, Tommy H. and J. Frank Kenney. 1986. *The Hare Krishna Character Type: A Study of the Sensate Personality.* Lewiston: Edwin Mellen.

Price, Marie Daly. 1985. "Rajneeshpuram and the American Utopian Tradition." (Discussion Paper No. 87.) Syracuse University, Department of Geography.

Reinccke, William. 1982. "Marching With the Avenging Angels." *Today/Philadelphia Inquirer,* January 31, p. 1.

Rochford, Jr., E. Burke. 1985. *Hare Krishna in America.* New Brunswick, NJ: Rutgers University Press.

Suttles, Gerald D. 1968. *The Social Order of the Slum: Ethnicity and Territory in the Inner City.* Chicago: University of Chicago Press.

de Tocqueville, Alexis. [1848] 1945. *Democracy in America,* edited by Phillips Bradley. New York: Knopf.

Wilson, James Q. 1968. *Varieties of Police Behavior: The Management of Law and Order in Eight Communities.* Cambridge, MA: Harvard University Press.

PART II

Critical Perspectives

Chapter 5

RATIONALITY AND EMOTION
Homage to Norbert Elias

THOMAS J. SCHEFF
University of California, Santa Barbara

MOST THEORIES AND METHODS in social science discount emotions and the possibility that they play causal roles in human conduct. The seminal work of Norbert Elias provides an example of the systematic study of emotions. His theory allows for parity between the elements in causal chains: emotion, perception, thought, and behavior, between individual behavior and social structure. His method of analyzing verbatim texts in their social and historical context may restore meaning to the study of human conduct.

The rationalist attitude is a key component of modern civilization. It has two components: One emphasizes thought and reason, the other discounts emotions. Modern rationalism is an outgrowth of the Enlightenment, the development of modern philosophy and science in the 17th and 18th centuries. The roots of rationalist attitude are best exemplified by the thought of Spinoza ([1678] 1954), who furnished what might be considered a motto of the Enlightenment: *Non ridere, non lugere, neque detestari, sed intelligere* (Do not smile, do not lament, nor condemn, but understand) (Cassirer 1932, p. xi). Spinoza was justifiably concerned that intense emotions can interfere with reason. He was hardly discounting, however, the role of emotion in all human conduct. Like other writers of his time, he treated emotions as important components of human experience.[1]

With the growth of modern civilization, however, the rationalist attitude narrowed to the point of excluding emotions by fiat. In some ways, the study of emotions has devolved rather than evolved. The work of Descartes, Locke, Bentham, and Mill proposes not only that we *should* be ruled by reason, which is a good point, but also assumes that humans *are* ruled by reason, which is not. Emotions gradually disappeared from many of the most serious discussions of the human condition. The danger of this attitude is that it overemphasizes human self-control and awareness, ignoring an entire side of human behavior: impulsiveness, lack of awareness, and loss of control.

The image of human action underlying rationalism is that decision makers consider a wide range of options and the consequences of taking and not taking each option. Although in some situations this image fits well with reality, in many others it does not. Important decisions often are made impulsively, taking into consideration few if any of the possible options, and considering few or none of the consequences. Many of the most important decisions individuals make may have this character, such as choosing a spouse or a career. Collective decisions also may be irrational: Stock market panics, famines, and wars often begin with impulsive, unaware, and/or out-of-control behavior.

The danger with the rationalist attitude is that it may obscure real flaws in ourselves and in our civilization. If we are all so majestically rational, then we need not reform ourselves and our society. Rationalism arose as a justifiable protest against the irrationality of the status quo that ruled the Middle Ages. Thought and action were dominated by substantive rationality, which often meant whim and caprice. The rationalist attitude in turn has come to idealize formal rationality, which often means blind adherence to rule and mechanical formula. Rationalism has come to be the dominant attitude in our present status quo, the social arrangements that go without saying in our society. One such arrangement is the suppression of emotions.

SUPPRESSION OF EMOTIONS
IN MODERN SOCIETIES

In a recent study, Sterns and Sterns (1986) have shown that attitudes toward anger shifted from the 18th century to today. They found that in advice manuals before the 18th century, anger was not condemned in toto, only excessive anger. Righteous anger even was encouraged. Beginning gradually in the 18th century, however, a tendency grew to condemn all anger. I believe that their findings apply to all emotion, not just to anger. Modern societies have a strong tendency to suppress not only excessive emotion but all emotion. The suppression of sexuality in the 19th century is a familiar and obvious example of the denial of basic human attributes. The suppression of emotions is even more pervasive but much more subtle.

The denial of emotion is institutionalized in our very language. For example, instead of speaking of our embarrassment directly, we say, "It was an awkward moment for me." This statement is a verbal defense against acknowledging an emotion. It was not I who was embarrassed (denial), but the moment that was awkward (projection).

Most theories of human behavior use one or another device against acknowledging emotions. The most candid approach has been to deny categorically that emotions have a causal role. B. F. Skinner (1969) has stated in print that emotions are not causes but effects of other causes. Proposing that all behavior is built on stimulus-response chains, he decided by fiat that only the stimulus side was causal, as if human responses, perceptions, thoughts, and feelings were secondary. Similar a priori thinking is involved in Marx's doctrine that the mode of production is the causal element in social change. Like Skinner, Marx ruled by fiat that one element in a causal chain was cause, the other effect.

Another approach in social theory is to acknowledge briefly the role of emotions but only abstractly and perfunctorily. In their general theory of action, Parsons and Shils (1951) named *affect* as one of the four basic components of social action. In this volume and in all of his subsequent work, however, Parsons never named specific emotions and never showed their role in action sequences. For Parsons, emotions functioned as a residual and virtually unused category for causes that were not rational. The same device can be found in many other theories: For Durkheim, the *social emotion* was a crucial ingredient of solidarity. Because he never named the concrete components or described their indicators, however, emotions had no actual role in any of his formulations.

A recent attempt to introduce emotions into economic thinking (Frank 1985) suggests how difficult it is to undo the habit of suppressing emotions. The author recognizes that status is an important element in economic behavior, acting independently of strictly monetary calculations. But rather than dealing with the underlying emotions of pride and shame, he translates them into behavior: the quest for status. This tactic obscures the very emotions he seeks to uncover and thereby continues the habit of suppression and denial. Frank has the desire to reintroduce emotions into social science, as indicated by his *Passion Within Reason* (1988), but his work as yet lacks the vocabulary of specific emotions to enable him to do so.

Another approach to diminishing the role of emotions in behavior is to recognize only a single composite emotional state without spelling out the specific emotions that it subsumes. In most variants of behaviorism, for example, specific emotions and their indicators seldom are named; reference is made instead to the composite state called only *emotional arousal*. Another variation on this approach is found in psychoanalytic theory. In these discussions, several specific emotions are recognized (anger, grief, and guilt), but most others are subsumed under the composite rubric of *anxiety*. These practices are less reductive than those found in Parsons and in Durkheim but still suppress the role of emotions by treating most of the specific emotions only in terms of a broad residual category.

Still another common resort in social theory is to ignore emotions altogether. This is the tack taken in rational choice theory. Neither the theory nor the method allows for the inclusion of emotions as elements in human behavior. Theoretical discussions make no mention of emotions, favoring gains and losses, positive and negative outcomes, utility curves, and other highly abstract concepts. The methodology of most studies in this framework guarantees the exclusion of emotions. Such studies typically use such easily available data as paper-and-pencil answers in laboratory experiments and surveys, and the public information produced by organizations, in order to be "objective." Actually these tactics exclude indicators of emotions and therefore determine the findings. In our civilization, neither individuals nor organizations are in the habit of making public their emotional states except under unusual circumstances.

Like many approaches in the human sciences, most rational choice studies favor the armchair approach over "hands-on." In his study of surgeons, Bosk quotes one of his subjects, a very senior supervisor:

> Surgery is a . . . contact sport. . . . You can't be a good armchair surgeon. If I want to know if my resident is doing a good job, I have to be in the operating room watching him. I can't tell what kind of a job a colleague has done from just looking at his patient. I may have suspicions, but unless I was there and know what kind of situation he was presented with, I can't really say anything. (Bosk 1979, p. 13)

Bosk goes on to demonstrate that social science is also a contact sport. By observing surgeons directly over a long period of time, he found that they taught ethics by relentlessly punishing surgical errors, especially those due to moral rather than technical lapses. Bosk criticized the studies in the sociology of medicine that claimed to have found a lack of ethical training for physicians (Barber et al. 1973; Crane 1975; Gray 1975). Their results, Bosk argued, are determined by their method—surveys and interviews—rather than direct observation. If rational choice and other theories of decision making are going to progress, some changes in methodology may be needed. Perhaps it will be necessary to obtain hands-on knowledge of a setting first, via ethnographic studies and/or discourse analysis, in order to assess the extent to which hidden emotions are involved, before generating experiments and surveys.

The taboo against emotions is so strong in modern social science, however, that even hands-on studies often manage to ignore their existence. In a precise and useful study of the dispute styles of inner-city boys and girls, Goodwin (1990), like Bosk, directly observed her subjects for several years. Getting even closer to her data than Bosk, she audiotaped the disputes and subjected them to microscopic, word-by-word analysis.

Goodwin found that the boys and girls had very different styles of disputing. Typically the boys were aggressively and insultingly confrontative, calling each other derogatory names and using ritual insults. The girls, on the other hand, had very little direct quarrelling. They specialized in behind-the-back innuendo. Both boys and girls, she argued, had dispute styles that were rejecting and insulting.

Goodwin's discussions of these disputes, however, is entirely behavioral. She focuses on the stimulus side of the chain of events involved in the quarrels but ignores the responses—the thoughts and feelings of the subjects. She discusses the ridicule, degrading, insulting, rejecting, and excluding that went on but not the possibility that the children were angry and hurt. In one dispute, one boy says to another: "You shut up you big lips" (Goodwin 1990, p. 85).

This utterance is insulting in two different ways. It is an aggressive and insultingly direct command that is rude and rudely stated, and it also ridicules the other boy's appearance. Since both boys are black, ridiculing the size of his lips is probably a racial slur.

The dispute style of the girls does not involve direct confrontations but "she said that you said" intrigue of the type that Bowen (1978) called *triangling*. Conflict that is this indirect usually results in rejection and exclusion. Yet the author virtually ignores the resulting emotions. The only feelings that are mentioned directly are jealousy and righteous indignation. No mention is made of anger, grief, fear, shame, or embarrassment. Goodwin instead uses the phrase *affect displays* as if to distance herself from the possibility that the children might have been suffering pain. So strong is the denial of emotions in social science that even a study as microscopic as Goodwin's manages to avoid giving them serious consideration.

The overwhelming majority of discussions and studies of human behavior avoid emotions and feelings by using one or more of the devices mentioned: categorical dismissal, as in Skinner; token mention, as in Parsons; broad categories like anxiety in psychoanalysis; or most commonly, simply ignoring emotions, as in rational choice studies and conversation analysis. Because social theories use ordinary language, and ordinary language imputes emotions to human being, most social theories imply but do not make explicit a role for emotions in conduct. It may take considerable ingenuity to bring these implications to the surface, as Collins (1990) has done with Durkheim, Goffman, and Garfinkel.

Another tradition in social science, however, considers the importance of emotions. Like Spinoza, Hume ([1740] 1978) recognized that under certain conditions, emotions can be causes and not just effects. Hume is not categorical, however. He does not claim that emotions are always the wellsprings of behavior, as Skinner states that they never are. His formulations are contingent and subjunctive (I am indebted to Don Brown, who brought this statement to my attention): "When I receive any injury from another, I often feel a violent passion of resentment, which makes me desire his evil and punishment, independent of all considerations of pleasure and advantage to myself" (Hume [1740], p. 464). Hume goes on to specifically contradict utilitarian doctrine, the progenitor of modern rational choice theory: "Men often act knowingly against their interest: For which reason the view of the greatest possible good does not always influence them. [But] men often counter-act a violent passion in prosecution of their interests and designs" ([1740], p. 464). Hume's comments are much more poised and complex than those of the Utilitarians or of Skinner. His image of human action is broader, in that it allows for both rational and irrational action, for the affect of resentment, for behavior that is determined by resentment, and finally for behavior that resists being determined by resentment. Hume sought to understand the relationship among reason, passion, and behavior in a way that most modern social theories do not. Darwin (1872), Nietzsche (1886), and Scheler ([1912] 1961), following in the same tradition as Hume, considered resentment and other emotions as causal components in a wide range of human behavior.

SHAME THRESHOLDS AND RATIONALITY: ELIAS'S APPROACH TO MODERNITY

A modern inheritor of the tradition of Spinoza, Hume, Nietzsche, Darwin, and Scheler is Norbert Elias, whose studies of what he called *the civilizing process* emphasize the role of emotions in modern societies, especially the role of shame. His methodology, although not clearly described by him, points toward an objective approach to studying emotions implied in verbatim texts.

Although Elias is beginning to be appreciated, virtually no notice has been given to his methodology. In a very generous appreciation of his work, the French historian Chartier (1988) provides an extremely detailed chapter on Elias's theory and method (Jon Cruz called this chapter to my attention). But Chartier glosses what I consider to be the most important feature of Elias's method in a single sentence: "[Elias used] a procedure that established the laws for the functioning of social forms on the basis of detailed examination of one instance of their realization in history" (Chartier 1988, p. 73).

Chartier's formulation is too brief and abstract to catch what may be the basic core of Elias's method—part/whole analysis: micro-macro interpretations of verbatim texts in their situational or historical context (Scheff 1990). In a display of unparalleled virtuosity, Elias grounded every analysis of historical process and social structure in the fine details of concrete examples, seeing the big picture in the part and the way the part fits into larger and larger wholes. This is the same method that Goethe used in his botanic and other scientific work, relating the micro- and macro-cosms (Goethe, [1785] 1963):

> In every living thing what we call the parts is so inseparable from the whole that the parts can only be understood in the whole, and we can neither make the parts the measure of the whole nor the whole the measure of the parts; and this is why living creatures, even the most restricted, have something about them that we cannot quite grasp and have to describe as infinite or partaking of infinity. (Goethe, quoted in Farley 1963, p. 195)

Elias's method offers to restore the unity of part and whole that has been sundered by excessive specialization in modern science, the rigid separation that is increasingly taking place between theorists, methodologists, researchers, and practitioners (Scheff 1990; Scheff and Retzinger 1991).

A discussion of Elias's methods requires raising the whole issue of objectivity in the human sciences. Elias is not content in his historical studies to describe outer events, as is true in many historical studies and in most current social science. He insists rather on interpreting meaning, that is, both outer events (behavior) and inner events (thoughts and feelings). Does any objective way of interpreting meaning exist, or are such interpretations necessarily subjective?

In my view, Elias's methods point the way toward objective interpretations. His method involves arriving at interpretations of meaning through close consideration of verbatim texts in their historical context. To understand that his method can be objective, it is helpful to consider the general nature of human expressions and to compare the way these expressions usually are interpreted in typical qualitative and quantitative studies.

As studies in language, philosophy, and anthropology have shown repeatedly, human expressions are inherently complex and ambiguous. Each human expression has many possible meanings, so the actual meaning can be understood only in context. Schutz (1962) pointed to what he called the *indexicality* of expressions. Any given word or sentence indexes many possible meanings. Each human communication is embedded deeply in the particular context in which it occurs and can be understood only in reference to that context. For example, the particular reference of a pronoun like *him, her, it,* or *their* can be understood only in context. These words are "blank checks"; only keen attention to the context in which they are used can lead to detecting their meanings. Pronouns are extreme examples of the blank check nature of human expressions. But when one closely examines actual communications, it turns out that all expressions have this kind of ambiguity, not only pronouns (Scheff 1990).

Steiner (1975) has provided a brilliant explication of the inherent complexity and ambiguity of human expressions. Although focused on the problem of translating texts from one language to another, Steiner shows that all texts are extraordinarily ambiguous, requiring prodigious efforts of what he calls *interpretive decipherment*. He avoids the current pose of poststructuralism, however. He does not say that all meanings are relative and irretrievable. By providing examples of poems well translated from one language to another, he shows that decipherment is possible, given the skill, talent, imagination, dedication, and resources necessary to do the job.

In this respect, human communication is fundamentally different from that of all other living things. The expressions of other animals have meanings fixed by genetic inheritance; in ants, for example, one chemical given off by an individual unambiguously means "member" to other ant inhabitants of its nest, and "enemy" to all ants that are not. As reference to any dictionary in any language will disclose quickly, all commonly used words have more than one meaning. It is not unusual for frequently used words to have a large number of meanings, some of them surprisingly contradictory or disparate.

How do quantitative studies typically deal with this problem? One technique is to avoid interpreting meanings altogether, sticking to external behavior. Another technique is to gloss over ambiguities, the method most frequently used in surveys, interviews, and paper-and-pencil tests. These studies depend entirely on the *reliability of their procedures,* following rules, to warrant the validity of their findings. But using repeatable procedures does not solve the problem of indexicality; it only guarantees that the studies will either ignore the particular meanings of each utterance or repeat the same errors in interpreting them.

The typical qualitative study makes the opposite error, depending entirely on the *validity of interpretation,* with no concern for reliability. In the usual ethnographic study, for example, the investigator freely interprets the particular meanings of expressions. Because the ethnographer seldom provides the verbatim text of the expressions being interpreted, however, the reader can only accept the interpretations on faith or reject them out of hand. There does not seem to be any middle ground.

If we leave academic research, however, many approaches may be used to interpret ambiguous texts. In courts of law, for example, disputants freely interpret verbatim texts. But these interpretations are neither discounted as being merely subjective nor accepted on faith. Rather they are considered merely as one step in a round of interpretations and counterinterpretations, a round that will continue until consensus is reached.

A trial at law involves serial cooperation among many participants. In the first round, the prosecution presents a case, which is a verbatim text (the evidence) and his or her interpretation of that text. The case for the defense is the second round of interpretation. The defense does not dismiss the prosecution's interpretation out of hand because it is "subjective," or accept the whole of it on faith. Rather the job of the defense is to criticize the initial interpretation, agreeing with some of it, disagreeing with the rest.

The succeeding steps follow the same procedure. After the defense comes the third round—the jury or judge. Still further rounds may involve appeals to higher courts. Because the evidence is brought forward to all subsequent steps, initial interpretations that are in error can be corrected.

The essential difference between legal procedures and those in mainstream social science is that in legal process, the meaning of texts is always retrievable both in theory and in practice. Even if earlier interpretations are in error, later trials or appeals can correct earlier errors because the verbatim texts are always presented. In qualitative studies in social science, the texts are seldom presented at all. A field-worker or ethnographer seldom makes available a verbatim text on which her or his interpretations are based. Quantitative studies have only one round of interpretation—the initial coding of the text. After that, the initial text vanishes, hidden behind layers of aggregated summations. In some ways, mainstream social science studies are conspiracies against arriving at accurate interpretations of meaning.

Elias's method, in my opinion, closely resembles the first step in a lawlike procedure. Unlike the typical quantitative study, Elias does not ignore the meaning of expressions or interpret them according to rigid rules. He interprets texts freely, in their historical context. But unlike the typical qualitative study, Elias only interprets verbatim texts, which gives the reader an opportunity to evaluate the interpretation. Elias's procedure, it seems to me, points toward a kind of rationality that Weber did not foresee, a substantive-formal rationality.[2] In this respect, Elias infuses with life what was only an idea in Mannheim's formulation, the possibility of an intelligence that is free floating.

ELIAS ON MODERNITY

Elias undertook a historical analysis of what he calls the *civilizing process* (1978, 1982, 1983).[3] He traced changes in the development of personality from the onset of modern civilization to the present. Like Weber, he gave great prominence to the development of rationality. Unlike Weber, however, he gave equal prominence to emotional change, particularly to changes in the threshold of *shame:* "No less characteristic of a civilizing process than 'rationalization' is the peculiar moulding of the drive economy that we call 'shame' and 'repugnance' or 'embarrassment' " (Elias 1982, p. 292). Using excerpts from advice manuals over a very long historical span—the last five centuries—he outlined a theory of modernity. By examining instance after instance of advice concerning etiquette, especially table manners, bodily functions, sexuality, and anger, he suggests that a key aspect of modernity involved a veritable explosion of shame.

Although he uses somewhat different terminology, Elias's central thesis concerning modernity is closely related to my own

(Scheff 1990). Elias ([1970] 1978) invoked physical changes to explain the decrease in awareness and predictability of action because of the increasing *number* of parties to social process and the decreasing *power* differentials between them. In my analysis of modernity, I point to what I consider the alienating consequences of these changes for social relationships: decreasing shame thresholds at the time of the breakup of rural communities, and decreasing acknowledgment of shame, which also may have had powerful consequences on levels of awareness and self-control.

The following analysis suggests the power of Elias's method and findings. He first presents a lengthy excerpt from a 19th-century advice book, *Education of Girls* (von Raumer 1857), which advises mothers how to answer the sexual questions their daughters ask:

> Children should be left for as long as it is at all possible in the belief that an angel brings the mother her little children. This legend, customary in some regions, is far better than the story of the stork common elsewhere. Children, if they really grow up under their mother's eyes, will seldom ask forward questions on this point . . . not even if the mother is prevented by a childbirth from having them about her. . . . If girls should later ask how little children really come into the world, they should be told that the good Lord gives the mother her child, who has a guardian angel in heaven who certainly played an invisible part in bringing us this great joy. "You do not need to know nor could you understand how God gives children." Girls must be satisfied with such answers in a hundred cases, and it is the mother's task to occupy her daughters' thoughts so incessantly with the good and beautiful that they are left no time to brood on such matters. . . . A mother . . . ought only once to say seriously: "It would not be good for you to know such a thing, and you should take care not to listen to anything said about it." A truly well-brought-up girl will from then on feel shame at hearing things of this kind spoken of. (von Raumer in Elias 1978, p. 180)[4]

This text suggests three different puzzles about decision making:

1. Why is the author, von Raumer, offering the mother such absurd advice?
2. Why does the mother follow his advice (as most did)?
3. Why do the daughters (as most did)?

Modern feminist theory might respond quickly to the first question, that von Raumer's advice arises from his position: He sought to continue male supremacy by advising the mother to act in a way that is consonant with the role of women as subordinate to that of men; the woman's role is *Kirche, Kueche, Kinder* (church, kitchen, children). Keeping women ignorant of sexuality and reproduction would help continue this system.

This formulation is probably part of a complete answer, but it does not attend to the other two questions: Why do the mothers and daughters submit to ignorance? Elias's formulation provides an answer to all three questions without contradicting the feminist answer. Each of these persons, the man and the two women, is too embarrassed about sexuality to think clearly about it. It could be true that von Raumer's advice is part of his male chauvinist position and that he is too embarrassed to think about the meaning of his advice. Thoughts and emotions are both parts of a causal chain.

Elias's commentary on this excerpt is masterful. First he interprets the repression of sexuality in terms of unacknowledged shame:

> In the civilizing process, sexuality too is increasingly removed behind the scenes of social life and enclosed in a particular enclave, the nuclear family. Likewise, the relations between the sexes are isolated, placed behind walls in consciousness. An aura of embarrassment, the expression of a sociogenetic fear, surrounds this sphere of life. Even among adults it is referred to officially only with caution and circumlocutions. And with children, particularly girls, such things are, as far as possible, not referred to at all. Von Raumer gives no reason why one ought not to speak of them with children. He could have said it is desirable to preserve the spiritual purity of girls for as long as possible. But even this reason is only another expression of how far the gradual submergence of these impulses in shame and embarrassment has advanced by this time. (Elias 1978, p. 180)

Elias raises a host of significant questions about this excerpt, concerning its motivation and its effects. His analysis goes to what he considers a basic causal chain in modern civilization—denial of the emotion of shame—and of the threatened social bonds that cause and reflect the denial.

Elias analyzed the causal process in repression, the arousal of shame, and the denial of this arousal:

> Neither "rational" motives nor practical reasons primarily determine this attitude, but rather the shame of adults themselves, which has become compulsive. It is the social prohibitions and resistances within themselves, their own superego, that makes them keep silent. (Elias 1978, p. 181)

Elias's study suggests a way of understanding the social transmission of the taboo on shame and the social bond. The adult, the author von Raumer in this case, is not only ashamed of sex, but he is ashamed of being ashamed and probably is ashamed of the shame that he will arouse in his reader. The mother responding to von Raumer's text in turn probably will react in a similar way, being ashamed, and being ashamed of being ashamed, and being ashamed of causing further shame in the daughter.

Von Raumer's advice is part of a social system in which attempts at civilized delicacy result in an endless chain reaction of unacknowledged shame. The chain reaction is both within persons and between them, a "triple spiral" (one spiral within each party, and one between them; Scheff 1990). A graphic picture of such a three-spiral can be visualized in the Kelley et al. (1983) diagram of what they call *meshed intrachain sequences* (MIS).

In a shame-shame loop (in Lewis's [1971] terms a *feeling trap*), one spiral involves one party's internal responses to his or her own responses, the second involves the other party's internal responses, and one involves the response of each party to the other's external actions. Shame-shame loops of any length occur only when shame is denied.

Certainly Elias understood the significance of the denial of shame in the way that I do: Shame goes underground, leading to behavior that is outside of awareness and compulsive:

> Considered rationally, the problem confronting him seems unsolved, and what he says appears contradictory. He does not explain how and when the young girl should be made to understand what is happening and will happen to her. The primary concern is the necessity of instilling "modesty" (i.e., feelings of shame, fear, embarrassment, and guilt) or, more precisely, behavior conforming to the social standard. And one feels how infinitely difficult it is for the educator himself to overcome the resistance of the shame and embarrassment which surround this sphere for him. (Elias 1978, p. 181)

His analysis suggests some of the negative, indeed destructive, effects of secrets and secrecy in a way that directly contradicts Simmel's (1960) famous essay. I believe that understanding the dynamics of unacknowledged shame will lead to exact models of repression and precise and reliable methods of understanding behavior that is unconsciously motivated and compulsive. Elias's analysis of this particular text is part of a larger study of changes in advice over the centuries.

In his demonstration of the change of mood concerning manners, Elias followed advice manuals from the Middle Ages to the present, showing an extraordinary change in the content and manner of advice about matters that now would be considered too tasteless (embarrassing) to write about.

In the 15th and 16th centuries, advice on courtesy and politeness, personal grooming, and so on was almost entirely a matter of adult-to-adult discourse that was frank and by modern standards blushingly explicit. Even Erasmus, perhaps the greatest scholar of his time, had no qualms or self-consciousness about writing an advice manual in which he described in precise detail the proper way of blowing one's nose, personal cleanliness, and so on.

In this era, the advice usually was justified, in no uncertain terms, as showing respect for other persons. Erasmus and the other counselors were not ashamed to talk about matters that are today considered too shameful to talk about. Virtually none of the matters that were discussed openly in these earlier books is even mentioned in current books of etiquette.

At the risk of embarrassing my reader, I mention that Erasmus did not hesitate to instruct *his* reader that in blowing one's nose in a handkerchief, one should turn one's head aside, not blow loudly, and not examine the contents afterward, "as if looking for pearls." Note that I have led up to this detail by first alluding to it abstractly in the last paragraph, hoping in this way to avoid abruptness and the consequent embarrassment to my reader. In our current alienated state, all are caught in a net of denial, denial of denial, and so on.

In the late 17th and early 18th centuries, a change began to occur in advice on manners. What was said openly and directly earlier begins only to be hinted at or left unsaid entirely. Moreover open justifications are offered less and less. One is mannerly because it is the right thing to do. Any decent person will be courteous; the intimation is that bad manners are not only wrong but unspeakable, the beginning of repression.

The change that Elias documents is gradual but relentless; by a continuing succession of small decrements, the manuals fall silent about the reliance of manners, style, and identity on respect, honor, and pride, and avoidance of shame and embarrassment. By the end of the 18th century, the social basis of decorum and decency had become virtually unspeakable. Unlike Freud or anyone else, Elias documents step by step the sequence of events that led to the repression of emotions in modern civilization.

By the 19th century, Elias proposes, manners are inculcated no longer by way of adult-to-adult verbal discourse in which justifications are offered. Socialization shifts from slow and conscious changes by adults over centuries to swift and silent indoctrination of children in their earliest years. No justification is offered to most children; courtesy has become absolute. Moreover any really decent person would not have to be told, as suggested in the text interpreted above. In modern societies, socialization of most children may *automatically* inculcate and repress shame.

SUMMARY

Elias's analysis of lowering thresholds and increasing denial of shame could explain why Spinoza and Hume wrote freely about emotions; they had not yet learned to be ashamed of them. By the late 19th and early 20th centuries, Darwin, Nietzsche, and Scheler were less free. Although they discussed emotion, they did so in a way that was less candid and more indirect than Spinoza and Hume. In all of Freud's vast corpus of writings on emotions and feelings, there is virtually no mention of shame, humiliation, or embarrassment.

By our time, perhaps Durkheim, Parsons, and Skinner had learned their lessons so well that most emotions were completely repressed, disappearing from their work and from their lives. To the extent that social scientists are loyal members of their culture, in which emotions are uniformly suppressed, they may unthinkingly suppress them in their studies. The suppression of emotion in social science is both a cause and an effect of the predicament of our civilization.

To correct what may be a significant flaw, it may be necessary to make two basic changes in mainstream social science. The first would involve theory, to consider the possibility that emotions may function as causal agents. As already indicated, Elias was the great pioneer of this approach. Several recent beginnings also have been made. Although he did not make emotions explicit, Elias's great contemporary certainly invoked them in his essay on crowds (Canetti 1962). This discussion reeks of the blood and blood lust that has been staining the earth in our time. By contrast, Skinner's work is redolent only of experiments in a quiet laboratory, and Parsons's of committee meetings in the Harvard Faculty Club.

The study of the economics of status by Frank (1985) already has been mentioned. In my own work, I have been investigating the role of collective emotions in large-scale political process, as in Hitler's appeal to the Germans (Scheff and Retzinger 1991) and in the rise of modern nationalism, as in the war fever that led to the catastrophe of 1914 (Scheff, Forthcoming). Although these studies are only provisional, they may point the way for new directions in social theory. They suggest that mutual pride is the binding force that holds families, communities, nations, and civilizations together, and that hidden loops of shame the explosive force that destroys them.

The second direction involves research methods. In order to avoid conducting studies in which design of the study determines the findings, it may be necessary to begin with micro-macro, part/whole investigations of a setting before generating experiments and surveys. T. S. Eliot said, "We had the experience, but we missed the meaning." Using a lawlike approach, such as that employed by Elias, might help social science regain the meaning of *human conduct.*

Recognizing and investigating the role of emotions, particularly the role of pride and shame in behavior, restoring them to parity with the other important components, such as perception and thought, might lead to advances in our understanding and control of our destiny, or at least in slowing down our descent into chaos.

NOTES

1. It is ironic that Spinoza's writings would become one of the roots of the rationalist dismissal of emotions; he gave a more considered and systematic treatment to emotions than most current experts. He named many specific emotions,

defined each one carefully, and offered a series of propositions concerning their sources and consequences (Spinoza 1678, pp. 211-250).

2. The procedure suggested here may integrate the quest for evidence in the positivist tradition with the interpretive turn in the rhetoric of inquiry. For summary statements of this latter direction, see John S. Nelson, Allan Megill, and Donald N. McCloskey (Editors), *The Rhetoric of the Human Sciences*. 1987. Madison: University of Wisconsin Press. (Charles Bazerman called this text to my attention.)

3. This section is based in part on pages 9-12 of Scheff and Retzinger (1991).

4. From *The History of Manners* by Norbert Elias, translated by Edmund Jephcott. English translation copyright © 1978 by Urizen Books. Reprinted by permission of Pantheon Books, a division of Random House, Inc.

REFERENCES

Barber, Bernard, John J. Lally, Julia Makarushka, and Daniel Sullivan. 1973. *Research on Human Subjects*. New York: Russell Sage.

Bosk, Charles L. 1979. *Forgive and Remember*. Chicago: University of Chicago Press.

Bowen, Murray. 1978. *Family Therapy in Clinical Practice*. New York: J. Aaronson.

Canetti, Elias. 1962. *Crowds and Power*. New York: Farrar Straus Giroux.

Cassirer, Ernst. 1932. *The Philosophy of the Enlightenment*. Boston: Beacon.

Chartier, Roger. 1988. *Cultural History*. Ithaca, NY: Cornell University Press.

Collins, Randall. 1990. "Stratification, Emotional Energy, and the Transient Emotions." Pp. 27-57 in *Research Agendas in the Sociology of Emotions*, edited by T. D. Kemper. Albany: SUNY Press.

Crane, Diana. 1975. *The Sanctity of Social Life*. New York: Russell Sage.

Darwin, Charles. 1872. *The Expression of Emotion in Men and Animals*. London: John Murray.

Elias, Norbert. [1970] 1978. *What Is Sociology?* London: Hutchinson.

———. [1939] 1978. *History of Manners*. New York: Pantheon.

———. [1939] 1982. *Power and Civility*. New York: Pantheon.

———. [1969] 1983. *The Court Society*. New York: Pantheon.

Fairley, Benjamin. 1963. *A Study of Goethe*. Oxford: Clarendon.

Frank, Robert H. 1985. *Choosing the Right Pond: Human Behavior and the Quest for Status*. New York: Oxford University Press.

———. 1988. *Passions Within Reason*. New York: Norton.

Goethe, Johann Wolfgang. 1785. *Philosophical Studies*. Quoted in Fairley, Benjamin. 1963. *A Study of Goethe*. Oxford: Clarendon.

Goodwin, Marjorie. 1990. *He-Said-She-Said*. Bloomington: University of Indiana Press.

Gray, Bradford H. 1975. *Human Subjects in Medical Experimentation*. New York: John Wiley.

Hume, David. [1740] 1978. *Treatise on Human Nature*. Oxford: Oxford University Press.

Kelley, Harold et al. 1983. *Close Relationships*. New York: Freeman.

Lewis, Helen B. 1971. *Shame and Guilt in Neurosis*. New York: International Universities Press.

Nietzsche, Frederich. 1886. *Ecce Homo*. London: Foulis.

Parsons, Talcott and Edward Shils. 1951. *Toward a General Theory of Action*. Cambridge, MA: Harvard University Press.

Scheff, Thomas J. 1990. *Microsociology*. Chicago: University of Chicago Press.

———. Forthcoming. *Bloody Revenge: Nationalism, War, and Emotion*.

Scheff, Thomas J. and Suzanne M. Retzinger. 1991. *Violence and Emotions*. Lexington, MA: Lexington.

Scheler, Max. [1912] 1961. *Ressentiment*. Glencoe, IL: Free Press.

Schutz, Alfred. 1962. *The Problem of Social Reality*. The Hague: Martin Nijhoff.

Simmel, Georg. 1960. *The Sociology of Georg Simmel*. Chicago: University of Chicago Press.

Skinner, B. F. 1969. *Contingencies of Reinforcement*. New York: Appleton-Century-Crofts.

Spinoza, Benedictus. [1678] 1954. "The Origin and Nature of the Emotions" and "The Psychology of the Emotions" from *Ethics*, Chapters 12 and 13 in *The Philosophy of Spinoza*. New York: Modern Library.

Steiner, George. 1975. *After Babel*. New York: Oxford University Press.

Sterns, Carol and Peter Sterns. 1986. *Anger: The Struggle for Emotional Control in America's History*. Chicago: University of Chicago Press.

von Raumer, Wilhelm. 1857. *Education of Girls*. (cited in Elias, 1978).

Chapter 6

RATIONALITY AND ROBUSTNESS IN MULTILEVEL SYSTEMS

MICHAEL T. HANNAN
Stanford University

PROPONENTS OF RATIONAL CHOICE THEORY argue for explaining large-scale social processes as implications of rational choice at lower levels of analysis and some form of aggregation. Because macrostructures are built of (partially) nested levels of analysis, social theorists can choose among several lower levels. Rational choice theorists virtually always regard natural persons as the only relevant lower level actors. This view is quite restrictive, and persuasive arguments exist for treating formal (or constructed) organizations as lower level actors in explaining macrosociological dynamics. Interestingly, different aspects of Coleman's (1990) formulation of a rational choice program treat both persons and organizations as rational actors in explaining macrostructures. This feature of his effort to build foundations for a rational choice sociology adds considerably to its realism and to its appeal to sociologists. It also greatly complicates analysis, however. It seems clear both that persons often build and join organizations to accomplish their goals and that organizations often act to achieve specified goals. But treating the actions of both kinds of actors as rational raises awkward theoretical problems.

AUTHOR'S NOTE: Preparation of this chapter was supported by National Science Foundation grant SES-9008493. It builds on joint work with Glenn Carroll. Discussions with James N. Baron, James S. Coleman, Susan Olzak, and Elizabeth West helped sharpen the argument.

120

This chapter argues that contemporary sociological theories, including those built on rational choice processes, lack a consistent set of principles for embedding rational choice in partially nested systems of more than two levels. The current state of the art is that modeling the implication of rational action in multilevel systems is extremely complicated.

Recognition of this complexity dulls the force of the now common claim that theories whose elementary units are collective actors fall short by definition. Such claims assume (usually without explicit attention) that (a) microprocesses are much better understood than macroprocesses, (b) aggregation relations are either trivially simple or complicated but well understood, and (c) no special theoretical complications arise in treating the actions of constructed actors, such as formal organizations, that stand intermediate between natural persons and macrostructures. There is good reason to doubt each of these implicit assumptions in the case of most sociological problems. If this is so, then the strategy of building tight links between microtheories and macrotheories loses much of its appeal. Instead it makes sense to build macrotheories that are robust in the sense of depending as little as possible on the details of the microprocesses at various levels and the exact mechanisms of aggregation.

PERSONS, ORGANIZATIONS, AND SOCIAL STRUCTURE

Most interesting macrosociological problems involve processes at three (or more) levels of analysis. This chapter concentrates on situations involving natural persons, organizations, and macrostructures. These levels are only partly nested because individuals and organizations interact in creating outcomes at the level of social systems. More precisely, the actions of individuals as they affect macroprocesses cannot be summarized by the actions of the organizations they construct and maintain, as would be the case in a fully nested system. Hence theories of macrostructure that build on microprocesses need to direct attention to actions at both lower levels.

Available sociological theories do not appear to be capable of dealing successfully with more than two (partly nested) levels of analysis. Most theory and research on macrostructures elides distinctions between levels, tacitly converting multilevel processes into two-level ones. Most commonly, the problem is reduced to one involving persons and macrostructures (see the many examples discussed by Kiser and Hechter 1991); that is, the distinctive effects of organizational processes receive little explicit attention in macrosociology, including that built on aggregation of rational choice processes.

Yet almost all collective action takes place in organizational contexts, and organizations are the main vehicles for action in modern society (Coleman 1990; Hannan 1986a). When interest groups, social classes, and ethnic groups take collective action, they do so in today's world by constructing and shaping such special-purpose organizations as political parties, occupational associations, and labor unions. Consider, for example, Charles Tilly's summary of the changing shape of collective action in France over 400 years:

> Back in the seventeenth century, a large share of all collective action went on in the context of routine, authorized gatherings such as markets, fairs, processions, festivals, hangings, and local electoral assemblies. As the twentieth century approached, the relative importance of routine, authorized public gatherings declined. Instead, deliberately called meetings, rallies, strikes, demonstrations, and other prepared actions became common means of getting together to act on shared interests . . . centralization of power tended to demobilize ordinary people and to make their ordinary routines irrelevant and ineffective as means of collective action. (Tilly 1986, pp. 75-6)

In the modern world, individuals encounter institutional constraints principally in formal organizations. Their experiences with constraints imposed by the state take place in schools, armies, bureaus of taxation, and so forth. They experience the economy as employees of firms, as seekers of jobs located in firms, and as customers of firms. As a consequence of the centrality of organizations in mediating individuals and institutions, efforts at social reform seek mainly to change such intermediary organizations as schools, employers, and government bureaus.

Few sociologists deny that organizations play pivotal roles in modern social change and in relating individuals to macrostructures. Nonetheless few sociological theories pay more than lip service to organizational processes in accounting for macrostructure and change. Indeed many prominent analyses of social change make no reference to modern theory and research on organizations. This is true even of theory and research, like Tilly's (1978, 1986), that emphasize the importance of constructed organizations in shaping processes of collective action.

Most sociological theory treats organizations as simple and unproblematic machines that link individuals or collectives to large-scale processes. Research that begins at the system level tends to assume that organizations implement the dictates of the state and the larger economy in more or less mechanical fashion in affecting individuals. Research that begins with individual actors, like that motivated by rational theories of social action, likewise tends to conceive of organizations as passively reflecting the interests of their members or elites; that is, in order to simplify linkages between persons and macrostructures, sociologists tend to assume that organizations merely implement goals set by members or elites (micro level interests) or institutional rules and constraints (macro level constraints) but do not otherwise affect either the direction or timing of change in society.

These simplifying assumptions do not fit well with our knowledge of the organizational world. For one thing, constructing a permanent organization is a very expensive solution to problems of collective action or institutional control (Hannan and Freeman 1989). Building an organization requires mobilizing and investing time and resources. Because the "overhead" costs of maintaining organizations are typically high, only a small fraction of the resources invested in an organization goes into a final product or collective action. Not only is reliance on permanent organizations expensive, it also can reorient collective action in unanticipated ways. The very processes of building and sustaining organizations can alter a group's goals, strategies, and tactics, as Michels ([1915] 1949) argued.

The operative agendas of organizations tend to diverge from their public goals and from the intentions of those who ostensibly control them. Such divergence has the consequence that organizations tend to develop their own idiosyncratic dynamics. Responses by organizations to changing interests of their members and of their institutional controllers is often halting at best. Inertia weakens links between intentions of individuals and collectives and outcomes in the organizations that they control, which complicates processes of large-scale change.

For these and related reasons, Tilly (1978) and Baron and Bielby (1980, 1984), among others, argue that sociological analyses that relate individuals and macrostructure in the modern world must attend explicitly to organizations. Coleman (1986, 1990), Kiser and Hechter (1991), and others argue that theories about the functioning of social systems should be based on explicit models of individual action (and unspecified process of aggregation). Suppose that both lines of argument are correct. Then we face a challenging theoretical and methodological question: How should we model actions at three partially nested levels of analysis?

RATIONALITY IN MULTILEVEL SYSTEMS

In order to make these issues concrete, I confine attention to the interesting case in which actions of natural persons are presumed to reflect rational choice processes, and properties of macrostructure are to be derived as implications of the aggregation of individual actions.

The concrete strategic issues in this context involve decisions about how much capacity for rational action to impute to social units at the different levels of analysis. Social science work ranges over all possibilities on these choices. Some theorists assume that both individuals and organizations are flexible and purposive (even maximizing) adapters to changeable external conditions. This seems to be the main point of view in contemporary economics, which regards both the persons who found organizations (or the principals who possess rights over organizations) and the organizations they build to be flexible optimizers over a broad range of external conditions.[1]

Other theorists assume that persons are flexible and substantively rational in pursuing their interests but assume that the organizations resulting from their joint, self-seeking behavior are highly inflexible and limited in substantive rationality. Selznick (1948) proposed the imagery of organizations as *recalcitrant tools*. Much recalcitrance and inflexibility reflects the operation of organizational culture in which precedent takes on a moral character and of organizational politics, especially processes of coalition formation.[2]

Some sociological work makes the opposite assumption, namely that individual actors cannot conduct their affairs rationally but that organizations can and do. Stinchcombe (in an interview reported by Swedberg 1990), for example, espouses this position and attributes it to Weber. He argues that organizations develop special expertise in gathering information and in making decisions that allow them to overcome the limitations on individual capacities.

Meyer (1983) disagrees with these views and argues instead that social systems differ little in how much rationality they exhibit but differ greatly in where they locate rationality. Moreover cultural stipulations that locate rationality in one kind of actor cause other kinds of actors to depart systematically from substantive rationality. In particular, the more that rationality is invested in persons, the less rational will be the set of corporate actors that they construct, and vice versa. In this view, either individuals or corporate actors might behave rationally, but not both.

Coleman (1990) argues for reliance on a two-level approach in which properties at one level are explained in terms of processes at a lower level and processes of aggregation. The levels of aggregation are not specified substantively. The higher level might refer to some properties of national social organization, and the lower level refers to its set of collective actors (e.g., organizations). Alternatively the properties of the collective actors might be the higher level phenomena, and natural persons the actors at the lower level. Clearly the rational choice perspective might be used in either case. In the first example, the corporate actors are assumed to behave purposively in interacting with others, with the result of their interactions yielding a macrostructure. In the second example, purposive action by persons yields properties of a corporate actor.

For present purposes, the key feature of Coleman's strategy is that:

> No assumption is made that the explanation of systemic behavior consists of nothing more than individual actions and orientations, taken in aggregate. The interaction among individuals is seen to result in emergent phenomena at the system level, that is, phenomena that were neither intended nor predicted by the individuals. (Coleman 1990, p. 5)

He goes on to suggest that explanation of systemic behavior need not be taken all the way to the level of individuals but may stop usefully at some level below that of the system but above the level of the individual. This argument suggests that an appropriate strategy for building theories of large-scale social systems is to reduce to the level of organizations as actors and to treat organizations as rational actors (in the way that most of economics treats firms as simple optimizers).

The potential difficulty with this approach follows from the tendency of rational choice theorists to emphasize actions of the persons who construct and maintain organizations—this is almost a defining property of the approach. From the perspective of natural persons, organizational outcomes are ordinarily neither intended not predicted. In other words, as long as one thinks of natural persons as relevant actors, a theoretical tension—perhaps even an inconsistency—is involved in treating organizations as simple rational actors in constructing models of macrostructure.

The theoretical tension becomes readily apparent when the specification of the process holds that (asymmetric) interactions of persons and organizations yield the higher level systemic behavior. If one tries to follow Coleman's strategy, it makes sense to treat persons and organizations as two kinds of rational actors in interaction. But this produces an inconsistency with what one would assume in considering just the two-level system composed of persons and organizations, with organizational actions regarded as an unintended consequence of the combination of individual actions; that is, one's assumptions about the rationality of organizational action and its relations to persons differ, depending on whether one also considers a third level (a larger social system in this case). This means that the theoretical strategy cannot proceed in a simple hierarchical manner, first working out the relations of individuals and organizations and then taking the worked-out theoretical structure as a building block in a theory of action at a more aggregated level.

ROBUSTNESS OF MACROTHEORIES

Most contemporary sociology assumes the desirability of a tight fit between levels; that is, it is commonplace to assume that good theoretical strategies contain close correspondences between micro behavioral assumptions and macroprocesses (perhaps at several higher levels). A preference for tight links motivates the considerable amount of work by sociologists on the "micro-macro problem" in recent years. This preference is so ingrained that many assume without reflection that sociological theories that do not direct explicit attention to natural persons are inherently flawed.

While the idea of building tight links across levels of analysis has broad appeal for sociologists, this strategy of theory building does not necessarily yield useful macrotheories. This is especially true when as much confusion exists about multilevel theories as in contemporary sociology. Tying macroprocesses to microassumptions makes sense as a general strategy when microprocesses and aggregation relations are understood with great clarity. If processes at different levels are linked tightly, then changing the details of assumptions about microprocesses and aggregation alters the specifications of macroprocesses—the macrotheory lacks robustness.

The general ecological-evolutionary approach provides an interesting cautionary tale. The core of this theory provides a vivid example of the advantages of loose coupling across levels when certainty about nature of microprocesses and aggregation relations matches the uncertainty about macroprocesses. A major source of the power of Darwin's theory of evolution by natural selection lies in its extreme decoupling of the form of macroprocesses from the precise specification of the relevant microprocesses: genetic mixing and transmission. As is well known, Darwin assumed what turned out to be the wrong model of genetic transition—blending inheritance rather than particulate (Mendelian) inheritance. Yet he got the macroprocesses right in the sense that his theory continues to serve as the main unifying framework in virtually all modern biology. Consider what would have happened had he built tight links between his macro-evolutionary theory and his genetics: The macrotheory would have become obsolete with the victory of Mendelian genetics.

I do not mean to diminish the importance of specifying the genetic mechanisms underlying a process of biotic evolution. This task surely is important, and completing it has been the major preoccupation of modern evolutionary population biology. But the example of Darwin makes clear that one can arrive at the correct macrotheory (and, in particular, identify the important macromechanism—natural selection in this case) with incorrect microfoundations *if the macrotheory is made sufficiently robust.* This example suggests that robustness with respect to changes in microfoundations is an important goal in developing macrotheories. This strategy makes sense, given considerable uncertainty about the precise forms of the microprocesses and of the great difficulty in specifying theories with action at more than two levels of analysis.

A further reason for preferring robustness concerns uncertainty about aggregation relations, about how actions of different actors combine to produce system level (unintended and unforeseen) consequences. Simon (1962), in an essay that shaped my thinking on the subject, points out that aggregation relations in physical and social sciences are usually more complex than the processes at either micro or macro levels (see Hannan 1991b). Recent work on game-theoretic economics is very informative on this score. A major result is that slight variations in the rules of the game produce very large differences in equilibrium outcomes (see Kreps 1990). I suspect that this result would hold generally in sociology, that slight variations in the institutional frameworks that combine individual actions would alter greatly the relation between patterns at different levels of analysis.

THE EXAMPLE OF ORGANIZATIONAL FOUNDING PROCESSES

Brief discussion of the bearing of these issues on current theory and research on the population ecology of organizations may help clarify my argument. This theoretical approach explains the structure and change in populations or communities of organizations in terms of interactions among the individual organizations that comprise populations and communities (Hannan and Freeman 1989). So the macro level is the organizational population (or community), and the micro level is the individual organization. This theoretical approach has been criticized for not giving prominence to a third level—natural persons. Does adding the complexity of a third level of analysis improve one's ability to construct and test macrotheories of organizational change?

Glenn Carroll and I have discussed these issues in the context of the theory of density-dependent organizational evolution (Carroll and Hannan 1989c; Hannan and Carroll 1992). This theory explains patterns in the evolution of organizational populations as implications of opposing processes of legitimation and competition.[3] In the context of this theory, *legitimation* means that an organizational form acquires the status of a "taken-for-granted." *Competition* refers to constraints arising from the joint dependence of multiple organizations on the same set of finite resources for building and sustaining organizations. One core idea is that rates of founding and mortality vary as functions of legitimation and competition. Founding rates rise and mortality rates fall as the legitimation of a population increases. Conversely, founding rates fall and mortality rates rise as competition within and among populations intensifies.

The second core idea is that legitimation and competition are affected by changing levels of *density,* defined as "the number of organizations in the population." Increasing density conveys legitimation in the sense of taken-for-grantedness, but the process has a ceiling, which means that the effect diminishes as density grows large. Competition also grows with density, according to the theory, but at an increasing rate.

Combining the two main ideas (and some technical boundary assumptions) yields a qualitative theory of density dependence in rates of organizational founding and mortality. Research has concentrated on three of its testable implications: (a) Founding rates have an inverted U-shape relation with density, (b) mortality rates have a U-shape relation with contemporaneous density, and (c) high density at the time of an organization's founding produces a permanent increase in mortality rates.

Within the context of this theory, the issue of links between natural persons, organizations, and organizational populations arises in a potentially interesting way in considering processes of organizational founding. In order to develop a theory of the causes of variations in organizational foundings, one must identify the social unit that can experience foundings. One possible choice of unit, used in much earlier research, is the organization observed to be founded. But this is not a useful specification of unit because "non-events" (the absence of foundings in some period) are as important as observed foundings in providing information about founding rates (for further discussion, see Delacroix and Carroll 1983; Hannan and Freeman 1987, 1989; Carroll and Hannan 1989b). A second possible choice is the organizational population, which can be thought of as experiencing increments and decrements to its stock of organizations. This choice, now a standard one in organizational ecology, makes it easy to express relations between social system properties and founding rates in explicit and testable ways.

Yet this choice turns out to be controversial for reasons that bear on the themes of this chapter. Zucker (1989) rejects this choice of unit and suggests that theoretical attention must focus on the potential founder. In the simplest case, the potential founders are all just natural persons. Then the risk set (the set of all actors who might found an organization) consists of all persons in the relevant social system. Narrowing the set to those who attempt to found organizations would create selection bias and make it impossible to provide informative tests of theories about the causes of variations in foundings. How would this play out in research like that by Hannan and Carroll (1992) on variations in founding rates of newspapers over two centuries in Argentina, Ireland, and the San Francisco region, banks in Manhattan over two centuries, and so forth? Considering the set of all potential founders and all potential organizational sponsors in these and other relevant cases would require collecting information on the millions of Argentines, Irish, and Americans who did and did not start newspapers during the 19th and 20th centuries, on the set of all possible bank founders in Manhattan, and so forth.

Furthermore, attempting to specify the set of actors at risk of founding a newspaper would require considering itinerant printers who could and did migrate to cities or nations and did begin newspapers; specifying the set of actors who might begin a banking organization in a city must include all foreign banks that might decide to do so. The latter example makes clear that not all potential founders are natural persons because partnerships and collectives start firms. So one must consider all pairs, triplets, and so forth. The size of the risk set so defined is impractically large. This is the main reason why studies of founding processes generally take the *population* as the unit of action and forego the opportunity to make links to the actions of potential founders.

Carroll and I conjecture that the theory of density-dependent legitimation and competition is robust with respect to variations in assumptions about microprocesses (Hannan and Carroll 1992, Chap. 9). For instance, it is consistent with rational utility maximization by entrepreneurs. When legitimation of an organizational form increases due to growing density, potential founders may come to believe that gains may be made from starting such an organization; that is, legitimation may affect the formation of beliefs about possibilities for profitable investment and thereby shape efforts at founding organizations. When competition intensifies due to increasing density relative to resources, potential founders postpone or cancel efforts to found organizations. Both responses would be rational for profit-seeking actors with some understanding of the market and industry.

What other models of individual action are compatible with the theory? For present purposes, it is most useful to observe that the theory is consistent with cases of apparently nonrational behavior. To see this, it is important to recognize that environments affect rates of organizational founding in two general ways. First, changes in environmental conditions affect the rate of attempts at founding an organization around a particular activity, using a particular organizational form. Second, environments also affect flows of foundings by altering the odds of success of organizing attempts.

Images of rationality in organization building highlight the first element in the process, the factors that shape attempts to start organizations. Resources sometimes become available and opportunities get identified in a manner consistent with common images of rational entrepreneurship. At other times, the exact causes of attempts to start organizations can vary enormously from person to person (or group to group) in a way that can be well described as random (with respect to expected probabilities of success, rates of return, and so forth). For instance, studies of attempts at entrepreneurship reveal that individuals can be prompted to try to start a business (or some other kind of organization) by many other kinds of environmental events, such as a spell of involuntary unemployment, forced retirement, or a change in working conditions (see Mayer and Goldstein 1961; Cooper et al. 1989; Evans and Leighton 1989).

Every organizing effort must pass through these initial steps, but many efforts fail before a functioning organization results. Hannan and Freeman (1989, Chap. 4) emphasize the importance of processes of selection during periods of "gestation" in shaping the organizational world. In some kinds of environments, entrepreneurs typically make many attempts to organize but with little success.

Under other conditions, the success rate of those attempting to organize may be high in that most of them actually get an enterprise off the ground and begin operations. The types of factors likely to induce success in opening a "business" presumably differ from those affecting the rate of organizing attempts.

Variation in organizational founding rates reflects both types of selection processes, and these might work at cross-purposes. High rates of founding attempts can be coupled with low rates of success in organizing, and vice versa. The same observed level of founding might be the result of very different environmental forces. Moreover, rationality may characterize only one of the two portions of the founding process; that is, the apparent rationality of a founding process might reflect the rationality of selection operating on randomly generated founding attempts.

Such possibilities further confound the interpretation of entrepreneurial action even at the collective level. When a high observed founding rate reflects the actions of large numbers of entrepreneurs attempting to enter a market and experiencing a high success rate in doing so, their behavior may well be rational. When a high observed founding rate reflects massive numbers of attempts and many failures, however, making the case for rationality at the level of individual founders proves more difficult.

Clearly, interesting opportunities exist for experimenting with microfoundations of organizational ecology, including processes of density-dependent legitimation and competition. The analytic issues involved are exceedingly complex. Moreover, efforts to build microfoundations and to assess their relevance are sure to be hampered by a general lack of data on the crucial preorganizing processes because we lack data on the rate of attempts to build organization and thus on selection processes that operate at this point in the general process of founding. Given the complexity of the analytic issues and the absence of necessary data, the strategy of building macrotheories and models with great robustness regarding microassumptions has great appeal.

DISCUSSION

Rational choice theorists, especially Coleman (1986, 1990) and Kiser and Hechter (1991), have provided a telling challenge to macrosociologists—telling because much macrosociological work in recent years has recoiled from the challenge to explain macrostructures as outcomes of general sociological processes. Addressing this challenge will almost certainly help reduce murkiness in macrotheories even if the proposals of the rational choice theorists ultimately are not accepted.

This chapter seeks to deepen discussion of the issues raised by this challenge. It has two main points. The first is that the proposal for a rational choice reconstruction of macrosociology has not yet worked out a consistent approach to modeling the implications of interactions of natural persons and constructed organizations for macrostructure. The problem is that actions of constructed organizations are viewed as at least partly unintended and unforeseen from the perspective of the natural actors who build them. In other words, at least some organizational action is nonrational from the perspective of the human actors involved. Once interest shifts to a more inclusive system that contains both natural actors and organizations in interaction, however, organizations are to be viewed as rational, purposive actors.

I suspect that the solution to this inconsistency in the treatment of constructed organizations in practice will be to continue to elide the distinction between individual and organizational actors, to convert three-level structures into two-level structures in which the issue does not arise. In other words, the likely impact of the rational choice proposal for a new macrosociology will result in a deemphasis of the distinctive character of the interactions between natural persons and constructed organizations analyzed by Coleman (1982).

The second main point is that macrotheories that rely on selection mechanisms have potential value when links between individuals and social structures are complex and/or obscure. The main idea here is that natural persons do indeed create and maintain organizations whose actions cannot be characterized well as rational (from the perspective of the persons involved). When organizational outcomes are (partly) decoupled from the motivations of natural persons, it can be helpful to think of organizational outcomes as random and subject to environmental selection (see Hannan 1986a; Hannan and Freeman 1989).[4] This does not mean that selection theories are rivals to rational choice theories generally, though this certainly will be the case in some instances.

Theories of organizational ecology as currently developed are certainly consistent with the view that rational behavior of natural persons creates a tendency for organizations to depart from simple notions of rationality and that change in the world of organizations is therefore shaped by selection. More generally, rationality at one level generates selection at a higher level. It may turn out that this is an interesting way to think about multilevel systems. The macrotheory, robust as it is, however, does not rise or fall on its links to microprocesses.

NOTES

1. Much relevant work is not explicit on this issue, allowing some possibility of adaptation by individual organizations and selection. For example, Williamson (1975, 1985) typically argues that organizational boundaries that minimize transaction costs will "obtain" in equilibrium.

2. Consider, for instance, Arrow's (1951) impossibility theorem on collective choice. The result is that collective decisions that result from the rational choices of individuals cannot satisfy the axioms of rational choice if the decisions are unconstrained. To the extent that organizations operate as committee decision structures, it follows that their preferences deviate from the axioms of rational choice even when each member has preferences that do agree with these axioms.

3. The theory was proposed originally by Hannan (1986b, 1989) and has been extended by Carroll and Hannan (1989a), Hannan (1991a), and Hannan and Carroll (1992).

4. It strikes me as ironic that Kiser and Hechter (1991) acknowledge the potential power of selection mechanisms but suggest that the conditions under which selection operates hold infrequently. The irony is that this is the main objection of most sociologists to rational choice theory: Many sociologists find rational choice plausible in only a very small fraction of human interactions.

REFERENCES

Arrow, Kenneth J. 1951. *Social Choice and Individual Values.* (Cowles Commission Monograph 12). New York: John Wiley.

Baron, James N. and William Bielby. 1980. "Bringing the Firms Back In: Stratification, Segmentation, and the Organization of Work." *American Sociological Review* 45:737-65.

———. 1984. "The Organization of Work in a Segmented Economy." *American Sociological Review* 49:454-73.

Carroll, Glenn R. and Michael T. Hannan. 1989a. "Density Delay in the Evolution of Organizational Populations: A Model and Five Empirical Tests." *Administrative Science Quarterly* 34:411-30.

———. 1989b. "Density Dependence in the Evolution of Newspaper Populations." *American Sociological Review* 54:524-41.

———. 1989c. "On Using Institutional Theory in Studying Organizational Populations (Reply to Zucker)." *American Sociological Review* 54:545-8.

Coleman, James S. 1982. *The Asymmetric Society.* Syracuse, NY: Syracuse University Press.

———. 1986. "Social Theory, Social Research, and a Theory of Action." *American Journal of Sociology* 91:1309-35.

———. 1990. *Foundations of Social Theory.* Cambridge, MA: Harvard University Press.

Cooper, Arnold C., Carolyn Y. Woo, and William C. Dunkelberg. 1989. "Entrepreneurship and the Initial Size of Firms." *Journal of Business Venturing* 4:289-332.

Delacroix, Jacques and Glenn R. Carroll. 1983. "Organizational Foundings: An Ecological Study of the Newspaper Industries of Argentina and Ireland." *Administrative Science Quarterly* 28:274-91.

Evans, David and Linda Leighton. 1989. "Some Empirical Aspects of Entrepreneurship." *American Economic Review* 79:519-35.

Hannan, Michael T. 1986a. "Uncertainty, Diversity and Organizational Change." Pp. 73-94 in *Social and Behavioral Sciences: Discoveries Over Fifty Years,* edited by Neil Smelser and Dean Gerstein. Washington, DC: National Academy Press.

———. 1986b. "A Model of Competitive and Institutional Processes in Organizational Ecology." Technical Report 86-13, Cornell University, Department of Sociology, Ithaca, NY.

———. 1989. "Competitive and Institutional Processes in Organizational Ecology." Pp. 388-402 in *Sociological Theories in Progress: New Formulations,* edited by Joseph Berger, Morris Zelditch, Jr., and Bo Andersen. Newbury Park, CA: Sage.

———. 1991a. "Theoretical and Methodological Issues in the Analysis of Density-Dependent Legitimation in Organizational Evolution." Pp. 1-42 in *Sociological Methodology 1991,* edited by Peter V. Marsden. Oxford: Basil Blackwell.

———. 1991b. *Aggregation and Disaggregation in the Social Sciences.* Rev. ed. Lexington, MA: Lexington.

Hannan, Michael T. and Glenn R. Carroll. 1992. *Dynamics of Organizational Populations: Density, Legitimation, and Competition.* New York: Oxford University Press.

Hannan, Michael T. and John Freeman. 1987. "The Ecology of Organizational Founding: American Labor Unions, 1836-1985." *American Journal of Sociology* 92:910-43.

———. 1989. *Organizational Ecology.* Cambridge, MA: Harvard University Press.

Kiser, Edgar and Michael Hechter. 1991. "The Role of General Theory in Comparative-Historical Sociology." *American Journal of Sociology* 97:1-31.

Kreps, David M. 1990. *Game Theory and Economic Modeling.* Oxford: Oxford University Press.

Mayer, Kurt B. and Sidney Goldstein. 1961. *The First Two Years: Problems of Small Firm Growth and Survival*. Washington, DC: Government Printing Office.

Meyer, John W. 1983. "Institutionalization and the Rationality of Formal Organizational Structure." Pp. 261-82 in *Organizational Environments: Ritual and Rationality*, edited by John W. Meyer and W. Richard Scott. Beverly Hills, CA: Sage.

Michels, Robert. [1915] 1949. *Political Parties*, translated by Edward Cedar Paul. Glencoe, IL: Free Press.

Selznick, Philip. 1948. "Foundations of the Theory of Organization." *American Sociological Review* 13:25-35.

Simon, Herbert A. 1962. "The Architecture of Complexity." *Proceedings of the American Philosophical Society* 106:67-82.

Swedberg, Richard. 1990. *Economics and Sociology: Redefining Their Boundaries: Conversations With Economists and Sociologists*. Princeton, NJ: Princeton University Press.

Tilly, Charles. 1978. *From Mobilization to Revolution*. Reading, MA: Addison-Wesley.

———. 1986. *The Contentious French: Four Centuries of Popular Struggle*. Cambridge, MA: Harvard University Press.

Williamson, Oliver E. 1975. *Markets and Hierarchies: Analysis and Antitrust Implications*. New York: Free Press.

———. 1985. *The Economic Institutions of Capitalism*. New York: Free Press.

Zucker, Lynne. 1989. "No Legitimacy, No History (Comment on Carroll and Hannan)." *American Sociological Review* 54:542-5.

Chapter 7

RATIONAL CHOICE THEORY
A Critical Assessment of Its Explanatory Power

RICHARD MÜNCH
Heinrich-Heine-Universität Düsseldorf, Germany

INTRODUCTION

RATIONAL CHOICE THEORY has been extended enormously in its application to social phenomena outside the economic realm in the narrow sense in the recent years of its expansion in sociology. In this process, it has attained the position of a paradigm which has been claimed to function as a core of theorizing in sociology as a whole. Indeed, one of the most acclaimed recent publications from the camp of rational choice theory, James Coleman's *Foundations of Social Theory* (1990), has been advertised as having a potential today for synthesizing sociological theory from a great variety of approaches similar to that of Parsons's *The Structure of Social Action* in 1937 (see Münch 1987, 1988). This centrality given to Coleman's approach calls for an examination of its real potential for explaining social phenomena outside the economic realm because this is the test for a theory that claims comprehensiveness and applicability to a wide range of phenomena in the social world other than economics in the narrower sense. In the following pages, I shall conduct such on examination by turning to Coleman's attempts at applying rational choice theory to the worlds of power and conflict, trust, solidarity, norms and the human self, culture, communication and legitimacy, the micro-macro link, and modern society in toto.

The common core of Coleman's (1990, pp. 13-9, 27-44) approach is his notion of social interaction as basically an economic transaction that is guided in its course by the actor's rational choice between alternative outcomes of an action taken in terms of its benefits and costs: An actor will rationally choose an action that promises to maximize benefits and minimize costs, or more precisely, that promises a net gain of benefits minus costs, or still more precisely, that promises the highest product of the net benefit to the actor and the probability of its occurrence.

The above-mentioned phenomena are analyzed according to the economic transactions of this kind that are involved in all of them all the time. We will see whether this provides a full understanding and explanation of what goes on in the social world.

THE WORLD OF POWER AND CONFLICT

In Coleman's rational choice view, *power* is on the one hand a structural condition within which economic transaction proceeds; on the other hand, it is itself shaped by economic calculations and transactions (Coleman 1990, pp. 58-9, 63, 65-90, 132-34, 139, 145-74, 214-15, 689, 701, 728-29, 780-82, 799-800, 933-97). Unequal power is, for example, a structural condition that results in unequal benefits in an interactive relationship.

The more one actor is superior to another in terms of power, the greater will be the gap between his or her benefits and the other's benefits. Nevertheless their relationship will continue to exist as long as both parties are better off by maintaining it than by withdrawing from it or by putting up resistance to the point of engaging in revolutionary activities. The subordinated party will engage in resistance and revolution only inasmuch as it expects greater benefits from such action, compared to the continued submission to existing authority. Because such expectations are vague and are mainly uncertain, revolutionary activities occur only rarely in extraordinary historical situations (Coleman 1990, pp. 489-99).

This is all very well insofar as we understand it as an economics of power. This is, however, by no means the whole reality of power, which is much more complex in its nature. One needs first to consider the internal character of power itself. Then a normative structure of power and a symbolics of power exist, just as an economics of power exists. Let us look at them more closely.

The Power-Relationship

In economic terms, any social relationship lasts as long as both parties draw more benefits from staying in the relationship than from withdrawing from it, and it runs smoothly as long as the less powerful of the two does not expect greater benefits from resistance or even revolutionary action against the more powerful party.

In political terms, this view is misleading because it presupposes that both parties have a choice of this kind and that they make it in this way. An *economic transaction* is by definition a voluntarily chosen act and implies a voluntary relationship. This is by no means the case in the power-relationship precisely because this is a relationship in which the party that is subjected to the power of another party has no choice and can be forced to carry out or to refrain from an action that he or she otherwise, under the condition of free choice, would not perform. Superior power forces the party subjected to that power to continue with a relationship that results in nothing but costs and no benefits, whereas any alternative would provide better results. The party subjected to power might try to withdraw in order to receive some benefits but cannot because the power-holder forces him or her to stay. The power-holder can do so physically but also symbolically by indicating to the power-subjected party that any attempt to withdraw from the relationship will result in even higher costs than those of staying in the relationship. The power-holder is in a position to shape the power-subjected party's objective situation or his or her subjective perception of that situation in such a way that any alternative action other than complying with his or her commands is or appears more costly. The sources of such power can be physical force, exclusive access to individual and collective goods and services needed by the other party, control over affective bonds that cut off the other party from alternative relationships, or the possession of knowledge that shapes the other party's perception of the situation.

Any explanation of why a social relationship continues to be upheld by both parties, although one party enhances its costs continually, needs more than one step. The first step remains on the economic level and shows that the party that only enhances its costs will incur even higher costs by withdrawing from the relationship. What I explain here is the continuation of a costly action because any alternative way of acting would be even more costly. It is the economics of the power-subjected party that is under scrutiny here. This is the level of the power-subjected party's action that is explained by rational choice theory.

Without stepping to the political level, however, such an explanation would be incomplete. On this level, we have to show that the first party in the relationship is capable of placing the second party—either objectively or in its subjective view—into a situation in which any alternative action other than complying with the commands of the first party is still more costly even though the chosen way of acting is itself costly enough.

When it comes to explaining this level of the action we are concerned with, rational choice theory does not tell us anything. What we need to explain here is why the second party is in a situation in which he or she has no better alternative than continuing with an action that only enhances his or her net costs. The theoretical proposition applied to this level of action tells us that one party in a social relationship will be in the situation of having only the choice of continuing with a costly form of action in the face of even more costly alternatives in as much as the other party has the availability of superior physical force, goods and services the first party needs, exclusive affective bonds, or superior knowledge. This is the level of action explained by a theory of power that cannot be reduced to the level of rational choice theory. It is a completely independent theory that needs as much elaboration as rational choice theory itself. That is the first indicator that tells us that rational choice theory has only limited explanatory power and cannot serve as the exclusive core of a truly comprehensive theory of action.

The other side of the picture that needs to be examined is the economics of the power-holder's action. Whether this party will make use of its power and to what extent it will do so depends on its utility calculations. It will make use of its power and force the other party to comply with its commands and to stay in the relationship provided that more benefits can be drawn from such an action than from any alternative way of acting. A point can be reached at which the threat or application of power becomes too costly, for it may undermine the motivation, cooperation, and loyalty of the power-subjected party and/or provoke resistance and rebellion. The more the power-holder party depends on such motivation, cooperation, and loyalty, which is mostly the case, the more it has to renounce the blunt threat or application of power and to make use of incentives to enhance motivation, of affective bonds to enhance cooperation, and of persuasion and legitimation to enhance loyalty.

This is a situation in which the power-subjected party has at least some alternatives open to it, even if that does mean no more than complying with little self-interested motivation, little confidence, and little conviction, which leaves the power-holder party worse off than if there had been more self-interest, confidence, and conviction on the part of the power-subjected party.

At this point, we have to go again beyond the economics of the power-relationship and to enter the level of its politics in the strict sense, thereby applying a theory of power. The power-subjected party may have no alternative outside the relationship, but he or she may have such alternatives within the relationship, and which one he or she chooses may have effects on the utility outcome of the power-holder party. The more this is the case, the more the second party in the relationship also has power over the first one and not only the other way round. This may extend to the point at which both parties have equal power over each other. The extent of that power depends on how few alternatives to that relationship the two parties have or how much either party is able to narrow down the objective or subjective situation of the other party so that staying in the relationship is less costly than leaving it. This situation varies from the point at which both parties have little power over one another to the point at which both have a lot of power over each other. At the first point, both may withdraw at any time, bringing the relationship close to an economic transaction on a free market. At the second point, the two parties cannot withdraw from the relationship at any time. Here we do not have a market, and hence the structural precondition for turning social interaction into economic transaction from which both parties draw benefits is not fulfilled. It is a closed, mutual power-relationship that continues to persist even though both parties continually increase their costs by mutually harming each other. This is the situation of a couple, for example, that continue to maintain their relationship though it may be extremely costly for both partners. The longer they have lived together, the more they will be cut off from alternatives objectively and/or subjectively. It is also the situation of neighboring groups and states that cannot simply move away in order to withdraw from a harmful neighboring relationship. Similarly it is the case with political parties and interest groups that are knit together in a conflictual relationship.

The Conflict-Relationship

The mutually closed power-relationship is very much prone to provoke conflict, which also runs counter to the aims of economic transaction. The more the two parties have their own interests, the more frequently they will clash with each other. In economic transaction, both parties draw benefits from the relationship; otherwise they would not engage in such activity. In conflict, one party's gain to a certain degree results in the other party's loss to the same degree. Because they cannot leave the situation in order to escape potential loss, they have to face the situation and try to overcome the resistance of the other party. What each needs in order to do that is power over the other party. The more one party's power outgrows the other party's power, the more it will be able to attain its goal at the cost of the other party's goal attainment. The more they have equal power over each other, the more both will tend to attain their goals halfway, like the sports game that finishes in a draw.

Conflict settlement in its pure sense does not entail economic calculation and transaction in the first instance. A conflict arises inasmuch as two actors are committed to pursuing a specific goal and cannot both attain that goal at the same time and to the same degree. The goals may be the same—as in the case of two opponents who want to win a match, but only one can be victorious—or they may be different—as in the case of two political parties, one advocating a tax increase, the other pursuing the opposite. In both cases, conflict arises because one party's goal attainment rules out the other party's goal attainment. The conflict arises all the more, the less the parties calculate their potential gains and losses economically. The economically calculating actor is never committed to one single goal that he or she tries to attain, independently of the losses he or she might incur, including the possibility that the goal might not be attainable at all because of the overwhelming resistance of other parties. This is what characterizes the political actor who is committed to a goal and does not negotiate easily about that goal. Otherwise the politics of goal attainment would dissolve into the economics of negotiation.

The more we have truly political actors with firm convictions and specific goals in the political arena, the less the course of political decision making will proceed according to economic laws and the more it will proceed according to the laws of power politics in the Machiavellian sense, including the threat and application of power, and the mobilization of power by way of military force, political support through tax payments, affective bonds, and claims to legitimacy. A sufficient explanation of events occurring in politics has to refer to such factors of successful power politics. Negotiation and corresponding economic calculations and transactions have no place in pure power politics. The parties in conflict will succeed or be defeated, or will be caught in a stalemate where none reaches its goal. This is the unique nature of the political game that cannot be reduced to the features of the economic game.

This of course does not rule out the fact that aspects of negotiation exist in real politics. In this case, we have a penetration of economic calculation into the realm of real political decision making. Such a development, however, has a precondition. The real political actors must not be overly committed to a specific non-negotiable set of goals, the whole process of politics has to include a plurality of decisions, and the political actors must not have a firm position on them or must not be interested in all of them to the same degree. Coleman (1971) specifies these preconditions for turning the power game into a bargaining process in an earlier article. He does so, however, in order to demonstrate the working of economic rational choice explanations in collective decision making. He does not follow back the same link to the other side of the coin, the realm of power politics per se without economic transactions.

Under the conditions set out for the political bargaining process, a mixture of political goal attainment, compromising, and negotiation occurs. The actors do not play the game of all-or-nothing but are willing to make concessions in order to make some gains at least, or they make concessions at one point in order to make gains at another point. At the end of such a bargaining process, they would be worse off than if they had succeeded in an all-or-nothing power game, but they would be better off than if they had been the losers of that game. Whether the actors play the all-or-nothing game or the bargaining game is not a matter of rational choice but a matter of the actors' characters and of the situational structure as outlined above. The course of the bargaining process is determined by the actors' commitment to specific goals, power, and incentives.

The less a party is committed to specific goals and the greater the number of its goals, the more flexibly it will act in the bargaining process and the greater the gains it will draw from that process and vice versa. The more it outranks the other party's power, the more it will succeed without having to make concessions and without having to be flexible in its goals and vice versa. The more a first party's opponent is committed to specific goals and correspondingly acts less flexibly, the more that first party will itself have to resort to power in order to make some gains and vice versa. The more flexible both parties are, the more both will increase their gains by way of making concessions (losses) at one point in order to make gains at another point, leading up to a greater net gain on both parts from the total game. In the pure power game, the greater gain comes with greater power; in the bargaining game, the greater gain comes with greater incentives that depend on a party's ability and willingness to make concessions. The more wealthy but also more flexible party will be able and willing to make more concessions that turn out to work as incentives for the other party. On the other hand, a party could not make gains in this way if it were the only one to show flexibility, because it would give away things without receiving anything in return. This shows that the bargaining process will proceed only under the condition of relatively equal power and equal flexibility; otherwise it will slide into the power game in which actors resort exclusively to power.

What we have to learn from these considerations on conflict is that a unique nature and mechanism of conflict settlement can be conceived and explained only in terms of a theory of power and not in terms of rational choice. The latter works only on preconditions that introduce an economic element into conflict settlement and turn it into a bargaining process that is only an economic variant of conflict settlement.

Power and Collective Authority

According to the view of rational choice theory, a collective authority will be established and will persist the greater the number of actors in a system who draw benefits from such an institution. The larger a system of authority grows, the more those in authority (principals) will be interested in delegating part of their authority to agents. Principals and agents will identify with each other, trust each other, and cooperate more, the more both partners draw benefits from their cooperation. The more systems of authority delegate responsibility to small units interacting directly with affected people, and the more small units are directly accountable, the more effectively the system of authority will work, which is contrary to a hierarchically organized bureaucracy (Coleman 1990, pp. 553-78).

This is the economics of authority that should not, however, be falsely identified with the uniquely characteristic nature of authority itself. The latter cannot be reduced to economics but always involves power with its own unique qualities. Authority is established and persists on the basis of power. Military conquest and even democratic election are primarily an act of exerting power to establish authority, as can be experienced when those who fought or voted against a government are nevertheless subjected to that established or elected government. Furthermore, the more powerful the established or elected government, the less its decisions will have to provide benefits for any individual actor who is subjected to its authority in exchange for continued compliance and support, and the less its persistence will depend on such utility calculations and economic transactions. A strong and powerful government is not like an economic actor who has to please everybody, but it has the capacity to enforce decisions that are harmful for nearly everybody, at least in the short run. To do so, the government may draw its power from various sources. It simply may enforce decisions by threat or application of physical force; it may use its reputation in order to silence possible opponents and in order to motivate people to make sacrifices; and it may use its legitimacy in order to define the situation so that no alternative seems to be possible.

In a society in which problems are great and are growing in complexity, a government that lives on the immediate return of benefits for popular support will soon slide into insolvency and lose its position. This is the case in very unstable political systems in which governments are unable to solve the great collective problems because they have not enough power or are the victims of enormous power-inflation. The understanding of government as a give-and-take between the government and its supporters (the military, established groups, or voters) helps provoke such a situation. In contemporary modern democracies, we witness the difficulties governments have in solving the problems created by our growing disruption of the ecological balance on the earth because they are established too much on the basis of short-lived economic transactions, namely governmental services in exchange for votes. They do not mobilize enough power in order to establish long-term ecological programs against the shortsighted interests of voters. Nor do they use their power in order to make decisions in the long-term interests of restoring ecological balance. Instead they compromise in the interest of the shortsighted securing of votes. Governments are also insufficiently active in mobilizing power by working on reputation and on legitimacy in terms of far-reaching cultural values: The reputational and discursive production of power is neglected, compared to the shortsighted economic mobilization of power by pleasing voters with governmental services. In this context, we have to take into account that power does not reside only on physical force or economic solvency but also on reputation and legitimacy. These are the non-political and noneconomic sources of power. A comprehensive theory of power must refer to the internal production of power and to its external production as well.

Our consideration of collective authority tells us that it would be very shortsighted to identify its own characteristic nature with the economic transaction of governmental services in exchange for political support. Some of the greatest problems of weak governments in our time result from just such a tendency in real politics. Simply deriving the theory of collective authority from such empirical observations, particularly from United States politics, blinds us to the complexities and the unique nature of collective authority. An economics of authority exists, to be sure, but it is disastrous to take that part for the whole.

The Nonpolitical Sources of Power

My preceding remarks on the nonpolitical sources of power tell us that an explanation of action within a power-relationship, in conflict settlement, and in the establishment and continuation of collective authority not only must include the levels of power politics and economic transaction but also the levels of solidarity-relationships and legitimacy, which have their own laws. How much power is available for an individual actor, a group, a party, or a government depends on its ability to produce and mobilize power.

The first aspect to consider is that of access to the means of physical force, which is the basis to which power ultimately has to resort. This access is accompanied by control over the people who apply such means—a well-organized military and police, and a functioning legal system, administration, and government with agents who carry out the political decisions. This is the internal production of power. In addition, power is produced externally.

A powerful government needs financial means in order to remunerate its agents and to carry out ambitious programs. For that, it depends on a prosperous economy from which it can draw the financial resources needed via tax payments. An intelligent economic policy is therefore a precondition for the economic production of governmental power. This production requires rational economic action on the part of the government.

A powerful government also needs support, loyalty, and cooperation by its agents and by the people. To achieve that, the government is dependent on relatively undivided respect within a relatively undivided population. The more sharply divisions are drawn in the societal community, the more any case of decision making will involve polarization with weak support for the government and thus little power. In terms of power, this means that the government cannot count on the undivided support, loyalty, and cooperation of agents and people when it tries to enforce its decisions. Such support, loyalty, and cooperation are needed, however, in order to make such attempts to enforce decisions effective. In this case, potential deviants have less chance of escaping enforcement.

This production of power via mobilization of support, solidarity, loyalty, and cooperation does not work in political terms or in economic terms. Such activities can be enforced by power or purchased by money only to a very limited degree, namely inasmuch as there is a politics and an economics of support, solidarity, loyalty, and cooperation. Genuine support comes as a product of collective sentiment. Inasmuch as a government wants to rely on such support, it must take the lead in a collective enterprise that aims at solving the collectivity's urgent problems. That means such a government first must open the people's eyes to their common problems beyond the particular problems of each group and individual member of the societal collectivity. Second, it must demonstrate its commitment to the common goals and its ability to attain them in exemplary actions. The people must see that this is a government that does not only serve particular interests but also takes care of the societal collectivity as a whole and in the long run, beyond shortsighted and particular interests. This is the climate for the emergence of trust, support, solidarity, loyalty, and cooperation. The government acquires a good reputation with which it can mobilize those activities in order to carry out its programs with enhanced power. Unbridgeable divisions in the societal collectivity, exploitation of governmental power in the service of particular interests, short-lived power politics, and conducting politics in terms of economic transactions undermine this reputational production of power.

Quite another form of producing power is the creation of legitimacy. This question relates to the legitimacy of the governmental system and also affects the whole process of political decision making. A government that acts on firm foundations of legitimacy acts with more power. It can better justify its decisions, which leaves potential opponents and deviants with fewer means of resistance because they will lack consent by other people. Creating legitimacy means that a government has the ability to play a leading role in political discourse and to lead that discourse in such a direction that a certain consensus on the definition of the situation, on the importance of certain values at stake, on the major problems that must be solved in that context, on certain programs for solving these problems, and on their consistency with the values at stake ensues.

A government that does not actively shape this political discourse and leaves it to free-floating intellectuals and journalists will be weak on grounds of legitimacy and thus will have only a small amount of legitimacy-power at its disposal. It will not receive the consent needed to carry out ambitious political programs and thus provoke resistance in terms of both harsh criticism and deviation legitimated by that criticism. It will not be able to overcome such resistance because of the lack of legitimacy as a source of its power and thus will fail if it cannot compensate its deficit in legitimacy by other sources of power. Such sources, however, will never produce consent and legitimacy as an important cultural source of power that secures the cultural success and persistence of a government.

Summing up, rational choice theory has only limited explanatory power concerning social phenomena that mostly include levels reaching well beyond economic transaction. My analysis of power has shown that an economics of power indeed exists. A complete explanation of what goes on in power-relationships, conflict, and collective authority, however, must step beyond such an economics of power to the levels of its politics, "solidarics," and symbolics.

THE WORLD OF TRUST, NORMS, AND THE HUMAN SELF

As there is an economics of power, there are also an economics of trust and commitment to norms, and rational choice theory has something to tell us about them.

Trust

The first component the theory has to offer is its treatment of trust as a phenomenon that parallels risk-taking behavior (Coleman 1990, pp. 91-115, 175-96): The likelihood that I will trust someone's advice, action, or lead increases with the product of the value he or she has for me and the probability with which I expect him or her to realize that value in the particular case involved. Whether I believe in a physician's therapy and cooperate or in a politician's program and support it depends on how valuable it is for me and how likely I feel that it will be successful. The resulting interaction is an economic transaction of trust in exchange for benefits.

To be sure, such an economically rational aspect of trust is found in a great proportion of behavior in modern life. This aspect is far from being all that is involved in trust and particularly does not represent the uniquely characteristic core of trust, which is different from pure economics and has a nonrational, emotional basis.

The primordial form of trust, or its opposite—mistrust— emerges in close relationships between mother and child or in the family and other primary groups for which a clear-cut differentiation between in-group and out-group is characteristic. The in-group is, on the one hand, a safeguard against any dangers coming from the outside world; on the other hand, the outside world will appear all the more dangerous the more the in-group cuts its members off from it. This is the origin of the individual's differentiation between the familiar and the unfamiliar, and the first differentiation between trust and mistrust is parallel to that differentiation. Trust goes to people who are perceived as belonging to one's own, first in a direct, and subsequently also in an indirect, way if people of one's own mediate to introduce strangers and to make us familiar with them. The transmission of trust to a wider group of people or to individuals who are outside our range of direct day-to-day contact proceeds by means of such networks of mediation. My trust in a doctor whose service I call on for the first time is mostly mediated by a person with whom I am familiar and who has my trust.

Such mediated trust-relationships may take on complex forms. For example, in modern politics, trust in politicians comes and goes in waves according to how trustingly the media talk about them and how much confidence my friends say they place in them, which is itself related to media talk. What goes on in this process is a transmission of feelings. In the last instance, trust is a feeling rooted in a personal history of such feelings which cannot be completely rationalized though it may partly undergo such a rationalizing process. A feeling of trust or mistrust is present at the moment of the first encounter with another person, dependent on my accumulated feelings of trust and mistrust. And it will depend very much on this trust at first sight whether I trust the advice, action, or lead of that person. My first-sight trust determines my evaluation of his or her talk and my cooperation, which again determine the success of his or her advice, action, or lead, and that success in turn serves as an instance on which my further trust resides. Thus trust works very much in a self-fulfilling way, as does mistrust. If I enter a relationship with trust, the probability of being confirmed in this attitude is great. If I enter the relationship with mistrust, many things will serve as corroborations of that feeling and will strengthen it further.

All this works before I begin to calculate benefits and costs and actually shapes my cost-benefit calculations. In that respect, we have to acknowledge a uniquely characteristic core of trust that does not work according to the laws of economics but according to the laws of feelings of familiarity and unfamiliarity, to which feelings of trust and mistrust are related. This does not mean that our trusting behavior cannot learn in a rational way. New experiences may call into question earlier trust or mistrust and may result in a redirection of such feelings. Any such process, however, has to overcome barriers of feelings that may block any learning in this direction. Only in a process of continuously stepping beyond the boundaries of one's own group will such barriers be broken down eventually and will trust be moved away from a pure feeling toward a more complex phenomenon that includes aspects of economic and other forms of rationality, such as moral or discursive rationality. Breaking down the barriers of primordial trust and mistrust is one of the most arduous processes on the way to modernity, and that dimension of modernity develops slowly and incompletely.

The emergence of citizenship and the breaking down of the barriers of group particularism and hostility between primordial groups is the greatest problem in building the modern world, as we may witness with the outbreaks of conflict between national, ethnic, racial, religious, regional, and other groups in developing and even developed societies, leading to civil war in those societies in which such conflicts had been artificially suppressed or stirred up by communist or other totalitarian rule. Turning mutual mistrust into trust in the process of building up a citizenship that includes a plurality of groups first necessitates long-lasting processes of redirecting emotions by an outstanding, charismatic leader who can attract the trust of a plurality of otherwise hostile groups because he or she demonstrates in an exemplary way the importance of the whole in contrast to the many parts. Only on such a basis will the processes of learning work gradually, demonstrating the economic benefits of cooperation, compared to confrontation, the moral validity of equal rights for everyone and hence reaching beyond one's own primordial group, and the political effectiveness of larger communities, compared with smaller ones.

Norms

Trustful relationships are also the characteristic milieu in which action is regulated by norms that are borne consensually. This is the very core of the regulation of behavior by norms, and it lies outside the visual range of rational choice theory. Again we can frankly admit that an economics of norm-regulated behavior indeed exists that is the legitimate subject of rational choice theory. According to Coleman (1990, pp. 45-64, 67, 241-341, 503-28), such an economic approach to norm-regulated behavior involves such assumptions as the following:

The greater the number of external effects in a system of action, the greater will be the demand for norms. The more the beneficiaries of norms are linked by social relationships, the more likely it is that norms will be established and upheld by zeal in sanctioning deviations either incrementally or heroically. The more norms are internalized by actors, the less external sanctions have to be applied. The more the socializee identifies with the socializing agent, the more likely it is that he or she will internalize the norms represented by the socializing agent. The greater the benefits experienced by the socializee as coming from the socializing agent, the greater will be his or her identification with him or her, based on identical interests. The larger the number of socializing agents with whom one identifies grows, the greater the number of interests that one develops. The more the individual's self grows, the more the object self, which sets the interests, and the acting self, which administers resources and carries out the actions, will engage in an economic transaction between principal and agent. The larger the systems of action grow, the greater will be an interest in regulating action by positive law set by an authority to which rights to act have been transferred. The greater the benefits that one draws from established social relationships (social capital), the more likely it is that one will uphold these relationships.

It is true that all such economics work in regulating behavior by norms. The existence of norms and conformity to norms make life easier. Traditions and frames for action liberate the individual from arduous and frustrating disputes and conflicts, and they reduce uncertainty. The individual thus will welcome such regulations of behavior that allow him or her to concentrate on pursuing his or her substantial ends instead of wasting energy disputing over the preliminaries. The same is true of existing traditions and frames, and these will be maintained as long as any change might result in uncertainty in general and uncertain benefits in particular. It is also true that it is more beneficial to stay with one's friends with whom one is familiar and with whom one knows where one stands, instead of making new friends with costly investments and uncertain results. Establishing a collective authority that regulates action by positive law is also more beneficial than having to dispute every step one takes in everyday life. Furthermore socialized persons who have norms internalized make social life easier and more beneficial for their fellows, who therefore are interested in providing such socialization. In the process of socialization, identification of the socializee with the socializing agent furthers the transmission of norms, and this identification grows with the benefits drawn from the relationship.

This is not, however, the whole story concerning the regulation of behavior by norms. It is only the economics of norms. Moreover calculating orientation to traditions, frames, and other norms contradicts part of their original nature. A calculating use of a tradition is no longer a tradition in its true sense because the latter's effect is exactly the setting of limits to calculation by taking out some basic norms and placing them beyond such calculation. They exist before calculation begins and shape calculation. Inasmuch as human life does not display order by coincidence alone and has some stable core, it cannot result purely from calculation because the latter can start only if at least some unquestioned and uncalculated givens exist.

In social life, such unquestioned and uncalculated givens must be shared because otherwise everybody would start from different premises, and dispute and conflict would prevail. People do not, however, live such an isolated life. They grow up with other people in groups who share the same life-world and back each other up in their view of the world day by day. This makes it easier for them to live in consensus about the essentials of social life. Their differentiation from the outside world, the differentiation of in-group solidarity, familiarity, and trust and out-group hostility, unfamiliarity, and mistrust contribute to establishing such a primordial consensus. Within such a solidaristic community, any deviation from norms will result in uniform negative sanctioning that reconfirms the binding character of the norms so that no uncertainty about norms emerges.

This is the truly characteristic core of the existence of norms, of the commitment and conformity to norms that is completely uncalculated in character. It is the nonrational basis of norm regulation. Only from this core might more complex and rationalized forms of normative regulation emerge. The expansion of normative regulations beyond primordial ties in large societies requires that differentiation between in-group solidarity and out-group hostility be broken down. That will happen only if social ties are established that reach beyond primary groups in order to expand the societal community that serves as the source of the binding power of social norms in the greater society. We know that it takes a long time to establish such ties and to break down barriers between hostile groups. It is, however, a development in its own right that cannot be replaced by other developments. This is the emergence of citizenship on an ever broader foundation. Inasmuch as economic transactions, cultural communication, and political legislation expand, they first will contribute to this development only inasmuch as they involve the knitting of new social ties. Only in a secondary way will their primary character contribute to the development of the societal community inasmuch as economic transaction replaces confrontation by cooperation, cultural communication replaces moral particularism by moral universalism, and political legislation replaces primordial norms by formal law.

At one point, Coleman touches the importance of social ties for the undivided regulation of behavior by norms when he speaks of the necessary links between the beneficiaries of norms in order to establish norms and to sanction deviations with zeal. He does not recognize enough, however, that this calls for the development of a much more complex theory of social action that reaches much beyond rational choice theory. Economics is but one element in the complex development of citizenship as the basis for the binding character of social norms in modern societies.

Socialization and the Human Self

A similar criticism relates to the economic view of socialization. To be sure, a beneficial relationship between socializee and socializing agent helps identification. The origin of that identification, however, lies elsewhere. It is rooted in the differentiation between in-group and out-group that strengthens the identification with one's own and the separation from people in the outside world. The major problem for the socialization process in modern societies is therefore one of breaking down the differentiation between in-group and out-group and expanding identification to an ever wider group of people parallel to the development of modern citizenship.

The conceptualization of the human self as an economic transaction between object self (principal) and acting self (agent) is but one dimension of the complex nature of the human self (Coleman 1990, pp. 503-28). The object self also sets goals and applies power to ensure they will be carried out by the acting self; it makes norms binding by committing the acting self to a community; it refers to ideas and values to which the acting self has to justify its proceedings. These are all important aspects of what is going on in the human self that cannot be reduced to economic transactions.

THE WORLD OF CULTURE, COMMUNICATION, AND LEGITIMACY

An economics of culture, communication, and legitimacy (Coleman 1990, pp. 325-70) also exists. Values, ideas, cognitions, and information are not only discussed in debates but also are disseminated in markets according to economic calculations. People take up values, ideas, cognitions, and information because they hope to receive benefits, and they turn them down if their maintenance becomes too costly.

This is not, however, the entire picture of the cultural world. It has its unique nature too, which cannot be reduced to economics. In order to take up an idea, I have to understand its meaning, and what I do with it depends on how I interpret this meaning. In this process, I establish a meaning relationship between my frame of interpretation and a particular instance of a cultural text. Consistency is the criterion for including the particular instance in my frame of reference. Ideas also claim validity for themselves, and this increasingly has to be proven against criticism the more an open discourse on such ideas occurs. Whether a certain right claimed by citizens, governments, oppositions, and other groups in a society can be justified as legitimate and maintained against contradictory statements determines whether those groups are allowed by the other groups to proceed in accordance with the right they claim. To be successful in such a discourse, one must be able to sustain one's validity claims with broadly accepted reasons. In this process, individuals and groups might try to sustain their economic interests in increasing benefits and decreasing costs on the strength of good, broadly accepted arguments. Nevertheless, whether they will succeed in doing so is not dependent on this relationship of interests to reasons but on their ability to point to such more generally valid reasons beyond their particular interests. Part of the argument might appeal to the economic interests of other individuals and groups, and other parts might appeal to more widely held general values. Nevertheless, it is still the ability to sustain a claim by citing more generally accepted reasons that determines whether an action can be carried out successfully. This is an aspect that we have to include in any explanation of an ongoing action that is not covered by rational choice theory.

Here is an example. Coleman (1990, pp. 1-23) refers to Max Weber's ([1920-21a] 1972a, [1920-21b] 1972b, [1920-21c] 1971) famous explanation of the rise of the capitalist spirit because of the emergence of the Protestant ethic in the Western world. In his preoccupation with the aspect of rational choice, he explains this relationship as a macro-micro-relationship in the following way: In the context of the Protestant community, it was more beneficial for the capitalist to accumulate wealth through hard work and reliable behavior without becoming addicted to the vices of a luxurious life-style because such behavior was rewarded by the members of that community with social approval and the acknowledgement that one belonged to God's "Elect," whereas any deviation from this path was punished by disapproval and by being grouped among the eternally condemned. It is no question that such economic calculations might have played their part and are worth being included in an explanation of what happened. For Weber, however, this was a minor and simple part of the explanation that did not call for major efforts on his part. What was much more important for him and what needed much more arduous work was to prove that a consistent relationship indeed existed between the meaning of the Protestant ethic and the meaning of the spirit of capitalism. This proof of the adequacy of meaning in his explanation, in contrast to his brief introductory remarks on the adequacy of cause (overrepresentation of Protestants in the groups of entrepreneurs and higher professionals and the rise of modern rational capitalism in Protestant areas), attracted his efforts overwhelmingly not only in the study on the Protestant ethic but in his entire comparative work on world religions and the rise of the Western world.

It is only a very small part in Weber's explanation, and an unimportant one because of its self-evident nature, that is touched by rational choice theory. Its explicit introduction does not add any new information. The greater part of the explanation involves enormous efforts in reconstructing cultural meaning-relationships, a task for which rational choice theory has no sensitivity at all because it does not seem to exist for rational choice theorists. Culture cannot be reduced to a variable in a deductive-nomological explanation. It needs much more interpretive work in order to understand the meaning of what happened rather than to explain it causally. Here the shortcomings of rational choice theory would result in a disaster if sociology were to follow its lead.

THE WORLD OF THE MACRO-MICRO LINK

In terms of rational choice theory (Coleman 1990, pp. 1-23), the relationship between macro and micro phenomena is seen unidimensionally as one in which outside given conditions are taken into account by rational actors in their choice of the most beneficial way to act.

Such a view overlooks the fact that the relationship between the macro and the micro is much more complex in reality. It includes the meaning-relationship between a cultural text and an action, as an individual instance and as a particular contribution to writing or rewriting that text. It includes the binding relationship between a community's group solidarity and an individual act of solidarity, support, cooperation, and loyalty that involves transmitting a collective sentiment from the community to an individual and back to the community. It includes the power-relationship between a leader representing a group who commands in the name of the group and the servant who obeys. These are all macro-micro-relationships that cannot be understood in terms of their unique character if they all are interpreted simply as a rational choice in the face of certain external conditions.

THE WORLD OF MODERN SOCIETY

Coleman (1990, pp. 421-50, 531-664) is concerned with the uncontrolled growth of large corporations (corporate actors) in modern society. According to Coleman's economic view, they grow inasmuch as it is more beneficial for individual actors in large systems to delegate rights to some acting bodies than to retain such rights for themselves.

This is a Hobbesian argument (Hobbes [1651] 1966) that does not take into account the fact that such corporations can be established by powerful actors simply by using their power regardless of the benefits to other actors.

The same economic bias accompanies Coleman's argument for better control of large corporations. For him, this is nothing but a question of how individuals can make sure that the corporations do not act against their interest in increasing benefits and avoiding costs. As Coleman says, global viability (responsibility) of large corporations produces a great many negative external effects for many people who have no chance of exerting control by advocating their interests against such corporations. What is needed, in Coleman's eyes, is the revitalization of independent paired viability of small units by decentralization and the control of corporate actors by the internal and external participation of affected people in decision making that will lead to the internalization of the external effects generated by corporations.

This is all very well as long as we are concerned with liberty in the economic sense and with the coordination of rights to liberty of self-interested individual actors in society at large. This is not, however, all about the complex framework of modern society. Decentralization has its negative effects too because it sharpens inequalities between the districts and regions in the decentralized system. The inequalities between rich and poor districts and regions will be strengthened. We can see this by taking only one short glance at the decentralized systems of education and crime control in the United States. Large societal systems of our time that are increasingly outgrowing the nation-state cannot be governed without the central-ization of power. Its control, however, necessitates institutions that are different from those of a decentralized liberal society in which everybody tries to look after his or her self-interest. It requires extended judicial control by a strong legal system; it requires com-petition between government and opposition; and it requires control by public discourse and intellectual criticism.

Such large societal systems particularly have to overcome group particularism and have to establish a citizenship that entails a plu-rality of groups with equal rights. They also have to work on citizens' rights that are justified and controlled in a permanent public dis-course. These features of modern society are as important as eco-nomic liberalism but reach much beyond the identification of mod-ern society with liberal society in the narrow sense of the coordinated liberty of economically self-interested individuals. We cannot solve the problems of contemporary world society with recipes from the outdated kitchen of an old-fashioned economic liberalism (see Münch 1986, 1991).

CONCLUSION

Rational choice theory is a welcome advance in sociological theory. It contributes to improving its explanatory power inas-much as we are concerned with the economics of social life. We can also freely admit that economics is everywhere, particularly in our modern social life, where economic rationality penetrates virtually every sphere of society. For this reason, it is easy for rational choice theorists to demonstrate the working of their approach with reference to a wide array of social phenomena beyond the economic sphere in its narrower sense. They fail, however, inasmuch as they take this demonstration to represent the whole story of social life. In this process, they simply reduce the whole complexity of social life to terms of economic calculation and transaction, the complexity of modern society to the simplicity of liberal society. Rational choice theory covers only a limited realm of social life. Its explanatory power is limited to the economic dimension of that life. A comprehensive sociological theory must interconnect rational choice theory in a greater framework with theories that are more adequate to deal with the realms of social life outside the economic sphere (Münch 1992). This is what I have tried to demonstrate in this chapter.

REFERENCES

Coleman, James S. 1971. "Collective Decisions." Pp. 272-86 in *Institutions and Social Exchange*, edited by H. Turk and R. L. Simpson. Indianapolis: Bobbs-Merrill.
———. 1990. *Foundations of Social Theory*. Cambridge, MA: Belknap.
Hobbes, Thomas. [1651] 1966. *The English Works of Thomas Hobbes*. Vol. 3, *Leviathan*, edited by W. Molesworth. Aalen, Germany: Scientia.
Münch, Richard. 1986. *Die Kultur der Moderne*. 2 Vols., Frankfurt: Suhrkamp.
———. 1987. *Theory of Action*. London: Routledge.
———. 1988. *Understanding Modernity*. London: Routledge.
———. 1991. *Dialektik der Kommunikationsgesellschaft*. Frankfurt: Suhrkamp.
———. 1992. *The Discourse of Sociological Theory*. Chicago: Nelson-Hall.
Parsons, Talcott. [1937] 1968. *The Structure of Social Action*. New York: Free Press.
Weber, Max. [1920-21a] 1972a, [1920-21b] 1972b, [1920-21c] 1971. *Gesammelte Aufsätze zur Religionssoziologie*. 3 Vols., Tübingen: Mohr Siebeck.

Chapter 8

WEAKNESSES IN RATIONAL CHOICE THEORY'S CONTRIBUTION TO COMPARATIVE RESEARCH

DAVID SCIULLI

Texas A & M University

THE GREAT STRENGTH OF RATIONAL CHOICE THEORY is that as its proponents endeavor to account for social order and group solidarity, they resist as long as possible appealing to actors' supposed internalization of shared norms. The central defect of the Parsonian tradition was precisely that its proponents too readily took this tack instead of first exhausting all other explanations. Indeed, rational choice theory emerged in American sociology in the late 1940s and early 1950s largely in response to Talcott Parsons's social theory (e.g., Homans 1950; Collins 1988, p. 339). In American political science, public choice theory had emerged a generation earlier in response to the then dominant *institutional approach,* but it became influential only after World War II (e.g., Downs 1957; Buchanan and Tullock 1962; Niskanen 1971). In both disciplines, proponents today insist that their concepts and assumptions are more "realistic"—less normative or idealistic—than those of the theorists they are challenging.

AUTHOR'S NOTE: Extracts from *The Foundations of Social Theory* by James S. Coleman have been reprinted by permission of the publisher, Harvard University Press; copyright © 1990 by the President and Fellows of Harvard College.

FIVE ASSUMPTIONS
OF RATIONAL CHOICE THEORY

Instead of appealing to actors' purportedly internalized norms or to the purportedly ideal workings of American institutions, rational choice theorists operate explicitly on the basis of four background assumptions and then implicitly on a fifth. The first background assumption is that individual actors typically are dedicated to maximizing their own private "wealth,"[1] or whatever happens to interest them subjectively. Rarely if ever can they be relied on to contribute to any purported group good. Thus actors typically face Olson's (1965) "free rider problem":

> Indeed, unless the number of individuals in a group is quite small, or unless there is coercion or some other special device to make individuals act in their common interest, rational, self-interested individuals will not act to achieve their common or group interests. In other words, even if all of the individuals in a large group are rational and self-interested, and would gain if, as a group, they acted to achieve their common interest or objective, they will still not voluntarily act to achieve that common or group interest. (Olson 1965, p. 2) (See also Hechter 1987, p. 40; Coleman 1990, p. 14)[2]

The second background assumption is that actors' subjective interests or desired ends are ultimately "sovereign," both conceptually and in practice (e.g., Brennan and Buchanan 1985; Coleman 1990, pp. 531-32).[3] Actors need not justify their preferences, nor, for that matter, need they formulate their preferences consciously or consistently (e.g., Posner 1990, 353-54).[4] How or why actors arrive at their preferences and whether or why their preferences change over time are issues that they dismiss conceptually as unimportant. Instead, actors' subjective interests are treated conceptually as either given or random (Parsons [1937] 1968 attacked this conceptualization directly, and Münch 1981, Alexander 1982, and Lechner 1990 develop his lead).

Michael Hechter poses this assumption uncritically: "Rational choice theory is . . . grounded in the rational actor methodology of microeconomics . . . [whereby] individuals are regarded as the bearers of sets of given, discrete, nonambiguous, and transitive preferences" (Hechter 1987, p. 30). James Coleman does the same at first: "In general, throughout this book, except in Chapter 19, I assume that interests are unchangeable; in a theory based on purposive action *interests must be taken as given* [italics added] before a rational course of action in pursuit of those interests can be charted" (1990, pp. 156-57). Yet four pages later he acknowledges that problems exist with this assumption: "As observation makes clear, *although the theory does not have a way of reflecting this*, [italics added] interests are not arbitrary, to be shaped at the will of the individual, but are held in place by constraints" (1990, p. 161). Coleman seems to modify the tenet of sovereignty of subjective interests by using Loury's notion of *social capital* (Coleman 1990, Chap. 12). But it will be shown momentarily that this does not modify it.

The third background assumption is that any society's existing distribution of rights and duties is also given or random. The tenet of *private wealth maximization* refers to the maximization of the value of such a given distribution. Coleman presents this assumption forthrightly: "Just as in the case of economic efficiency, the social optimum is defined relative to an existing distribution of rights and resources. . . . If that distribution is highly unequal, this implies that the interests of some actors count for much more than do the interests of others" (1990, p. 262).

The fourth background assumption is that actors' normatively unfettered efforts to maximize their own private wealth are more likely to result in collective prosperity or social wealth than any effort to restrain these efforts by institutionalizing nonrational norms. For Coleman, "the criteria of optimality of constitutions . . . are based on the same conceptual structure as the criterion of economic efficiency" (1990, p. 354). And the latter is more the outcome of a hidden hand than of any design:

> The achievement of social efficiency in this case [of establishing a normative restraint] lies in a redistribution of rights of control over each action to the group as a whole. But with a group that is not homogeneous, it becomes more problematic to define social efficiency. (Coleman 1990, p. 260)

Hechter poses a skeptical question but yields to liberal complacency rather than provide an answer:

> If rational choice theorists have a Holy Grail, surely it is the concept of the invisible hand, which provides for the establishment of a self-sustaining

and—in some sense—ethically justifiable social equilibrium (Nozick 1974: 18-22). By transforming private vices into public virtues . . . this kind of equilibrium allows for the possibility of order among rational egoists without the necessity of formal controls. To what extent can an invisible-hand explanation account for compliance in large groups or for social order? (Hechter 1987, p. 73)

This leads to the fifth, more implicit background assumption of rational choice theory. Even the most pessimistic rational choice theorists (whether, for example, Buchanan or earlier liberals like Hayek and Oakeshott) adopt this assumption, and at times they state it explicitly:[5] Actors' relatively unfettered pursuit of their own preferences is more likely to yield and sustain a benign direction of social change—a stable, liberal-democratic society—than any effort to restrain this pursuit with institutionalized norms. Richard Posner puts this as well as anyone else:

The strongest argument for wealth maximization is not moral, but pragmatic. . . . we look around the world and see that in general people who live in societies in which markets are allowed to function more or less freely not only are wealthier than people in other societies but have more political rights, more liberty and dignity, are more content (as evidenced, for example, by their being less prone to emigrate)—so that wealth maximization may be the more direct route to a variety of moral ends. (Posner 1990, p. 382)

This background assumption is the source of rational choice theory's greatest weakness as a conceptual framework in comparative research. By focusing on whether actors maximize their private wealth or subjective preferences, rational choice theorists close themselves off from concepts that address changes in the quality of communication among rational actors. As a result, they fail to recognize, and clearly cannot explain or account for, changes in the major institutions and organizations of a civil society: Are these institutions and organizations restraining arbitrary exercises of collective power within civil society, or are they permitting and encouraging such exercises?

Once one challenges the assumption that the direction of social change yielded by actors' rational choices is somehow intrinsically benign, because arbitrariness within civil society is somehow restrained more or less automatically, the conceptual (and then empirical) limits of rational choice theory come to the fore. When its proponents actually are called on to account for the presence of a relatively benign civil society in the late 20th century, in the face of enormous systemic pressures to the contrary, they readily find that their core concepts and assumptions fail them. Instead of accounting for the nonrational restraints that account for the presence of relatively benign civil societies in the late 20th century, rational choice theorists skirt the issue. They assume conceptually—all historical evidence to the contrary notwithstanding—that the emergence of institutionalized normative restraints on arbitrary exercises of collective power is like the generation of social wealth: that it is yielded automatically, by a hidden hand, as actors endeavor to maximize their private wealth unfettered by nonrational norms of any kind. Thus they are unable to specify the institutionalized normative restraints on individuals' private wealth-maximization that simultaneously (a) frame heterogeneous actors' and competing groups' nonmanipulated and noncoerced communication, and thereby (b) resiliently restrain arbitrary exercises of collective power within civil society.

Coleman is as blunt about this failure as any other writer in this theoretical tradition:

> The notion of willpower, or the power to prevent short-term interests from overwhelming long-term interests, has no place in standard theory of rational choice. Yet it is a common element in the actions of natural persons. . . . The consequence is that a corporate actor is in a unique position to exploit weakness of will in natural persons, even to exploit the potential for such weakness by encouraging impulsive action. (Coleman 1990, pp. 548-9)

A PRELIMINARY CRITICISM: THE LIMITED SCOPE OF RATIONAL ACTION

The issue of directionality is discussed more methodically below. But one preliminary criticism of rational choice theory's conceptual framework sets the stage for this: When the costs and benefits of a social action are qualitative rather than readily quantitative or measurable, it is not possible to characterize any existing distribution of rights and duties as efficient or inefficient in general (e.g., Coleman's position in his earlier quote from 1990, p. 382).

It is useful to recall that neoclassical economics assumed the existence of competitive markets, and the latter in turn was marked by at least three characteristics: multiple producers, their ease of entry into and exit from any industry, and their production of goods and services that are indistinguishable other than by price. Thus worldly qualities and actors' efforts either to describe and explain them or to create and maintain them were explicitly bracketed conceptually from consideration. Consider how Coleman updates the assumption of competitive markets and thereby brings this conceptual bracketing from economics to sociology:

> [A] constitution will have an optimal allocation of rights if power in the postconstitution system of action is distributed in proportion to each actor's participation in the construction of the constitution. But because power in the postconstitution system is in part determined by the constitutional allocation of rights, a number of different constitutional allocations could be optimal, depending on who wins the constitutional struggle. (Coleman 1990, p. 355)

The particular point at issue here is that rational choice theorists, unlike neoclassical economists, typically fail to incorporate the criterion of quantitative ends into their very definition of *rational action*. This is why they so often overstate this concept's scope of application.[6] This is why rational choice theory leaves researchers to subjective descriptions of many social actions and to uncertainty regarding which particular social actions are rational and which are not.[7]

For example, Hechter's failure to specify explicitly that social action can only be labeled *rational* on the basis of its quantitative results leaves him in the nether world of fathoming the nature of actors' subjective preferences. As such, he concedes that ultimately any social action might be rational: "[Rational choice] theory treats individual preferences as sovereign, but if it is to yield testable implications about group behavior, these preferences must be specified in advance. Otherwise the theory is empty, *for any behavior can be viewed as rational with the advantage of hindsight*" [italics added] (Hechter 1987, p. 31) (See also Coleman 1990, p. 18). He goes on to note that "the preferences—which provide the motivation for all behavior—are exogenous to the theory, and therefore unexplained" (Hechter 1987, pp. 31-3, Note 22).

The broader theoretical point at issue here is that modern civil societies are comprised of heterogeneous actors and competing groups, and the latter experience great difficulty simply in recognizing and understanding in common what the outcomes of social actions are that cannot be reduced to quantitative indices. This difficulty is precisely why rational choice theorists are so wedded to their central concept: Actors' normatively unmediated or strictly instrumental and strategic efforts to maximize private wealth are the only actions that social scientists too are likely to recognize and to understand in common under modern conditions. This is why Olson, Buchanan, and Coleman all refer to actors' and groups' consensus regarding any given distribution of rights within any modern society (and presumably the duties that they share in maintaining this distribution): Such actors and groups can recognize and understand in common quantitative increases or decreases in efficient production or effective administration. Otherwise, however, they remain both fragmented in their normative beliefs and competitive in both formulating and pursuing their own subjective interests.

RATIONAL CHOICE THEORY
AND COMPARATIVE RESEARCH

Four other criticisms of rational choice theory elaborate the implications of its fifth background assumption, and these criticisms are tied directly to its (largely proposed) contribution to comparative research (e.g., Tsebelis 1990). These criticisms are posed rarely in the literature, and they may be listed in turn:

1. Rational choice theorists hypostatize either a benign, Lockean direction of social change (e.g., Hechter, Coleman) or a malevolent, Hobbesian direction of social change (e.g., Buchanan). They fail, however, to account conceptually for shifts in either direction in practice.

2. Rational choice theorists hypostatize markets, hierarchies, and corporations as the dominant institutional and organizational forms of modern civil societies. They fail to account conceptually for professions, universities, the research divisions of corporations, or other deliberative bodies.

3. Rational choice theorists correctly reject normative theorists' conjecture that modern actors share internalized normative motivations and that this accounts for social order. They fail, however, to distinguish institutionalized normative orientations and how the

latter account for a benign direction of social change by restraining the maximization of private wealth.

4. Rational choice theorists hypostatize actors' "rights" and their acceptance of the basic distribution of rights in civil society. They fail to account conceptually for either the presence or absence of institutionalized normative restraints on arbitrary exercises of collective power within civil society.

All four criticisms revolve around the first, and only the first can be elaborated here.[8] For present purposes, a *benign or non-authoritarian direction of social change* may be defined as one in which arbitrary exercises of collective power within a civil society are restrained institutionally. In turn, a *malevolent or authoritarian direction of social change* is one in which these exercises are not being restrained and are increasing.

Conceptualizing Institutional Outcomes: Hypostatization and Inconsistency

Rational choice theorists fall into two distinct camps when they address the issue of directionality: On one side, Buchanan, Hayek, and Oakeshott explicitly reject the assumption that directionality within liberal democracy is intrinsically benign; and they are thereby anxious Hobbesians. On the other side, Olson, Hechter, Coleman, and Posner all refuse to challenge this assumption explicitly; and they are thereby complacent Lockeans. Hechter explicitly accepts this assumption, whereas Olson and Posner do so implicitly (for Hechter, e.g., 1987, pp. 62-9, 183-86). Coleman is intriguing because he is at first inconsistent in his position, but then, as he reveals his Lockean sympathies, his work exposes several of the limitations of the rational choice conceptual framework as such.

Regarding Coleman's initial inconsistency (e.g., 1990, p. 16), on the one hand, he insists that because "the integration and organization of the system" is problematic, he avoids functionalism's teleological explanations for social order. He does not adopt the view, he says, that individual action contributes invariably to system integration (but see Posner 1990, p. 379, on how the rational choice framework does this conceptually regardless). Yet he nonetheless insists that "much of what is ordinarily described as nonrational or irrational is merely so because the observers have not discovered the point of view of the actor, from which the action *is* rational" (Coleman 1990, p. 18). Thus like Hechter, Coleman finds that any behavior can be labeled *rational* in retrospect.

These positions are inconsistent in that *if actors believe a system is rationally integrated or organized, from their point of view, then Coleman has no conceptual basis for suggesting that this may not be the case.* He also has no conceptual basis for simply bracketing the issue from view and claiming that tenets of value-neutrality somehow prevent him from declaring his complacency explicitly.

As one example of how the inconsistency affects his theory, Coleman rejects Weber's distinction between associative groups based on members' rational common interests and communal groups based on members' nonrational attachments. By his approach, both types of groups "are authority systems in which actors transfer authority without receiving an extrinsic payment" (Coleman 1990, p. 73). Coleman goes on to say that "this is a subjectively rational transfer of authority when it is based on the belief that the exercise of authority will be in the actors' interests" (1990, p. 73). Whether this belief is manipulated, controlled, or subtly coerced is something that rational choice theory cannot address conceptually. And yet this is an eminently sociological issue rather than a social-psychological one. Once the rational choice conceptual framework hypostatizes the sovereignty of actors' subjective interests, it already assumes system integration.[9]

After all, not only Coleman but even Buchanan posits a consensus among actors regarding the legitimacy of existing institutions, the existing distribution of rights within a civil society. Consider the following passages:

> The appropriate position for viewing the problem [is not "to take the perspective of a philosophy of natural rights" (1990: 333) but rather to hold that] rights originate with consensus and are nonexistent in the absence of consensus. Rights do not inhere in individuals but originate only through consensus; yet consensus itself requires recourse to individuals. (Coleman 1990, p. 334)

> The contractarian derives all value from individual participants in the community *and rejects externally defined sources of value,* [italics added] including 'natural rights'[10] . . . [S]ocietal or communitarian influences enter through modifications in the values that are potentially expressed by the individual and not externally. . . . [Thus], a contractarian 'explanation' of collective

order [is that] individuals will be led, by their own evaluation of alternative prospects, to establish *by unanimous agreement* [italics added] a collectivity, a polity, charged with the performance of specific functions, including, first, the provision of the services of the protective or minimal state and, second, the possible provision of genuinely collective consumption services. (Brennan and Buchanan 1985, pp. 21-2)

In short, the rational choice conceptual framework cannot accommodate any "externally defined sources of value" because this challenges the sovereignty of subjective interests. Thus whenever actors believe subjectively that exercises of authority are in their subjective interests, a rational choice theorist cannot question that they are integrated rather than controlled. For Coleman:

An implication of this reasoning is that the morally correct or ethical outcome is endogenously determined, by the members of the system itself. For example, if the members of the Jonestown community in Guyana knew what they were doing and went through the internal weighing process described above when they followed Jim Jones's directive to drink the poisoned Kool-Aid, the outcome was a morally correct one. (1990, p. 387)

But by what standard can Coleman or any other rational choice theorist know, in comparative perspective, when the members of any collectivity actually recognize and understand what is being expected of them by authorities?

Coleman's explicit capitulation to liberal complacency is manifestly evident in his discussion of *social exchange* (1990, pp. 37-43, 384-87). Here he addresses the concepts of *social equilibrium* and *social optimum,* ignoring the issue of whether the exchanges at issue take place within larger social settings that are themselves either malevolent or benign, authoritarian or nonauthoritarian.[11]

Coleman's liberal complacency is evident as he stakes out two positions. One position is his explicit dismissal of Hobbes's social contract theory in favor of his often-repeated Lockean consensus theory of rights. Aside from the quotation above, consider the following statement from Coleman:

Hobbes saw the problem [of bringing about order through a social contract] as more serious than it actually is. Here the consensual character of a right becomes extraordinarily useful, for the determination of who holds a right is not under individual control. . . . A right is inherently a social entity and . . . exists only when there is a high degree of consensus about where the right lies. . . . The result of this consensual character of a right is that each individual is not in an exposed position in giving up the right to control his own action. The individual actor already is not in full control of that right, for he holds it only at the pleasure of all those affected. . . . Thus the giving up of rights over individual control of actions is not a set of individual actions, each subject to a free-rider problem, but is an implicit collective decision about rights to act—a collective decision to transfer a set of rights from individuals to the collectivity. (Coleman 1990, p. 54)

Like Buchanan's positing of "unanimity" over "meta-rules" (Brennan and Buchanan 1985, pp. 17-32, 98-107), Coleman's positing of consensus over rights is slipped surreptitiously into the rational choice conceptual framework. Neither Coleman nor Buchanan makes room for this conceptually. Coleman holds, for instance, that his perspective "is that of actors who transfer rights or resources to others and thereby either give others authority over their actions or else vest rights of control in a particular position. I begin, conceptually, with a system in which no authority exists, but only individuals holding rights" (1990, p. 170). This is all well and good, but then where does the consensus come from regarding rights that Coleman so readily presupposes? Put differently, when can it be said that heterogeneous actors' and competing groups' communications regarding rights ever result in a consensus of opinion that is (a) unambiguous in their own eyes (or subjectively), and (b) clearly noncoerced, nonmanipulated, and nondistorted in the eyes of outside observers? The point again is that this is an empirical issue. It is not an issue that may simply be left to speculation.

The second position staked out by Coleman that reveals his liberal complacency is that when actors exercise their consensual rights, the result is not only efficiency or the maximization of their private wealth. It is also a largely self-policed social order, as opposed to a more coercive or malevolent social order (Coleman 1990, pp. 67-8). He offers neither empirical nor theoretical rationales for this grand assumption.

Implications of Rational Choice Theorists' Complacency

More than merely benign, actors' and groups' normatively unmediated competition within economic and political marketplaces is for rational choice theorists positively virtuous: It fosters individual diversity and innovativeness, economic and political adaptability, and ethnic and cultural tolerance (see McClosky and Brill 1983 for an unsuccessful effort to document this in survey research). These theorists acknowledge, of course, that particular sets of actors and groups may well benefit disproportionately from robust interest competition. They also acknowledge that neither systemic nor informal mechanisms of social control are ever displaced entirely by the impersonal sanctions of gains and losses of wealth within political and economic marketplaces.[12]

What is surprising, regardless, is that their unwarranted optimism or complacency stands largely unchallenged conceptually in the social sciences today despite Weber's pathos and that of many other classic theorists. For Weber, systemic pressures of rationalization yield breakdowns of meaning and then bureaucratic impositions of meaning to the point of authoritarian excess. They do not yield a consensus or shared meaning and a benign direction of social change. Within the context of the contemporary conceptual default, however, rational choice theorists are able to dismiss out of hand the significance of any and all imbalances of resources, power, and influence within political and economic marketplaces. The extent and intensity of social controls that corporate management exercises over research or legal divisions, for instance, are not an issue that the concepts expose to research (the massive literature on corporate crime notwithstanding). Their concepts direct them instead to exploring how incentives are structured within corporations in order to ensure that the agent (management) exercises these controls in the principals' (shareholders') interest. All hidden hand outcomes of exercises of collective power are for them of little significance as long as governments remain "democratic" and markets remain competitive or "free."

By substituting an atheoretical, empirically unsupported complacency for the classic social theorists' pathos regarding modernity, rational choice theorists dramatically alter the agenda of social theory and social research alike. Their conceptual framework eliminates the possibility of balanced critique. It encourages instead one-sided or unreflective apologetics for existing social arrangements. Unlike the classics' earlier concepts (rationalization, anomie, alienation), this conceptual framework fails to invite the development of new value-neutral concepts capable of identifying in comparative perspective when the direction of change is shifting within Western or non-Western civil societies.[13] For instance, by failing to explore whether and when the social infrastructure supporting a benign direction of social change is jeopardized by certain hidden hand outcomes of competitive markets and democratic governments themselves, rational choice theorists either posit optimistically that this can never be the case or else refuse complacently to address the issue.

> This thesis, that there is a progressive replacement of the natural environment by a purposively constructed one, is similar to Max Weber's thesis of a progressive rationalization of society.... [It] constitutes a qualitative change, as the very form of social organization changes. [But] this general approach to historical development is not one that allows prediction of the future state of the constructed environment. (Coleman 1990, p. 552)

The issue, of course, is not whether any rational choice theorist can predict the exact outcome of historical developments. The issue is rather whether any rational choice theorist can say the first word about shifts in the direction of social change.

Because this is not possible within the conceptual framework of rational choice theory, Coleman may define *responsible behavior* as "that which takes into account the interests and rights of others" (1990, p. 556). With this, he again substitutes liberal complacency for Weber's pathos: For Weber, when actors operate according to an "ethic of responsibility" within the context of systemic pressures of rationalization, the result is increased bureaucratization and susceptibility to authoritarianism. Weber was not predicting precise outcomes either. He was instead addressing shifts in the direction of social change and essentially calling on future generations of social scientists to specify what could account for the presence of more benign civil societies in the late 20th century despite systemic pressures of rationalization to the contrary. Rational choice theory's unargued complacency instead brackets a priori some of the most intriguing research issues unique to sociology or political science, as opposed to economics or psychology.

This great polarity between Hobbesian anxiety and Lockean complacency—between (a) Weber's pathos regarding breakdowns of meaning and bureaucratic impositions of social control, and (b) rational choice theorists' optimism regarding actors' consensus over rights and automatic sharing of meaning—can be escaped only by developing concepts that directly address the issue that they join: the quality of actors' communications within particular sectors, institutions, and organizations of particular civil societies. Here Lon Fuller's critique of legal positivism is particularly important as a point of departure.

The Importance of the Quality of Communication Within Civil Society

In Fuller's view, the emphasis that legal positivists (including rational choice theorists) place on the effectiveness of law enforcement in accounting for a stable social order is not so much mistaken as partial: It is certainly correct that social scientists can recognize whether rules (or shared social duties) are being effectively enforced by whether instances of law breaking are decreasing over time. Indeed, the effectiveness of enforcement may be converted into quantitative indices of law breaking of one kind or another. In this way, it is rendered consistent with other strictly rational or instrumental calculations of efficiency or optimality.

But Fuller's point moves beyond this. Whether rules (or shared social duties) are successfully recognized and understood by heterogeneous actors and competing groups cannot be reduced—by social scientists or actors—to quantitative indices of law breaking and the effectiveness of enforcement. Such indices fail to reveal whether such actors and groups are recognizing and understanding what the rules (or their shared social duties) are. After all, actors may purposefully disobey rules that are clearly understandable (as is the case, for example, with civil disobedience). Conversely when rules or duties are not understandable—as is the case, for instance, with "laws" that prohibit "threats to the State"—actors' disobedience may be altogether inadvertent. For that matter, enforcement may be uneven, and again inadvertently so.

In Fuller's view, it is only possible for heterogeneous actors and competing groups, as well as specialized enforcers themselves, to recognize and understand what the laws (or shared social duties) are when the latter are kept consistent with a specific set of procedural qualities (Fuller 1969, pp. 46-84): They must apply generally, they must be promulgated, prospective, clear (at least to those trained in such matters), noncontradictory, possible to perform, constant over time rather than repeatedly changed, and congruent with officials' actual conduct. This holds true, he insists, irrespective of (a) what the laws' (or duties') positive content happens to be, (b) whether a legitimate law-making body drafted the laws (or duties) in an acceptable way, and (c) whether both their content and their legitimacy are consistent with the public's expectations.[14]

Fuller saw that power holders on one side and actors on the other each face an unavoidable situation once law-making or law-enforcing bodies encroach against the procedural normative restraints just noted. On their side, actors find that no longer does any reasoned basis exist for them to feel a moral responsibility to obey "laws" or to bear shared social duties. They may continue to obey power holders out of fear, indifference, or ignorance, of course. But officials' acts of encroachment nonetheless demonstrate—behaviorally, empirically—that power holders are implicitly (or worse, explicitly) oriented by the following presupposition: Actors are incapable of reasoning about, or taking responsibility for bearing, their shared social duties. What other presupposition might account for power holders' failures to ensure that the shared social duties they are sanctioning are at least kept recognizable and understandable?

On their side, power holders must realize that they have indeed crossed a most significant formative threshold. Having encroached against these procedural restraints, they can no longer be reasoned in feeling any moral (or fiduciary) responsibility for honoring any other restraints on how they exercise collective power. Their only concern, at this point, is the strictly strategic restraints posed by competing power holders and social influentials. These are the restraints that rational choice theorists study.

Two Dead Ends of Rational Choice Analysis: Voting and Civility

It must be emphasized that, taken together, Fuller's procedures of interpretability are indeed normative or nonrational. Actors' fidelity to these procedures cannot be expected to result in their most efficiently producing goods or most effectively administering services or personnel. It can only be expected to draw attention to, and thereby to keep open the possibility for heterogeneous actors and competing groups to restrain, arbitrary exercises of collective power within any sector, institution, or organization of a modern civil society. By contrast, the four rules that Coleman believes these actors and groups may employ in common to evaluate a corporate body's actions (1990, pp. 374-75) fail to address whether it is wielding its collective power arbitrarily. Coleman indirectly acknowledges this:

> The free-rider problem that exists for any indivisible event tends to lead each individual in a large collectivity not to exercise his right to partially control the actions of the collectivity. One of the consequences of the free-rider problem is that it is irrational for an individual [even] to vote in any but the smallest collective decisions if the act of voting imposes a cost on him. (Coleman 1990, p. 375)

Indeed, rational choice theorists have never been able to account for what they call the *paradox of voting* in national elections: Why do so many people vote? Why does anyone vote? This is the first dead end of rational choice analysis.

If one begins with Weberian pathos rather than rational choice complacency, however, an explanation comes into view: The popular franchise has been associated historically—whether rightly or wrongly—with the institutionalization of normative (that is, nonrational) restraints on arbitrary government. The popular exercise of the franchise even today may well be a reflection of the public's reluctance to allow such restraints to atrophy or even to experiment with their removal. Thus many members of the public vote even when they are not remunerated and indeed even when they incur all costs for doing so. Rational choice theorists might counter that the popular franchise was not really critical to restraining arbitrary government historically and that it is certainly not critical to restraining arbitrary exercises of collective power within civil society today—and they may be correct. But rational choice theorists are obliged nonetheless to specify which institutions or organizations are critical to such restraints, and then they are obliged to work the latter into their conceptual framework. Voting is indeed not rational behavior. But only because rational choice theorists are complacent liberals can they consider this behavior paradoxical.

When enforcers encroach against the integrity of the procedural norms noted above, the laws or shared social duties that they are enforcing—however rationally—cannot be said to contribute intrinsically to a benign direction of social change. This cannot be said even if most actors believe subjectively at any given moment in time that these duties and their enforcement are legitimate. Instead these beliefs are manipulated, controlled, or subtly coerced, and as such they contribute, however incrementally, to a malevolent social order.

A second dead end of rational choice analysis comes to the fore in Coleman's (1988) examples of *social capital*, including actors' shared feelings of security in allowing their children to travel alone in familiar (and, by his examples, always ethnically or religiously homogeneous) neighborhoods. These examples rest on decidedly nonrational, internalized normative restraints on individuals' rational decision making. After all, if harassing children brings pleasure and possible material reward to an assailant, with low likelihood of pain or cost, on what rational grounds is an actor discouraged from this practice? Coleman turns to the idea of social capital precisely because the institutionalization of rational choice principles is so unappealing that it brings him to reappraise decidedly anachronistic alternatives. The same principles simultaneously close him and other rational choice theorists off from recognizing that contemporary professions, and even many corporations today, continue to institutionalize Fuller's nonrational procedural norms in practice.

NOTES

1. Wealth maximization avoids some of the hedonistic implications of utilitarianism. "Since utility is more difficult to estimate than wealth, a system of wealth maximization may seem a proxy for a utilitarian system, but it is more; its spirit is different. Wealth maximization is an ethic of productivity and social cooperation—to have a claim on society's goods and services you must be able to offer something that other people value—while utilitarianism is a hedonistic, unsocial ethic" (Posner 1990, p. 391). Lechner (1990, p. 96) ignores this distinction, but then Olson, Buchanan, Hechter, and Coleman all ignore it too.

2. Hechter goes so far as to reduce the intensity of "solidarity" to the utilities invested in it: "The greater the average proportion of each member's private resources contribute to collective ends, the greater the solidarity of the group"

(1987, p. 18). This is why Hechter reduces obligations within groups to a "membership tax" (1987, p. 41). His approach is reductionist because it fails to capture many of the most prized purposeful solidarities—those most prized when threatened. Hechter senses this: "There is no satisfactory individualistic account of how large public-goods-seeking groups can attain sufficient selective incentives to assure their survival" (1987, p. 36).

3. This is why American law normally enforces contracts irrespective of whether they are reasonable or fair: "[A] fully informed party is normally the best judge of his own utility or interest and, therefore, of the value to him of a bargained-for performance" (Eisenberg 1989, p. 1463). The legal issue, of course, is whether a party is indeed fully informed.

4. "The economic perspective is thoroughly (and fruitfully) behaviorist. 'Economic man' is not, as vulgarly supposed, a person driven by purely pecuniary incentives, but he is a person whose behavior is completely determined by incentives; his rationality is no different from that of a pigeon or a rat. The economic task from the perspective of wealth maximization is to influence his incentives so as to maximize his output. How a person so conceived could be thought to have a moral entitlement to a particular distribution of the world's goods . . . is unclear" (Posner 1990, p. 382).

5. Hechter (1987, p. 7) sees that the classical social theorists left rational choice theorists with three problems, but none capture the one under discussion: Can the source of individual wants be specified without referring to socialization? Is not much action nonrational and ritualistic? Why is social order so common rather than exceptional (also Lechner 1990, p. 99)? Hechter's response to all three questions is to recapitulate his definition of *solidarity* (see Note 2) without indicating whether solidarity is controlling or integrative, manipulative and coercive, or intersubjectively recognizable and understandable. Lechner's critique (1990, p. 103) of Hechter's definition of *solidarity* ignores this distinction and thereby follows Parsons, Münch, and Alexander in resting on an undiscussed alternative definition. All four theorists use religious collectivities and other ascriptive intergenerational collectivities (Lechner's phrase) as counterexamples to rational choice premises. But such counterexamples fail to challenge the latter premises conceptually, unless these four theorists can demonstrate that such collectivities are increasing in number today rather than decreasing.

6. This is what Lechner is driving at, I think, when he distinguishes "weak-but-broad versions of rational choice theory" (1990, p. 95). They are weak in their "relaxed assumptions about the rationality of actors" and broad in their scope of application. He draws this distinction, however, without stressing the intrinsic interrelationship between rational action and quantitative ends.

7. "[Rational choice theory] leaves unexplained many, possibly most, of the phenomena it sets out to explain, without providing any suggestions for how this large residuum of ignorance may be shrunk" (Posner 1990, pp. 371-2). Coleman notes that the "success of a social theory based on rationality lies in successively diminishing that domain of social activity that cannot be accounted for by the theory" (1990, p. 18). Posner is saying, of course, that rational choice theory has little prospect of claiming success by this standard. And Coleman himself sees the limits of rational choice theory. He sees that the "idea of maximization of utility . . . mak[es] precise what is meant by 'purposive action' " (1990, p. 18) rather

than leaving the latter more vaguely teleological. "Any teleological principle which specifies that some quantity is to be maximized or minimized is more powerful than a less specific principle. This predictive power . . . is somewhat vitiated when measurement of the quantity . . . is less unequivocal" (Coleman 1990, p. 18). For Hechter: "The specificity of goals is likely to vary across individuals, however, and, worse, it is not directly measurable. Thus there is a subjective element involved in specifying the individual's dependence [within any group]" (Hechter 1987, p. 54)

8. The other three criticisms are elaborated at length in two chapters of a 21-chapter book manuscript titled *Professions and Corporate Governance: Studies in Societal Constitutionalism.*

9. Coleman is unique among rational choice theorists (and pluralists and liberals) in attempting to incorporate the concept of *objective interests* into his social theory (1990, pp. 511-5). This effort is discussed in the full version of this chapter (see Note 8).

10. Buchanan opposes elevating any purported set of "natural rights" to a resilient normative restraint on actors' immediate subjective interests. Brennan takes exception to Buchanan's going this far in acceding to the sovereignty of subjective interests. Thus their collaboration nicely recapitulates the tensions riddling liberalism's Lockean and Hobbesian strands.

11. Coleman's most sustained discussion of disequilibrium may be found where he discusses collective behavior, contrasting the latter to "individual maximization of utility [which] leads to a stable equilibrium in many social situations" (1990, p. 202). The problem is that he never establishes earlier in the book why individual maximization tends toward stable equilibrium. As a result, it is unclear why he believes that collective behavior tends toward disequilibrium at the system level. He occasionally raises the issue of "abuses" of the taxing power (e.g., 1990, p. 344) and other manifestations of "corporate power" (e.g., 1990, pp. 356-7). But he fails to address how heterogeneous actors and competing groups might recognize such abuses in common, let alone restrain them institutionally. Instead he ultimately hinges the issue on a subjective judgment: Whether the entire economy expands sufficiently so that all groups acknowledge subjectively that they are better off (e.g., Coleman 1990, pp. 346-7).

12. Examples include Buchanan (1989, pp. 32-5) on norms and customs; Hechter (1987, pp. 62-73) on direct reinforcement, differential association, and reciprocity; and Coleman (1988, 1990) on social capital.

13. How do rational choice theorists explain the remarkable stability of American democracy, for instance, other than to attribute this to institutions of robust interest competition itself?

14. In the full version of this chapter (see Note 8), Fuller's procedural threshold of interpretability is used to distinguish situations of possible social integration from those of demonstrable social control. Brennan and Buchanan (1985, pp. 100-4) reduce law's legitimacy to ranges of expectations regarding acceptable behavior that actors happen to acknowledge at any given point in time. This is why they end up accepting that actors may agree to "meta-rules" that permit "legitimate lawmaking bodies" to make unannounced or secret changes in the law—as long as the changes do not challenge actors' existing expectations (Brennan and Buchanan 1985, pp. 107-8). Luhmann offers the same argument ([1972] 1985; 1982, pp. 90-137; 1990, pp. 187-202).

REFERENCES

Alexander, Jeffrey C. 1982. *Positivism, Presuppositions, and Current Controversies. Theoretical Logic in Sociology*. Vol. 1. Berkeley: University of California Press.

Brennan, Geoffrey and James M. Buchanan. 1985. *The Reason of Rules: Constitutional Political Economy*. Cambridge, UK: Cambridge University Press.

Buchanan, James M. 1989. *Explorations Into Constitutional Economics*. College Station: Texas A & M Press.

Buchanan, James M. and Gordon Tullock. 1962. *The Calculus of Consent*. Ann Arbor: University of Michigan Press.

Coleman, James S. 1988. "Social Capital in the Creation of Human Capital." *American Journal of Sociology* 94:S95-120.

———. 1990. *Foundations of Social Theory*. Cambridge, MA: Harvard University Press.

Collins, Randall. 1988. *Theoretical Sociology*. Orlando, FL: Harcourt Brace Jovanovich.

Downs, Anthony. 1957. *An Economic Theory of Democracy*. New York: Harper & Row.

Eisenberg, Melvin. 1989. "The Structure of Corporation Law." *Columbia Law Review* 89:1461-525.

Fuller, Lon L. [1964/1969] 1975. *The Morality of Law*, Rev. ed. New Haven, CT: Yale University Press.

Hechter, Michael. 1987. *Principles of Group Solidarity*. Berkeley: University of California Press.

Homans, George C. 1950. *The Human Group*. New York: Harcourt, Brace.

Lechner, Frank. J. 1990. "The New Utilitarianism." *Current Perspectives in Social Theory* 10:93-111.

Luhmann, Niklas. [1972] 1985. *A Sociological Theory of Law*. London: Routledge & Kegan Paul.

———. 1982. *The Differentiation of Society*. New York: Columbia University Press.

———. 1990. *Political Theory in the Welfare State*, Rev. ed. Berlin and New York: de Gruyter.

McClosky, Herbert and Alida Brill. 1983. *Dimensions of Tolerance: What Americans Believe About Civil Liberties*. New York: Russell Sage.

Münch, Richard. 1981. "Talcott Parsons and the Theory of Action, I. The Structure of the Kantian Core." *American Journal of Sociology* 86:709-39.

Niskanen, William A., Jr. 1971. *Bureaucracy and Representative Government*. Chicago: Aldine, Atherton.

Olson, Mancur. 1965. *The Logic of Collective Action*. Cambridge, MA: Harvard University Press.

Parsons, Talcott. [1937] 1968. *The Structure of Social Action*. New York: Free Press.

Posner, Richard A. 1990. *The Problems of Jurisprudence*. Cambridge, MA: Harvard University Press.

Tsebelis, George. 1990. *Nested Games: Rational Choice in Comparative Politics*. Berkeley: University of California Press.

PART III

Metatheory: Rational Choice Pro and Con

Chapter 9

IS RATIONAL CHOICE THEORY
A RATIONAL CHOICE OF THEORY?

PETER ABELL

London School of Economics: The Interdisciplinary Institute of Management
and The Centre for Economic Performance

INTRODUCTION

A VALID THEORY amounts to a rational conjecture about the
nature of a more or less latent mechanism that purports to account
for a puzzling "empirical" event or relationship. Such empirical
phenomena are themselves, however, theoretically described, in
the sense that the world does not inhabit our senses in a neutral
manner. So if I may be excused a wholly pretentious paraphrase,
the world is a totality of theoretically described facts! Thus the
relationship between an individual's socioeconomic status of origin and destination is an empirical one but one constructed out of
a prior descriptive theorization of socioeconomic status. If this
relationship is deemed puzzling, it in turn invites a conjectural
theory. The latter is clearly dependent upon the former, and this
may explain why much "theoretical" writing in sociology seems
to be preoccupied with getting the former right.[1] But we can only
find repose with descriptive theory if it provides us with "facts"
that are transparent and consequently fail to further puzzle us. It is
possible, of course, that today's conjectural theory might become
tomorrow's descriptive theory, in the sense that improved mea-
surement/observation may begin to elide the basic distinction.

AUTHOR'S NOTE: I should like to thank Stephen Hill for his help in improving
upon an earlier version of this chapter.

For example, we may conjecture that the covariation of SES mentioned above may be accounted for deductively by certain assumptions about individual motives/actions and the structure of competition in the labor market. These assumptions may, however, subsequently be tested directly rather than indirectly. In a world of costless and perfect information (theoretical conjecture under certainty!), all conjectural theories eventually would befall the fate of becoming descriptive. But social scientists, no less than the subjects they choose to study, have to accommodate rationally to the costs of acquiring information, so such an eventuality is effectively guarded against.[2]

Conjecturing a theory is patently a risky/uncertain business, for if it were not, there would be no need to attempt it. It is appropriate to ask which of the frameworks available to us, given the current state of our information/knowledge, is most likely to prove useful in revealing the nature of latent social mechanisms. We must, of course, assume that the likelihood depends upon past success and failure in this respect. Furthermore the degree of confidence we might place in any framework will decrease with the extent to which past success is accounted for by plausible alternatives to the framework. Clearly a given framework cannot be totally secure until no plausible alternative exists. What is our rational choice of framework?

PUZZLING EMPIRICAL RELATIONSHIPS

No doubt many productive ways of thinking exist about the sorts of puzzling empirical relationships that sociologists should address. I shall, however, adapt a scheme popularized by Coleman (1990); Figure 9.1 gives the bare bones. Following Parsons (1937), the concept of *individual action* is made to lie at the very heart of things. Despite heroic attempts to argue to the contrary, I see no good reason to depart from the view whereby the social world is propelled ultimately by the actions (and forebearances) of individuals. It is only because we do and do not do things (intentionally or otherwise) that things happen in the social world.

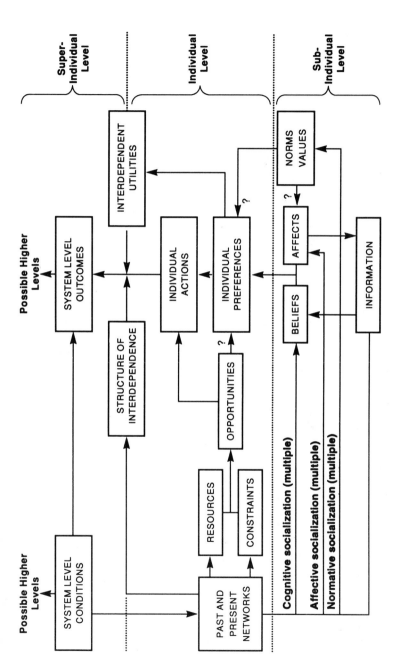

Figure 9.1. Puzzles

185

Accordingly a requirement of any descriptive theory (as I used this term above) is that it should warrant adequate descriptions of individual actions. This requirement should, however, be handled with some considerable care. The level of "adequacy" (the requisite descriptive detail) should be determined entirely by the need to locate the action within the ambit of the explanatory puzzles implied in Figure 9.1—particularly the individual-to-system puzzle that appears at the right-hand side. That is to say, the amount of detail sought in any descriptive theory of individual action should be no more or less complex than what is necessitated by our attempts to explain how individual actions are "structured" or combined into system level outcomes (the micro-macro inference). This point has to be made explicit because many descriptive theorists, particularly those working within or drawing upon the phenomenological tradition, have sought to provide something like exhaustive descriptive vocabularies of the "meaning of individual actions." Though sociological theories always must be compatible with (not inconsistent with) such descriptive theories (if accurate), they are in no way dependent upon them, no more than the bridge between thermodynamic and kinetic theories depends upon detailed descriptions at the molecular level. Indeed if social theorists had expended the same amount of time and effort in devising a vocabulary of social interactions as they have in trying to tie down all the nuances in the "meaning of action," then we would, theoretically speaking, be much better placed. The "Weberian Demon" has taken its toll, inviting us to grasp the full coordinates of individual action[3] (Lindenberg 1990).

The major empirical puzzle is how it is that interdependent individual actions produce system (or if you prefer, collective) level outcomes. Putting it another way, how it is that these outcomes can be explained by those self-same interdependent individual actions? The complexity of sociological theory in this particular domain is thus intimately associated with the nature of the interdependencies that can occur between the individual actions. Indeed if we were pressed to abstractly classify theoretical puzzles, then the most useful way of decomposing this domain would be in terms of (a) the types of interdependencies that can occur between individual actions, and (b) how they might be simplified in order to gain some theoretical traction (Coleman 1986). This is a dauntingly complex issue; the economists have, of course, made the most headway but only with rather simple sorts of actions and with heroic simplifying assumptions about the nature of the interdependencies.[4] Much of Coleman's work (1990) can be seen as an attempt to adapt and develop the economists' insights to wider sociological purpose. I have allowed in Figure 9.1 for interdependence to be built into the utilities or preferences of the actors (see later).

An additional issue exists. For certain purposes, one may take the interdependencies as exogenous, so the individual actions may be regarded as taking place within the framework (constraint/ facilitation) of the interdependencies. Certainly if this can be accomplished, it makes life easier. Of course, in many cases the pattern of interdependencies may be under the control of one or more of the actors involved; then they must in some way be rendered endogenous. The actors choose the structure of interaction (a system level outcome). Much descriptive theory has in effect invited us down this path but without giving us much guidance in the massively complex issues of constructing appropriate conjectural theories.[5]

If the concept of *individual action* lies at the heart of things, then individuals' goals/utilities/preferences[6] must inevitably feature. The second major empirical puzzle then is how these are themselves created/established. This is not the place to get involved in details, but in Figure 9.1 I have allowed for a subindividual (or multiple-self) level puzzle—namely, how possibly conflicting, or perhaps irreconcilable, elements (arguments) are coordinated into an individual level utility function or preference schedule. It seems to me useful to think in terms of individuals who are placed in various networks of relations with others, which provide the source of influence (socialization) in establishing certain beliefs, affects, and values (thus preferences for actions or arguments in utility functions). Just as a theoretical problem exists about how individual actions are structured (combined) into a collective outcome, a parallel problem exists about how the multiple, fragmented, individual sources of belief, affect, and value are (or are not) structured into coherent individual level utilities and preferences. It often has been remarked that it is the ambition of sociological, as opposed, for instance, to economic, theory to render utilities endogenous. If my opening remarks carry any conviction, this must be because we find puzzling the relationship between individuals' positions in various networks and the preferences for action they consequently acquire. As far as I am aware, we have little in the way of genuine conjectural theory of socialization. We should bear in mind here that the major sociological insight is to construe preferences (thus beliefs, affects, and values) as partially socialized (passively acquired or at least acquired as the unintended consequences of what we do) and partly self-made (rationally?).

One of the near standard assumptions in economic theory is to the effect that individual level constraints (e.g., prices), resources (e.g., income), and preferences are exogenous and determined independently of each other. In particular, opportunities (determined by constraints and resources) in no way determine preferences. Such an assumption certainly eases the burdens of the theoretician but is probably unacceptable to sociologists; opportunities may partially determine individual preferences.

Each of the arrows in Figure 9.1 may be seen as more or less puzzling and thus inviting some sort of conjectural theory. It most probably oversimplifies matters, but it provides a convenient starting point, and the arrows indicate explanatory issues that have been raised both by rational action theorists and by their critics. Those carrying a question mark are the most controversial.

ASSUMPTIONS OF RATIONAL
ACTION THEORY

If one is prepared provisionally to accept the sketch of theoretical puzzles that I have outlined, then which theoretical framework would furnish a rational choice in the construction of conjectural theory? I shall argue that despite all its limitations, rational action or choice theory (RAT) is what we are after. At least, it is where we should start. I am well aware that this is regarded in many circles as heterodox in the sense that sociological theory often is interpreted as an attempt to transcend rational choice. Two remarks: First, I think it would be unfortunate to set up stark oppositions. In adopting a RAT perspective, we must guard against throwing out all that has been achieved by way of criticism of RAT. The last thing sociological theory needs is an intellectual balkanization. The challenges are complex and technically demanding well beyond our present capabilities, and a certain mutual goodwill and tolerance is needed. Second, it is important to recognize that in choosing a theoretical way of looking at things, one is not going to entirely secure oneself against conceptual and epistemological criticism. Theoretical conjecture is usually a matter of choosing the least worst among a set of competing possibilities. To search for a theoretical vocabulary that is invulnerable to conceptual criticism, though often the apparent objective of some descriptive theorists (e.g., Giddens 1979), is not a rational way of going about things.

In order to make my case that RAT may be deemed the least worst starting point for the conjectural theorist, I shall examine its major assumptions. They are as follows:

Individualism—It is only individuals that ultimately take actions.

Optimality—Individual actions are optimally chosen.

Self-Regard—Provisionally, individuals' utility functions and actions are entirely concerned with their own welfare.

Paradigmatic Privilege—RAT itself is the necessary starting point with which to compare other types of theory.

Individualism

I do not want to rehearse here the lengthy debates about methodological individualism, reductionism, and associated issues because they have not, on balance, served social science very well [but for a contrary view see O'Neill (1973), Hindess (1988)]. It is perhaps significant, though, that even Etzioni (1988), who is the latest in a long line to argue comprehensively against RAT and reductionism, says, ". . . collectives, *per se* do not deliberate or decide" (p. 186), that is, in the terms used here, choose to act. In taking Figure 9.1 as an organizing framework, I have in all essentials embraced the first major assumption of RAT. As far as I can see, the assumption should cause no problems for the construction of conjectural theories as long as a number of issues are made explicit.

First, as Figure 9.1 implies, system level relationships (system conditions determining system outcomes) are a perfectly acceptable currency as long as they are ultimately construed as "shorthand" for the conjunction of relationships that run through the lower parts of the diagram. Indeed a conjectural theory about the (puzzling) connection between two system level variables must ultimately imply a mechanism involving individual actions. The theoretical question is precisely this: How has the system level relationship been generated by the (interdependent) actions of individuals? Needless to say, we may not be in possession of such a theory or currently have the prospect of arriving at one though we must accept that such a theory is in principle possible—individuals have through their individual (though interdependent) actions "made" the relationship. I think the assumption of individualism in RAT implies no more than this about the explanation of system or collective level empirical generalizations. And as such, it is entirely innocuous.

Second, no contradiction exists between the view being promoted here and the one that sees individuals' actions as "shaped" by their membership in a group (more generally a collectivity) (Hechter 1987). If, as some "structuralists" opine, an individual is often so circumscribed by internalized standards and external constraints upon his or her action that he or she has barely any choice at all, then this may call into question optimality and self-regard, but it does not undermine the assumption of individualism in the sense that it is still the motor power behind individual actions (albeit "programmed ones") that drives things along.

Third, and related to the previous point, the view often is promoted (e.g., most recently by Etzioni) whereby the collectivity is said to have "primacy" over the individual. If *primacy* is used to refer to the fact that individuals are socialized (affective, cognitive, and valuative) by priorly existing groups (networks), then this is perfectly consistent with the picture provided in Figure 9.1.[7]

Fourth, the involvement of sub- or intraindividual mechanisms might in some ways appear at odds with sociologists' assumption of individualism. This conclusion would be premature. The assumption requires merely that the individual may be deemed to have the capacity to act (can apply motor energy or form intentions) upon the basis of preferences. That is, some intraindividual mechanism exists for coordinating the possibly disparate components of motivation. These issues will be more fully discussed below. It is significant that the most analytically penetrating models of intraindividual coordination, self-control, and monitored selves have all been discussed with a RAT framework (e.g., Thaler and Shefrin 1981, Coleman 1990).

Some, largely in reaction to the economists' often-promoted assumption of preference stability, have sought to question the intertemporal permanence of the individual. I find no warrant for this if one is prepared to contemplate changing utilities (affects and beliefs—see below). Metaphysical debates about how we decide whether we are deemed to be the "same person" when our preferences change do not add significantly to the sociologists' armory, however much they may tantalize the philosophers.

The RAT assumption of individualism seems thus to be an entirely rational choice from the perspective of the conjectural theorist. Conjectural theories describe latent mechanisms whereby things happen and connections get made in the social world. Things happen in the social world because individuals do and do not do things, and they are the only things that do and do not do things. All statements that attribute "doing" to other things can, in principle if not in practice, be translated without loss into statements about individuals doing things.

Optimality

Although it is possible to rapidly become technical about the nature of optimality, it is not my purpose to do so here: This would not help.[8] Let us say, given a set of opportunities, an individual chooses optimally if no other action exists whose consequences he or she prefers to the chosen action. Clearly an actor's preference-driven action will in turn depend upon that person's (a) beliefs or reasoning about the consequences of the available actions, and (b) affect (desire for/against) for the consequences (and perhaps for the action itself).[9]

It may thus by derivation be possible to speak of optimal beliefs and affects (Elster 1989a). Davidson (1980, 1984), and his insistence that in the final analysis it is only by assuming optimality (rationality, in his terms) that we can begin to make sense of what others do (and do not do), is useful. That is, construct an account of actors' latent beliefs and desires (affects) upon the basis of their manifest behavior. If people were to act insistently in a way that is inconsistent with their preferences, then not only would the nature of social science be called into question but the very fabric of society would begin to crumble. Indeed, for Davidson, it is in essence the assumption of optimality that gives something rather like RAT its paradigmatic privilege (assumption 4). I will discuss this below.

The major alternative assumptions to the one under examination seem to be[10] as follows:

1. That individuals frequently do not act optimally in terms of their preferences.
2. That although individuals may act optimally in terms of their preferences, senses exist in which their preferences are themselves not optimally formed (nonoptimal beliefs and affects).
3. That individuals do not act upon choices but are driven by forces entirely beyond their control (structuralism).

In order to judge the warrant for the strong claims that the optimality assumption makes, it is useful to look at each of these alternatives in turn.

To maintain that, in the general course of things, actions are knowingly chosen so as not to maximize satisfaction is difficult. Certainly some cases are well documented, by Elster (1989) among others, in which "weakness of will" may be said to prevent people from acting in the way they would "really prefer"—that is, according to their better judgment. Furthermore at times we act impulsively, which in retrospect we find distasteful and for which we have no reasons to suppose our "real" preferences have changed in a short passage of time. We may be possessed also by our desires (in the grip of our emotions clouding our reason). We do find ourselves doing and not doing or being able to do what we want to do. Our preferences also may be imprecise or unclear, our actions entirely experimental or based upon wishful thinking, and more than one optimal choice may be available.[11] All of this and perhaps more must be acknowledged, and some actions may then in certain respects tax the optimality assumption of RAT, although in practice most of the problems upon analysis reduce to examples of point (2) above. Be this as it may, to elevate these issues to a place of prominence in our theoretical endeavors seems to me entirely counterproductive, not to say irrational. It is like fine-tuning before we have found the major wavelength. Is there any warrant for the theoretical strategy that would in effect exhort us to commence our inquiries with an assumption whereby most actions do not flow optimally from individuals' current preferences? I think not. Note that nothing that has been said so far holds one to the view that the "preferences" themselves would represent the individual's best, or any other, judgment were circumstances, including self-knowledge, to change or evolve; all of this comes later.

It is no doubt correct that when adopting the optimality assumption we assume also that people's "preferences" are in some sense accessible to them to act upon and that they actually cause their actions. One might regard these as rather innocuous assumptions, but for some the former is a bone of contention (e.g., Denzin 1990). It should be noted that we are not dealing here with knowledge of the process (ratiocination or causal) that eventuates in the preference pattern but with our derived preferences themselves. Denzin's point is (following Derrida) that language is our only but imperfect route to self-knowledge and it cannot guarantee self-access even to our most superficial dispositions. We cannot be deemed to act rationally upon what we do not know (or know whether we do know) about ourselves. I have to confess a certain irritation with this view, but I suppose the RAT response would be to model individuals' actions as a decision under risk of uncertainty with respect to their own preferences. At least I know of no other reasonable approach, so pending deeper insight into these matters, RAT still seems to be our rational choice of framework.

We must, if we rely to any extent in our analyses upon the testimony of subjects about their preferences, guard against being taken in by their post hoc rationalizations. This is obvious, and skills are called for in avoiding this pitfall, but to elevate the problem to the point where all personal accounts are claimed to be no more than rationalizations must be regarded as little more than perverse (Gilbert and Abell 1983). But neither do we have to go the full way with Becker when he says: "Decision units are [not] necessarily conscious of their efforts to maximize or can verbalize or otherwise describe . . . the reasons . . . [for] their behaviour" (Becker 1976, p. 44). This may be true sometimes, particularly when following an optimal rule, but surely the strength of sociology is in part based upon an understanding of what goes on between people's ears.

I turn now to the second alternative assumption—the nonopti-mal formation of preferences. Some take the view (particularly many economists) that preferences are not only stable (compared to constraints) but also are formed in ways that entirely resist the attentions of RAT. Their genesis is either uninteresting (changed constraints accounting for changed action) or beyond rationality. Sociologists almost unanimously reject the first view but find some sympathy for the latter. It is not infrequently claimed also that the idea of optimality is so weak, when taken by itself, as to constitute an affront to serious understanding—"people do what they most want to do," albeit in a constrained way. Indeed as is frequently observed, if we are to be permitted any sort of utility arguments, then actions may (certainly *ex-post facto*) always be made to look as if they are optimal. Of course, if we have indepen-dent evidence about the nature of utility function arguments, then this possibility is guarded against, as we are not then entirely dependent, when drawing conclusions, upon revealed prefer-ences. But in the context of the sorts of empirical puzzles I outlined above, it is more often than not the case that assumptions have to be made about utility functions/preferences because conjectural theories deal with complex latent mechanisms. How do we guard against the accusation that under such circumstances the assump-tion of optimality can be entirely protected against potential ref-utation? Clearly one route is by setting limits upon the nature of peoples' motives/utilities, and so on (I will consider this option below), but the problem can be addressed also by asking what meaning we might attach to the concept of subjective rationality and optimality and nonrational (nonoptimal) actions.

Boudon (1989), writing from a general RAT perspective, says: "We need a general model of the motivated actor in which the actor has good reasons (not necessarily valid reasons) for doing what he does and thinking what he thinks" (p. 24). Indeed, he equates "irrational" actions with those that are driven by forces within us that are subintentional; that is, with what I have termed *structuralism* (point 3 above). Thus technically for Boudon, *all* actions are "rational," albeit in a subjective way, and only behav-iors are deemed irrational.[12] I think this equation, however, does not provide the most helpful way of looking at things. It makes the concept of *subjective rationality* just too permissive (thus overprotecting the optimality assumption in RAT) and effectively nullifies the distinction between irrational and nonrational action.

It is probably more useful to work with a four-fold distinction along the following lines: (a) "objectively" optimal actions, (b) subjectively optimal actions, (c) suboptimal actions ("irrational"), and (d) nonoptimal behaviors (not rational).

Although it is perhaps not possible to offer watertight arguments for clear demarcations between these categories, this is by the way. What does matter is that they lead us in an intellectually productive direction.

The way in which I wish to make use of these distinctions cuts across the conventional demarcation between decisions (actions) under certainty, risk, and uncertainty. If merely for analytical convenience we think for a moment in terms of the classical "action × outcome (ends)" matrix of decision theorists, then preferences that range over the actions are a function of the beliefs about outcomes and the affect attached to the outcomes.[13] We may speak then of the following derivative optimality conditions (see Figure 9.1):

1. Actions are optimal with respect to preferences (the "best" action is chosen).
2. Preferences are optimally formed with respect to beliefs and affects.
3. Beliefs are optimally formed with respect to the information available.
4. Available information (collected/processed) is optimal with respect to affects.
5. Affects are optimal with respect to individual autonomy.[14]

I shall refer to conditions 2, 3, and 4 jointly as *cognitive autonomy* and to condition 5 as *affective autonomy*. Thus cognitive and affective autonomy guarantee optimal preferences (Abell 1977).

We may propose then that an action is objectively optimal when conditions 1 to 5 hold true. Such actions may take place under certainty, risk, or uncertainty, according to standard assumptions about the nature of beliefs. These assumptions are collectively very strong, and many social theorists maintain that it is only rarely if ever that actions will conform to this ideal pattern. This, it is suggested, is for two distinct reasons: (a) Individuals do not (or cannot), in practice, autonomously conform; the requirements

are just too stringent, and (b) individuals are systematically pre-
vented by others (not necessarily intentionally) from conforming.
Social interaction itself characteristically undermines optimality.
Any theory based upon RAT will thus, it is proposed, ultimately
prove predictively inadequate.

Because the optimality conditions run, as it were, backward
from 5 to 1, it is perhaps best to consider them in this order (see
also Figure 9.1). I shall not, however, inspect point 5 in any great
detail. The issue at stake is whether we may assume that affective
dispositions in some sense flow from a balanced or autonomous
personality. No doubt forms of behavior/actions exist that flow
from affective dispositions that are "irrational" or pathological.
When this occurs, it usually implies that individuals resist all
occasions to consider the opportunity costs of maintaining the
disposition (e.g., constantly striving for what is beyond their
grasp or manifestly damages them). I think a profound sense
exists, though, in which we can speak of people managing to bring
their affects (emotions) under a degree of autonomous control by
the way in which they examine the consequences of what they do,
but it may be that ultimately our likes and dislikes are beyond our
rational control (I cannot bring myself to not like rice pudding!)
and that their explanation consequently will escape the precepts
of RAT. It may nevertheless still be possible to interpret affective
dispositions as the outcome (albeit most probably unintentional
on all sides) of the interaction of the individual in question within
the context of his or her various socializing networks (Figure 9.1).
For instance, most double-bind theories are not resistant to an
assumption whereby the causally binding actions (e.g., of parents)
are rational—at least in Boudon's sense of the term. Heise's (1979)
affect control theory seems to offer a promising way forward upon
these matters.

It is points 2, 3, and 4 that have attracted most attention. I do
not want to rehearse here the well-known arguments and coun-
terarguments, but what is proposed is that preferences cannot be
optimally formed (cognitive autonomy guaranteed) for a variety
of reasons, prominent among which are the following:

- *satisficing:* Beliefs are not optimal with respect to information (Simon
  1983).

- *search:* No adequate theory of optimal search exists; therefore, once again beliefs are not optimal with respect to information, nor information with respect to affects (Winter 1971).

- *decision biases:* Preferences are not optimal with respect to beliefs and affects (Kahneman and Tversky 1979).

- *exclusions:* Not all possible actions are considered (Etzioni 1988).

- *limited deliberation:* Not all consequences of all actions are thought through (Hindess 1988).

- *received styles of reasoning:* These prevent optimal belief formation (Hacking 1982).

- *ritual/routine/habit/copying:* These systematically lead to exclusions and do not evolve optimally in an evolutionary sense.

All of these imply that actions are characteristically made upon a self-imposed information basis that is more limited than would be requisite for us to be able to speak unhesitatingly of objective optimality (upon the basis of full information). Furthermore the limits cannot themselves be explained away in RAT terms—or at least this is what is maintained by critics. In this restricted sense, RAT fails, or at least it is called into question.[15]

Nevertheless in each case a conceptual understanding of the apparent limitations of RAT is established in terms of the departure from full optimality and, notwithstanding my above remark, in all cases RAT-inspired models are available. This is one significant sense in which RAT can make a claim for paradigmatic privilege: It still serves, even in default, as a benchmark. Whether these models will prove entirely adequate is partly an empirical matter (they certainly push back the boundary in favor of RAT— e.g., rational search, processing copying models, etc.) but also no doubt partly conceptual. If ultimately no possibility of a rational theory of information gathering and processing exists, then a behavioral residual resistant to the precepts of RAT must exist (Nelson and Winter 1982). We may, though, speak of *subjective* optimality when we have an understanding of how either cognitive and/or affective autonomy fails to furnish full information. Individuals' preference-driven actions, given their beliefs/affects, are optimal though we have reason to suppose the latter are not themselves optimally fashioned. This is equivalent to saying (in respect to beliefs at least) that the action is rational, given the level of information.

I believe that one of the most useful theoretical devices available to us is to model the information environments of individuals (cf. Boudon 1989; also Friedman and Hechter 1988) and thus to comprehend their subjective rationality. If the conclusions of such an analysis suggest a unique optimal preference/action, then we are able (nontautologically) to depict what it is to act suboptimally ("irrationally"). Thus in contrast to Boudon, when subjective optimality fails, we are not precipitated into the realm of uncontrollable forces (and behavior as opposed to action). Rather we say an action is not optimal with respect to an independently described information environment.

Of particular sociological interest are those social interactions in which the information environment of individuals is (intentionally or otherwise) restricted by others rather than by their own failings. So a focal individual's beliefs about the consequences of actions and about feasible actions are not objectively optimal (see Abell 1977, where the idea of cognitive autonomy is placed in the theory of power, influence, and manipulation). Again, individuals, given their controlled information environment, may be seen (nontautologically) as acting optimally but in a subjective manner. Examples of this sort abound in social theory. The Marxist theory of hegemonic culture, for example, may be made to match this way of looking at things (Abercrombie et al. 1990). In all cases a question arises about the optimality of the actors who are manipulating/controlling the information environment, but no a priori reason exists to suppose their actions will evade the optimality assumptions of RAT. Indeed, much modern theory of the strategic manipulation of information in games fits in here perfectly well (Kreps 1990).

In conclusion, it might not be possible to adumbrate a perfectly watertight and predictive theory of optimality, but this is not what is ultimately at issue because we have to balance (rationally) the virtues of an imperfect theory against other theoretical approaches available to us. In this respect, the theory of optimal action must at the very least command our close attention.

Self-Regard

The standard version of RAT usually starts with the assumption that individuals act (optimally) in order to satisfy their self-regarding preferences (utilities).[16] That is, optimal actions are taken in a way that is indifferent to the welfare/utility/consumption of others, either considered individually or collectively. Although nothing intrinsic to the theory mandates this assumption, it is regarded frequently as a natural analytical starting point, only to be cautiously discarded if and when the facts speak otherwise.[17]

Furthermore, if other-regarding preferences are eventually invoked, it is not infrequently maintained that they must in some way be explained or accounted for, whereas self-regarding sentiments do not invite explanation, being in some way natural or self-explanatory. Much ingenuity also has been exerted in attempting to show how other-regarding sentiments can be explained by a deeper understanding of the interaction of self-regarding actors (e.g., the folk theorems in iterated game theory and the genesis of social norms as a product of externalities). In this sense, self-regard is given significant primacy in the scheme of things. What is more, where other-regarding sentiments do hold partial sway, the question sometimes is raised (Etzioni 1988) of whether the "utilities" (affects) of self- and other-regard are commensurate one with the other. Thus a number of issues can prove problematic from a sociological standpoint, notably the following:

> *The primacy question:* Should self-regard be given theoretical primacy? If so, why?
>
> *The genetic question:* Should other-regard be seen as either (a) explained by self-regard, or (b) if not, in need of special explanation (whereas by contrast, self-regard is self-explanatory)?
>
> *The commensurability question:* Can preferences for action be standardly constructed, in the presence of other-regarding sentiments, by balancing the utility/affect of each against the other?

The Primacy Question. Hard-line RAT theorists would give self-regard absolute primacy, reduce all other-regarding sentiments (altruism, malice, personal and moral norms) to self-explanatory self-regard, and detect no problem of commensurability (e.g., Becker 1976). It is this hard-line model against which many sociologists seem to inveigh.

Let us start with the primacy issue. This seems merely to imply that if and only if no evidence exists to the contrary, then assume self-regarding utilities. If, however, independent evidence exists for other-regarding internalized norms or whatever, it would be a mistake to ignore it. Indeed, to do so would often make the job of providing an explanation (e.g., of a collective outcome [Figure 9.1]) far more difficult than it need be.[18] We may go on to ask for an explanation of the source of the norms, but that is a genetic question (see below). I believe it is crucial to keep the two questions clear in one's mind; they often have been confounded in unfortunate ways in critical writing.

But why, given a *tabula rasa*, make self-regard rather than other-regard a first assumption? Is this a rational strategy for the conjectural theoretician? For a number of reasons, it might be.

First, although it is not often acknowledged, self-regard provides a neutral (least biased) assumption between positive (altruistic) and negative (malign) other-regard. Many sociologists find self-regard assumptions unacceptable in favor of assumptions about positive moral sentiments (e.g., most recently Etzioni 1988). As I have urged, in the face of evidence for the latter (which is often massive), no dispute at this juncture should arise between rational action theorists and others. The debate should shift elsewhere, to the genetic issues. But in the absence of independent evidence, self-regard might quite properly be regarded as our least innocuous assumption.

This leads to the second point. Just as we can make our theoretical work overly difficult (or at least mislocate it) by failing to take account of internalized norms, we can make it too easy by assuming preferences/utilities for what it is we wish to explain. Think for a moment in terms of the most profound sociological problem—the existence of social order. One way of emptying the question about social order of its theoretical interest is to assume that individuals possess a preference for that self-same social order. The ambition of Adam Smith was to explain partially the existence of social order in the absence of a private disposition toward this objective.[19] If individuals have a taste for social institutions (e.g., keeping promises, not betraying trust), then these institutions are theoretically unpuzzling.

I suspect many of those who find RAT difficult to accept would respond at this point by saying that the existence of internalized other-regarding standards has proven to be so ubiquitous in past analysis that it is just silly not to assume them in future inquiries. I have much sympathy with this reaction. It does push us back onto the genetic issue, but still a point remains to be answered. It is extremely difficult to specify the other-regarding utility functions for a set of interacting individuals that make other-regarding outcomes unproblematic. The notorious *reductio absurdum* of this is where two altruists fail to get through the door. Indeed, unless each of two altruists has an equal weighting for him- or herself and for the other party (they have identical utility functions), a problem of optimal coordination (collective outcome [Figure 9.1]) still remains.

At a more realistic level, Hechter's (1987) analysis of group solidarity brings out the same point. People may to a degree possess (internalized) a norm of group solidarity, but the issue of sanctions and second-order collective goods remains. It is in this sense that self-regard is awarded primacy. Collective outcome puzzles are puzzles precisely because self-regard will dominate in the analysis—even if utilities contain some other-regarding arguments.

The Genetic Question. The occurrence of other-regarding sentiments tends, as we have seen, to push queries back in the direction of origins. First, in this regard, I can find no clinching justification, once we entertain the possibility of other-regarding sentiments, for seeking an explanation for other- and not for self-regard. Arguments from primary socialization and infant studies might suggest we are ultimately selfish as a species—I am not competent to judge upon this matter—but I would have thought it judicious to keep an open mind, allowing that as a species we might be equally open to socialization in either a selfish or unselfish direction. In this sense, egoism or self-regard might be interpreted as a norm as much as altruism usually is. Of course, if other-regarding utilities can be shown theoretically to derive always from self-regard, then the issue will be settled once and for all. I know of no attempts to reverse the argument, that is, to derive self-regard from other-regarding motives (altruistic or malign). In this respect, self-regard does seem to be accorded some considerable genetic priority. Attempts to derive norms and so on from assumptions of self-regard and externalities (Arrow 1951, Coleman 1990) have proved theoretically productive. In the space available, I have not been able to consider the role of norms in Figure 9.1.

The Commensurability Question. As we have seen, nothing from the RAT perspective may prevent one assuming, if the evidence warrants it, any well-formed preferences schedule—self-regarding or not. Etzioni (1988), however, has by implication raised the issue of whether optimal preferences can be meaningfully spoken of when utilities range over both one's self and one's moral commitments (to others or society, etc.). Can the superego and the id be combined into a well-behaved ego? More specifically, following Thaler and Shefrin (1981), what happens if "the psyche contains more than one energy system" or if we have sources of preference not associated with being better off (Sen 1977) or if we have multiple preference rankings (also Hirschman 1982). Etzioni makes the point that when we are torn between our moral duty and our baser selves, then it is not merely, as utility theory (and RAT) would have it, that commensurable vectors have a resultant. We do not act morally because it, on balance, brings us mere pleasure (utility). Morality and utility are made of different stuff (question marks in Figure 9.1).

It is quite difficult to know what to make of these claims. Individuals do manage to act upon decisions when they are torn down the middle, but the point presumably is precisely that they are torn; and the decision whether to do their duty or to have their cake is fundamentally different from the decision to have their cake or a biscuit. In other words, to assume a smooth, well-behaved utility calculation in the former case is to miss the point. But why should we want to model such situations as distinct? Probably because in repeated plays the action will show a variability that will not be evidenced when the calculation involves a smooth optimization.

I think that (contra Etzioni) the best way of handling situations in which individuals face competing internal demands upon themselves is not to assume incommensurable "motivated energies" that could immediately invite us to desert RAT (or at least to adopt a randomizing model) but to postulate multiple internal utility functions with interdependencies (externalities) (Abell 1989). We then can view the individual as facing, for example, an internal prisoner's dilemma, in which the Pareto optimism is problematic but realizable through the agency of personal norms in repeated intraindividual interactions.[20] Indeed, returning to Figure 9.1, the intraindividual puzzles can in all likelihood be most expeditiously modeled in this manner. The impact of (socializing) networks is not to produce an individual with a simple unitary utility function but one with a complex of interdependent functions (see Coleman 1990 for a not dissimilar view). It may even be possible to envisage such "utility systems" as subject to catastrophic jumps (Fararo 1978).

Paradigmatic Privilege

In my earlier remarks, I have had repeated occasion to note that RAT, even where it might fail us, might still be allowed to set a standard in the sense that it is only what is left over when it has worked its best, a situation that invites the introduction of alternative theoretical frameworks. This is a stronger claim than one that would call for free competition among alternative frameworks. It is, however, not a claim for exclusivity, nor is it, more importantly, necessarily a claim of causal priority. As remarked ad nauseam, the standard RAT interpretation of competitive market functioning (general equilibrium theory) rests upon a prior specification and enforcement of property rights. Also, it is widely recognized that certain markets that could open, often do not (e.g., in blood, babies). It may be that there is no RAT interpretation of prior property rights (see Nozick 1974, though) or of which markets fail to open, but note that in each case the puzzle arises precisely because of an independently conducted RAT analysis.

The puzzle is clothed, if not manicured, by RAT. It is in this sense that we may speak of paradigmatic privilege. RAT appears to provide a point of departure. For these sorts of reasons, it should be accorded pride of place in our thinking. It is barely necessary to mention its achievements in economics and now in political science (Alt and Shepsle 1990). Furthermore, there is little evidence of any serious competitor. If we were to restrict our interpretation of RAT to individual objective optimality with exogenous preferences, then this might not take us too far. But as I hope I have indicated, we can add much fruitfully to this stark picture while staying within the spirit of the theory. RAT is indeed a rational choice of theory—it is at the moment our least worst choice of framework. It rests, as we noted at the start, upon four primary assumptions, each of which can be tampered with. In the final analysis, though, it is the assumption of optimality—people, given their information (and so on) choose a best course of action—that has to be preserved if the framework is to keep its cutting edge. Putting it another way, if the predictions of our theory fail, then we should at least initially assume that we have modeled the preferences incorrectly rather than assume a suboptimal choice. This in the final analysis is all that RAT requires of us.

NOTES

1. I am not wanting to suggest that descriptive and conjectural theories necessarily emerge in this order. The relationship between the two is complex; witness explanations of SES in, for example, Roemer's recent work (1982), where conjectural theory suggests descriptive theory. One of the consequences of a preoccupation with sorting out the nature of descriptive theory is to undervalue a deductive approach to theory building.

2. That is, a world of imperfect information will have a role for deductive theories with axioms that are not directly tested.

3. Readers will recognize the allusion to Laplace.

4. Notably abstracting away from the process of adjustment to competitive pricing so that prices are parametric.

5. The choice may take place within the framework of a prior structure of interdependence.

6. I shall until later in the chapter use these terms interchangeably.

7. That collectivities (e.g., societies) might have ontological and causal priority over any given individual (or set of individuals) should not be in dispute; the system conditions in Figure 9.1 permit this. The point is that the recursive use of Figure 9.1 always invites us to see these conditions as an outcome previously generated by individuals. A chicken/egg issue is clearly at work here. The assumption of individualism only requires that in principle (not in practice) the implied cycle can be broken by considering what individuals do!

I have further allowed in Figure 9.1 that the system level impacts upon the individual via a network (of individuals). Individuals encounter groups as a network of individuals (albeit as carriers of group culture, etc.). Technically this would mean, for instance, that contextual effects always could be replaced by an auto-regressive model deriving from a network. (See Anselin 1988, Friedkin 1990.)

8. Basically it is usually assumed that all the outcomes of the feasible actions can be compared in terms of a $\geq$ relation that is complete, reflexive, and transitive. No metric is required. I shall use the term *optimal* rather then *rational* because the latter often is used to cover a number of assumptions in RAT.

9. Although the action itself is not usually regarded as carrying utility, nothing in RAT precludes this (expressive actions).

10. In addition, it may be assumed that actions have unintended consequences that are functional for the system. Evolutionary functionalism might see these as competitively optimal. I shall not consider these issues here as I believe Elster (1989) has had the last word.

11. The theory then will not be determinate, inviting additional ideas about how the equally feasible alternatives are selected (e.g., multiple equilibrium in games).

Furthermore, if completeness (Note 8) fails, then incomparable courses of action may exist.

12. I use the distinction between *action* and *behavior* that is standard in the analytical philosophy of action. It is not one adhered to by many social scientists.

13. In terms of expected utility theory, *beliefs* are probability numbers and *affects* are utilities.

14. This may be regarded as a rather controversial idea. So for many RAT theorists, affects are taken as entirely exogenous.

15. Decision biases may have to be incorporated into the basic expected utility model (Arrow 1982). This may be particularly true of the micro-macro aggregation in sociological models in which competitive forces cannot drive them out (Frey and Eichenberger 1989).

16. I shall use the term *self-regard* rather than *self-interest* and contrast it with *other-regard*.

17. This constitutes a restriction upon the nature of utility functions and thus in part protects RAT against the accusation of tautology.

18. For example, in the voting paradox or with the problem of free riding and collective goods.

19. Smith was perfectly aware that competitive markets depended upon prior contracts about property rights.

20. Just as social norms are collective outcomes in Figure 9.1, we can think in term of personal norms as an intraindividual collective outcome (a unified individual).

REFERENCES

Abell, Peter. 1977. "The Many Faces of Power and Liberty." *Sociology* 11:2-24.
———. 1989. "Games in Networks: A Sociological Theory of Voluntary Associations. *Rationality and Society* 1(2):259-82.
Abercrombie, Nicholas et al. 1990. *Dominant Ideologies*. London: Unwin Hyman.
Alt, J. E. and K. A. Shepsle. 1990. *Perspectives on Positive Political Economy*. Cambridge, UK: Cambridge University Press.
Anselin, L. 1988. *Spatial Econometrics: Methods and Models*. Dordrecht: Kluwer Academic.
Arrow, Kenneth J. 1951. *Social Choice and Individual Values* (Cowles Commission Monograph 12). New York: John Wiley.
———. 1982. "Risk Perception in Psychology and Economics." *Economic Journal* 20:1-9.
Becker, Gary. 1976. *The Economic Approach to Human Behavior*. Chicago: University of Chicago Press.
Boudon, Raymond. 1989. "Subjective Rationality and the Explanation of Social Behavior." *Rationality and Society* I(2):173-96.
Coleman, James S. 1986. "Social Theory, Social Research and a Theory of Action. *American Journal Society* 91:1309-35.
———. 1990. *Foundations of Social Theory*. Cambridge, MA: Belknap.
Davidson, Donald. 1980. *Essays on Actions and Events*. Oxford: Clarendon.
———. 1989. *Inquiries Into Truth and Interpretations*. Oxford: Clarendon.

Denzin, Norman K. 1990. "Reading Rational Choice Theory." *Rationality and Society* 2(2):172-89.

Elster, Jon. 1989. *Solomonic Judgments: Studies in the Limitations of Rationality*. Cambridge, UK: Cambridge University Press.

————. 1989a. *The Cement of Society: A Study of Social Order*. Cambridge, UK: Cambridge University Press.

Etzioni, Amitai. 1988. *The Moral Dimension: Toward a New Economics*. New York: Free Press.

Farraro, Thomas. 1978. "An Introduction to Catastrophes." *Behavioral Science* 23:291-317.

Frey, B. S. and D. Eichenberger. 1989. "Should Social Scientists Care About Choice Anomalies?" *Rationality and Society* 1(1):101-22.

Friedkin, Noah E. 1990. "Social Networks in Structural Equation Models." *Social Psychology Quarterly* 53(9):316-28.

Friedman, Debra and Michael Hechter. 1988. "The Contribution of Rational Choice Theory to Macrosociological Research." *Sociological Theory* 6:201-18.

Giddens, Anthony. 1979. *Central Problems in Social Theory: Action Structure and Contradiction in Social Analysis*. Berkeley: University of California Press.

Gilbert, G. N. and Peter Abell. 1983. *Accounts and Action*. Aldershot: Gower.

Hacking, Ian. 1982. "Language, Truth and Reason." Pp. 30-49 in *Rationality and Relativism*, edited by M. Hollis and S. Lukes. Oxford: Blackwell.

Hechter, Michael. 1987. *Principles of Group Solidarity*. Berkeley: University of California Press.

Heise, David. 1979. *Understanding Events: Affect and the Construction of Social Action*. Cambridge, UK: Cambridge University Press.

Hindess, Barry. 1988. *Choice, Rationality and Social Theory*. London: Unwin Hyman.

Hirschman, Albert. 1982. "Rival Interpretations of Market Society: Civilizing, Destructive or Feeble?" *Journal of Economic Literature* 20:1463-84.

Kahneman, Daniel and Amos Tversky. 1979. "Prospect Theory: An Analysis of Decision Under Risk." *Econometrica* 47(2):264-91.

Kreps, David M. 1990. *Game Theory and Economic Modelling*. Oxford: Oxford University Press.

Lindenberg, Siegwart. 1990. "The Method of Decreasing Abstraction." (Mimeo). University of Groningen, Groningen, The Netherlands.

Nelson, Richard R. and Sidney G. Winter. 1982. *An Evolutionary Theory of Economic Change*. Cambridge, MA: Belknap.

Nozick, Robert. 1974. *Anarchy, State and Utopia*. Oxford: Blackwell.

O'Neill, John, ed. 1973. *Modes of Individualism and Collectivism*. London: Heinemann.

Parsons, Talcott. 1937. *The Structure of Social Action*. New York: McGraw-Hill.

Roemer, John E. 1982. *A General Theory of Exploitation and Class*. Cambridge, MA: Harvard University Press.

Sen, Amartya. 1977. "Rational Fools." *Philosophy and Public Affairs* 6(4):317-44.

Simon, Herbert A. 1983. *Reasons in Human Affairs*. Stanford, CA: Stanford University Press.

Thaler, Richard and H. M. Shefrin. 1981. "An Economic Theory of Self-Control." *Journal of Political Economy* 89:392-406.

Winter, Sidney. 1971. "Satisficing, Selection and the Innovating Remnant." *Quarterly Journal of Economics* 85:237-61.

Chapter 10

THE LIMITS OF RATIONAL CHOICE EXPLANATION

JAMES BOHMAN

Department of Philosophy, St. Louis University

MANY PHILOSOPHERS, sociologists, and political scientists defend the claim that rational choice theory can provide the basis for a unified and comprehensive theory of social behavior. In this chapter, I dispute such claims on both theoretical and empirical grounds. Certainly rational choice theory does provide empirically adequate explanations of certain social phenomena. But such explanations are adequate only under precise conditions, and many of the unresolved problems of rational choice theory as a research program result from extending its explanations beyond their proper, restricted scope. I illustrate this difficulty by contrasting successful rational choice explanations, such as the analysis of conventions, with unsuccessful ones, such as other norms of social cooperation. I conclude by recommending that the scope of rational choice theory be conceived of narrowly rather than broadly and that the theory be supplemented by other explanatory theories at both the micro level of models of rationality and the macro level of institutional structures.

From Durkheim to Parsons, sociology has attempted to distinguish its forms of explanation from those of psychology, particularly explanations inspired by utilitarianism. Whereas Durkheim showed that such explanations make implicit social assumptions, Parsons argued that all such explanations face irresolvable problems of the "randomness of ends," making it impossible for them to explain

AUTHOR'S NOTE: I would like to thank the Alexander von Humboldt Stiftung for their support while I was writing this chapter.

enduring social order. In light of the success of economics, however, rational choice theory has revived the attempt to formulate a comprehensive and unified social science that explains actions in terms of individuals' beliefs and desires or, in the terms of the theory, information and preferences.[1] Instead of mere randomly chosen ends, rational choice theory tries to explain *choice* as maximization within the constraints imposed by the choice situation (decision theory) and those imposed by the interdependent choices of others (game theory). In this chapter, I want to argue that although such constraints do provide the means necessary to explain certain forms of social action and behavior, the explanations consistent with those constraints are adequate only under precise conditions. Problems in rational choice explanations result from extending these constraints in ways inconsistent with the assumptions of this basic theory and thus beyond its proper scope.

A research program begins with the explanation of a "core" set of phenomena and develops by gradually expanding its scope from this successful, elementary core.[2] A research program reaches its limits, however, when this extension fails: The program then either produces inadequate explanations or begins to appeal to extratheoretical, auxiliary assumptions that do the explaining. I want to argue that rational choice theorists already have done both, insofar as they have either broadened their explanations in ways that are often inconsistent with their own core assumptions or have imported extratheoretical assumptions about institutional structure or alternative models of rationality from outside the theory. Both strategies reveal the incompleteness of the theory and the inadequacy of these broader approaches, as the examples of social norms discussed here will show. Two lessons can be learned from these failures: First, rational choice theory is limited in scope and hence is neither a candidate for a comprehensive social theory nor even a "benchmark" for extending sociological explanation; second, "narrow," economic versions of rational choice theory are superior to "broader," sociological ones because they remain within the clear scope of the core of the research program.

THE BASIC STRUCTURE
OF RATIONAL CHOICE EXPLANATIONS

Rational choice theory is the formal elaboration of the theoretical structure of decision- and game-theoretic constraints on utility maximizing actions. This structure gives the theory its quantitative features and explanatory adequacy even while basing its explanations on such "subjectively" defined conditions as preferences. Its explanations are adequate if and only if the constraints formalized in its theories can be shown to describe empirical choice behavior or actions. Most rational choice theorists, however, believe that this standard of adequacy does not in any way restrict the potential scope of the theory because all such situations may be formalized in some model or other.

For all its emphasis on constraints, rational choice explanations work by assuming that agents are rational in a very specific sense: that they are utility maximizers (although this may mean different things to different theorists). One of the legacies of interpretive approaches to social science was to clarify problems about the generality of norms and standards, including those of rationality. Rational choice theory tries to sidestep these issues by appealing to economics, the most formal and quantitatively successful of the social sciences, and specifically to the concept of *expected utility* as a way to unify a theory of economic behavior. Economic agents are maximizers who choose that action or set of actions having the highest expected utility with respect to their own preferences (whatever they happen to be). After much debate about how to measure preferences (whether cardinal or ordinal), marginalist economics avoided irresolvable problems of the indeterminacy of interpersonal comparisons by simply measuring preferences according to the ranking manifested in the pattern of the agent's choices; the concept of *revealed preferences* also makes it possible to avoid questions of the intrinsic rationality of beliefs and desires themselves and to focus on behavior. Preferences are simply taken as given, and all considerations of their rationality, other than their consistency or "transitivity," are irrelevant to the explanation of action. Consistent choice in this sense is always maximizing.

This assumption about maximization is crucial to the theory because it permits a quantitatively and qualitatively precise specification of how rationality can become a formal property of individual actions. As Jon Elster puts it, the rationality of an intentional action can be specified in terms of "the right relation between the goals and beliefs of the agent" (Elster 1986, pp. 12-6). This "right relation" has at least one specific formal property: *consistency,* or as it is put in relation to actions, *maximization.* All forms of rationality express some criterion of consistency. The rationality of *beliefs* consists in their logical consistency with each other, while that of *desires* consists in their transitivity: If one prefers A to B, and B to C, then one prefers A to C. Practical rationality is consistency of choice: It is rational to act in a way that is consistent with one's preference ranking, that is, in the best or maximizing way to realize one's preferences, given one's beliefs. Using these formal criteria of consistency to restrict the range of rational alternatives in intentional action, the theory acquires whatever predictive power it has. This same formal character may bring with it limits on the empirical application of the theory. For example, if an agent operates with several utility functions (and hence maximizes different preference orderings—say, one at work and the other at home), then the criteria of consistency become more complex and more difficult to make empirically significant, given reflective and changeable preferences. While all forms of rationality are identical with consistency of one sort or another, I will speak of maximization as distinct from other forms of consistency because it is the crucial assumption of rational choice explanations of action. This formal and simplifying assumption of maximization, I shall argue, is the source of both the limits of the theory and of the power of the theory within those limits.

Assuming maximization requires that a rational agent acts to achieve the best consequences and thus chooses the highest ranking alternative among the set of feasible actions and strategies. Powerfully predictive theories in the natural sciences employ similar assumptions about maximization as well; consider, for example, Newton's laws of motion as described by differential calculus and Darwin's survival of the fittest, understood as maximum reproductive success.[3] All these theories attempt to explain a domain of phenomena by showing how the maximization of a value, such as survival rates among offspring, explains everything in a domain. This assumption defines a research strategy: If we assume that the behavior of a system tends to maximize the value of some variable, and if our measurements of its value in an experiment are at odds with the predictions of the theory, then "we never infer that the system is failing to maximize the variable in question, but assume that our specification of the constraints under which it is operating is incomplete" (Rosenberg 1980, p. 82). Alternatively, when an action fails to maximize, the theory does not then explain it as irrational or nonrational but rather discovers "the point of view of the actor, from which the action *is* rational" in this sense (Coleman 1990, p. 18). For example, we might extend decision theory by introducing the theory of games, showing that choices in this context can be explained in terms of the constraints of the interdependency of choices made by other utility maximizing agents; or we may add Simon's conception of suboptimal choice, of *bounded rationality* under "satisficing" rather than optimizing conditions; or we might see that the agent is maximizing in terms of the best worst choice with a mini-max rule. Nonetheless consistent maximization (of some sort) is the key element of any minimal theory of rationality, in terms of which the rational choice theorist can try to predict how individuals will behave under certain conditions if they act rationally. In each case, rational agents adopt optimal strategies, seek efficiency with regard to information costs, or maximize the best worst outcome for decisions under risk.

For all the formal complexity of its theoretical models, rational choice explanations can be decomposed into basic elements that extend and formalize the basic features of ordinary explanations of intentional action. As a subspecies of intentional explanation, any rational choice explanation must have the minimal elements of intentional explanation that are part of its basic guiding assumptions (Statements 1 and 2 below) and that then are completed by a formal-minimal model of rationality (Statements 2-4). It is the application of this model (Statements 2 and 3) that gives the theory its explanatory power, not any inductive dispositional generalizations about "rationality" as philosophers like Hempel have thought. Following Hempel (1965), Davidson (1980a, 1980b), and particularly Elster (1985, 1986), we can reconstruct the basic assumptions of rational choice explanations in the following statements.

The Assumptions of Rational Choice Explanation

1. Rational action is characterized by the proper relation between the individual's beliefs (B), desires (D), and the action (A) performed. In light of B, A is the best way to satisfy D.

2. Rational actions must be voluntary, insofar as reasons must be real causes and not post hoc rationalizations: B and D cause A qua reasons and can be connected to the consequences of A.

3. B and D are internally consistent, and their relation to choice fits the idealizing assumptions of the model of utility maximizing rationality. These conditions make the choice fully rational: The means must be the best available, given information attainable by the agent.

4. Other conditions depend on the constraining features of the choice situation, including the choices of others, coordinating mechanisms, and other constraints that establish enduring patterns of action that are equilibrium states of a society. While the explanation of a rational action may refer to these conditions, they must in turn be explained as the aggregate consequence of individual rational action.

5. Given 2, 3, and 4, some course of action must be rationally decidable as the best among well-defined alternatives (if one exists). The theory cannot predict which among equally weighted alternatives will be chosen and is in this case indeterminate.

6. The actor does (A).

The specification of these conditions overcomes one of the empirical problems of a formal maximizing theory: Much as Wittgenstein said of rule following, any action can be seen as maximizing some sufficiently arbitrary set of beliefs and desires, much as any adaptation can always be seen as increasing fitness in some respect or another.[4] Rational choice theory, too, must avoid being Panglossian, seeing everything social as the outcome of maximizing-purposive behavior or its unintended effects, leaving no room for irrational and nonrational causes. A clear challenge for the theory, once it claims comprehensive scope, is that it merely stipulates definitions of certain types of actions so that they may be described, vacuously, to fit the intentional and maximizing assumptions of the theory (Bohman 1991, Chap. 2).

It is difficult to quarrel with some of these premises. Whereas Statement 1 is simply a general premise of any intentional explanation, Statement 4 in part simply assumes the interdependency of choices necessary for game theory. Both assumptions can become contentious when (1) is defined as a prescription for methodological individualism and (4) a restriction to aggregative mechanisms. The caveat in (5) shows clear predictive limitations of the theory that can to some extent be overcome in such multidimensional models as complex games. In what follows, however, my objections shall focus on Statements 2 and 3 of the form of explanation outlined above, which I shall call the *intentionality assumption* and the *maximization assumption.* I shall begin with some relatively trivial examples in which these assumptions do not hold and then go on to discuss examples that challenge the core claim that rational choice theory can be a comprehensive social theory: Its explanations of certain types of norms are simply too narrow, and when they are broadened, they become inconsistent with these very intentional and maximizing assumptions.

LIMITS OF THE INTENTIONAL
AND MAXIMIZING ASSUMPTIONS:
SOME PROBLEM CASES

First of all, some actions exist for which reasons cannot be the cause (and thus Statement 2 does not hold). As any insomniac knows, not all consequences can be made the goal of an intentional action. This is the case for outcomes of actions that are "essentially by-products," including such paradoxical phenomena as wanting to forget, to fall asleep, or to be spontaneous (Elster 1982, p. 21). In general, the model does not apply whenever any of the conditions do not obtain, as is the case not only for by-products of actions but also for some irrational behavior, some moral and social norms, addictive behavior, and much more (most of which also do not fit the rationality conditions of Statement 3). Such cases do not refute the theory but require the social scientist to look carefully at its scope and explanatory assumptions. Many of these cases appear to be explained as forms of maximization of some sort or another in light of preferences for heroin or honor. In both cases, some nonintentional and nonrational mechanism is at work that really does the explaining and that cannot itself be explained on the assumptions of the theory. To do otherwise would be similar to the error of explaining the maximizing phenomena of natural selection as a consequence of the rational choices of a reproducing species.

The core cases for the theory, however, are economic phenomena in the broadest sense. Consumer behavior shows how the assumptions may yield empirical hypotheses with predictive value, such as the way supply and demand relationships predict the movement of actual market prices to the equilibrium price. Neoclassical economics attempts to see such lawlike relationships as the aggregate of rational choices made by consumers and producers, all of whom conduct their transactions as utility maximizers. Prices in certain markets function as a coordinating mechanism and thus serve as the sort of constraint that I have in mind in Statement 4. A rise in price will cause a reduction of the amount demanded so that, for example, a tax increase on gasoline would cut consumption by rational consumers. If actors are truly maximizers, however, then prices may not function as stabilizing and equilibrating mechanisms in the way that the theory predicts. John Roemer, for example, has shown how Marx's analysis of capitalism has this consequence as well. The aggregate of all utility maximizing behavior of all capitalists results in the failure of the system as a whole to reach any equilibrium state (as is the case in games with multiple equilibria). By each capitalist seeking to maximize profits, the tendency is for each to follow such disequilibrating strategies as constant exploitation and technical innovation. This example raises questions about the stability of many gamelike processes, and I shall return to this problem again in discussing conventions and norms.

A more problematic case might reveal more about the nature and scope of the theory and how it guides empirical sociological research. Its application to political phenomena generally and to voting in particular is one such case, a case that challenges claims for the universal scope of the theory. As Elster notes, "Voting does seem to be a case in which the action itself, rather than the outcome it can be expected to produce, is what matters" (Elster 1986, p. 24). As the many discussions of the voter's dilemma show, it is pointless on maximizing grounds alone to vote in a large election with a secret ballot. Besides the large number of people in the social interactions that make up an election, one reason that the assumptions of rational choice explanations do not hold is that the causal condition (Statement 3) does not apply. In a large election, it is highly unlikely that any single voter will cast the decisive ballot; therefore, for a rational maximizer to invest any resources in voting, such as time, would be irrational. Some political theorists seem content to condemn all politics to irrationality and see participation as rational only if "selective incentives" exist, that is, rewards specific to individuals who vote, in the absence of any mutually advantageous mechanisms like those of the market. But rather than a "market failure" of the political system in coordinating and aggregating choices, these difficulties point to an explanatory failure of the theory when it is applied beyond the conditions of its validity. Voting is a rational action but only in a much richer sense that would include moral and self-expressive action, along with instrumental action, in its domain. It is surely an exercise of reason to try to convince others to change their beliefs and preferences in debate; but here rationality has little to do with maximization in any direct way, but rather with impartiality. Stinchcombe has called these uses of rationality *reason* and has used it to explain the standards of impartiality used in professions like accounting: The accountant does not maximize the firm's assets even if that might be a prudent strategy for the owners at any particular moment; nor does the judge apply the law to maximize anything for himself or herself or for the group.[5] I would argue that a similar notion of public reason is at work in democratic deliberation, debate, and voting.[6] Neither public impartiality nor deliberation can be accounted for without a broader notion of rational preferences and reflective preference formation.

Such cases of maximization "dilemmas" that lead to explanatory deficits could be multiplied so that the clear presentation of the conditions required to apply the theory entails rejecting the claim made by some theorists, such as Gary Becker, that a broad rational choice theory is a complete account of all human behavior (Becker 1976, p. 8). Whether we know it or not, according to Becker, the economic approach to human behavior is unlimited in explanatory scope and power: "All human behavior can be viewed as involving participants who maximize their utility for a stable set of preferences and accumulate an optimal amount of information and other inputs in a variety of markets" (Becker 1976, p. 8). Because we compete with others to satisfy these preferences, marketlike coordinating mechanisms provide part of the social explanation of how maximizers interact. For example, marriage choices can be explained as utility maximization in a market: "A person decides to marry when the expected utility from marriage exceeds that expected from remaining single or from the additional search for a more compatible mate" (Becker 1976, p. 10). The first problem is that this apparently lawlike statement has all the marks of a tautology. It is an easy and empirically vacuous trick to redescribe all of the motives that agents may have for marrying in terms of expected utility.[7] This empirical vacuity arises from the stipulative definitions necessary to expand notions like *utility* and *markets* to fit this domain.[8]

The deeper problem here again has to do with the intentional and maximizing assumptions of the explanation. The fact that actors do not have the intentions that these descriptions seem to ascribe to them does not bother Becker, nor does he recognize that rational choice theory does not require the same motivational assumptions as neoclassical economics: "The economic approach does not assume that decision units are necessarily conscious of their efforts to maximize, or can verbalize or otherwise describe in an informative way the reasons for the systematic patterns of their behavior" (Becker 1976, p. 7). Certainly laws of supply and demand do not require that actors choose in light of them. But Becker's remarks show that the generalization of rational choice models of explanation can be had only by abandoning the intentional assumption: the idea that the theory was supposed to give an account of how reasons cause actions. Instead the theory searches for nonintentional maximizing motives and market mechanisms, making the rationality of actors themselves less and less important as an explanatory condition. The problem is that without these assumptions, there is no reason to explain marriage choices in terms of *expected* utility. Becker must at least show how his explanation is dependent on the actual intentions of the actors involved; otherwise the explanation has no microfoundations, the supposed strength of rational choice theory as a research program. If intentions do not explain why agents are so efficient in their search for a compatible mate, then some other mechanism must bring it about. But here the broadened analogy to a market breaks down. In the absence of clear mechanisms of competition, one has little reason to believe that rational agents would be so efficient to reduce the costs of their choice behavior; even if we could say what reducing costs means in this context, it is hard to see why that increases agents' expected utility more than less efficient courting behavior. Because the explanation does not appeal to actors' intentions (maximizing or not) or to consequences of those intentions, it is not an explanation in terms of agents' rationality at all.

One result of the falsity of Becker's comprehensive claim is that the assumptions of rational choice explanation delimit conditions that apply only to a certain range of intentional actions. While any research program can test whether its core explanatory assumptions can be expanded beyond its elementary varieties, rational choice research itself shows that it is not a "complete theory of all human behavior" and that this imperial aim only entangles the theory in conceptual and empirical difficulties. More methodologically sophisticated proponents of the theory, such as Russell Hardin, argue that the theory simply makes stipulative assumptions about action and that it loses its explanatory power when the individual's calculus is expanded beyond the narrowest cost-benefit motivation. "To attempt a complete decision theory of human behavior would be absurd," Hardin argues, because a complete assessment requires an "extended calculus." Such calculations bring in too many additional variables and unmanageably pack "the context and much of the social history that has brought that context about into one's decision calculus" (Hardin 1982, p. 14).

Despite this modest approach, the theory's formal and stipulative assumptions have also been so often shown not to obtain that some, like Amos Tversky, have adopted a much more modest and empirical approach.[9] Others, like Amartya Sen, have questioned the usefulness of its model of rationality. Purely economic and utility maximizing agents, acting in some actual historical society, would not be competent actors but instead would be "rational fools." The reason, Sen argues, is that rational choice theory has "too little structure," particularly with regard to preference rankings (Sen 1979, p. 102). To overcome this lack of structure, Sen introduces an element entirely lacking from the maximizing, formal concept of rationality: *reflexivity,* or the capacity to consider the "rankings of preference rankings" (Sen 1979, p. 103). Rational agents do not simply choose in light of stable preferences but can ask the reflexive question, What type of preferences should I have? This reflexivity makes practical rationality of choice at least in part a matter of judgment about one's preferences themselves and how one ranks them, not just of maximizing one's given preferences. And as soon as *reflexivity* is introduced, so is *indeterminacy*: What is "best" is not univocal but relative to a variety of different rankings. Such second order preferences introduce considerations that could not be captured in the explanatory concept of maximizing rationality and so must make wider empirical assumptions about the relations of reasons to actions. It is indeterminate, however, insofar as even those additional empirical assumptions do not entail unique outcomes for a whole domain such as "marriage choices." Hence the rational choice theory would have to introduce even more auxiliary explanatory conditions, taken from other theories better suited to deal with the influences of social contexts on choices and the changing and indeterminate character of social actions. Such explanations make the same mistake as do theories with a single type of cause or causal mechanism, such as Parsonian internalization: Social actors are neither norm-following conformists nor maximizing fools, no matter how wide-ranging the behavior that can be deduced or described in terms of these mechanisms.

EXPLAINING CONVENTIONS AND NORMS

Next I would like to take these criticisms of the maximizing and intentional assumptions of rational choice theory a step further by examining an important area of social behavior that has given the theory enormous difficulty: the problem of social norms and rules. While certainly few areas of social life are governed by explicit rules, a variety of different instances of action and use of language may be called rule-governed in a looser sense. But it is unlikely that all of them can be made to fit a single concept.

David Lewis is correct in arguing that the idea of a rule is "a messy cluster concept" with many distinct senses (Lewis 1969, p. 105). These senses could all cluster around the assumptions of rational choice theory. I have shown already, however, that rules of accounting or legal reasoning do not fit the assumptions: They are not explainable in terms of rationality or agents' individual preferences. If reasons and preferences are not causal in the sense required by the theory, then neither are rules when they function as reasons. The different types of rules each test the limits of its claims to be a comprehensive and exclusive form of explanation, and some but not all rule-following actions clearly violate the intentional and maximizing assumptions of the theory; they may be reasonable, irrational, or nonrational.

In the explanatory models of rational choice theory, explicit rules must be explained as intentional, that is, in terms of the goals or purposes that the agent pursues in following a rule. Rulelike patterns of behavior also might be the unintended effects of individual utility maximizing behavior; in that case, agents are not following what they believe to be "rules" that are the causes of their behavior. Moreover, rule following must be rational in a utility maximizing sense and hence caused by consistent beliefs and desires. According to the Hobbesian variant of the social contract tradition, the only category of rules that can fulfill these desiderata is what David Lewis calls *conventions:* namely, intentional agreements and regularities of behavior that express a common preference and coordinate actions according to expected outcomes. The typical case of such a convention is driving on the left or right side of the road. Either rule will do, so long as we can expect that it will be followed in the future. No one will be better off by acting contrary to what others are doing: Because everyone wants to get safely where he or she is going, one or the other rule will be an equilibrium state for rational actors. Conventions are explained in rational choice theory as *coordination equilibria,* a regular pattern of behavior that satisfies the interests and preferences of each actor; they may function with or without explicit agreement although each actor expects that others will behave in a certain way for a convention to exist. Thus conventions are the solutions to certain coordination games in everyday life. Lewis quotes Hume's example of two rowers in a boat who fall into a smooth rhythm and develop the expectation that the other will also keep to it. The actions of each come to "have a reference to the other, and are performed on the supposition that something is to be performed upon the other part" (Lewis 1969, p. 44).

Lewis's defining condition for the existence of a convention may be used to specify when the rational choice model may explain rule following. Conventions exist if people conform to them because they believe that others will. What is important is neither the content nor the specificity of the rules but only an expectation about the future behavior of others. Lewis sets out the specific conditions for conventions in terms of preferences and beliefs:

> A regularity R in the behavior of members of a population P when they are agents in a recurrent situation S is a convention if and only if it is true that, and it is common knowledge that, in any instance of S among members of P: (1) everyone conforms to R (2) everyone expects everyone else to conform to R (3) everyone prefers to conform to R on the condition that others do, since S is a coordination problem and uniform conformity to R is a coordination equilibrium in S. (Lewis 1969, p. 58)

As required by intentional explanation, the agents' independent beliefs and preferences cause conformity to R. This description of *conformity* fits all of the conditions for applying the rational choice theory; it does seem to explain the persistence of some of the conventional aspects of social life. Indeed the more arbitrary and unenforced the convention and the less it is dependent on specific form and content, the better suited to this type of explanation it is. Certain coordination problems can be solved by either some explicit agreement or some widely recognized expectation, no matter what it is, so long as it is observed regularly and a common preference exists to resolve the problem.

As rational choice theorists recognize, however, not all rules are solutions to coordination problems and not all social situations approximate S, the solution to a coordination game. Some rational choice theorists attempt to solve the problem by explaining how different rules, such as rules of cooperation, also emerge out of different choice situations. In particular, following some such rules has costs to the agent: While driving on one side of the road or the other might go on even in the absence of sanctions, speed limits are followed only if they are enforced. One can better fulfill one's preferences by being a "free rider": If others follow the rule, an actor receives all the benefits with none of the costs; if they do not, then one is also better off not following the rule. Sanctions and incentives are one solution, but they too are costly and require that others sanction not only those who do not conform but also those who do not sanction, increasing costs even more (Elster 1989). Hardin and Axelrod have argued that repeated decisions or "iterated plays" within the prisoners' dilemma situation show the long-term rationality of cooperating (Axelrod 1984, Hardin 1982).[10] While this result is formally true, it clearly violates the maximization assumption, whether agents are narrowly self-interested or not. If each agent is a utility maximizer in any sense, repeated plays may not occur, and compliance or cooperation breaks down. Even sanctioned rules would not be carried out unless agents had independent, non-self-interested and impersonal reasons for enforcing them (because enforcing is not necessarily utility maximizing). Thus a reflective agent who considers alternative rankings for his or her preferences and who exercises "reason" in Stinchcombe's sense might be able to make judgments about the justice or legitimacy of such norms for each and for all and observe them despite the costs. One might preserve the maximizing assumption by positing the capacity to act in light of current long-term interests; but this question-begging notion "has no place in standard theory of rational choice" and is really only impartial reason by another name.[11] Derek Parfit has argued on convincing philosophical grounds that it is at least not self-evident that we should choose to maximize the utility of our future selves, particularly if my actual future interests significantly diverge from my current long-term ones, as is a common human experience. Thus maximizing rationality faces a new dilemma once repeated plays or temporality are brought in: Not only do "interpersonal dilemmas" exist, but maximization may be "intertemporally self-defeating" (Parfit 1984, p. 92).

These difficulties can be illustrated in the inadequacies of various attempts to explain rules or norms other than conventions in terms of maximizing behavior. For all the weaknesses of Parsons's own positive account of norms and social order, he is correct that the Hobbesian solution to these difficulties, the sanctions of "force and fraud," cannot create a social order stable enough for obligatory rule following. Hobbes was right to appeal to coercion, because all utility maximizing agents will cooperate if large sanctions are certain. But in the absence of ubiquitous sanctioning, stability is like any good that is in everyone's long-term interests. Indeed, as Hobbes noted, it is a precondition for some maximizing behavior such as commerce or for some desires like that for "commodious living"; but it is itself a public good that all share. What is required is only that others follow rules often enough that beneficial interactions tend to be repeated; any individual maximizing agent may free-ride and not contribute to the stabilizing, rule-following behavior. Thus stability through rule following is inconsistent with the assumptions of rational choice theory; it can be achieved only collectively and hence cannot avoid standard contributors' dilemmas. This implies that stability is a consequence of rule following and is not caused by agents maximizing their own utility; nor is it an unintended consequence because the consequence itself is inconsistent with rational behavior in this sense. Once an order stable enough to permit repeated interaction is in place, then it can become clear that following rules in the long run may be utility maximizing for all agents (including themselves). The simple fact that some rules have such a consequence does not causally explain their emergence, anymore than the fact that a norm serves a particular function of social integration. In the end, what is assumed is that cooperation and conventions are identical. Simple games do not capture all the dilemmas that a rational actor faces in cooperating with other rational actors; prisoners' dilemmas are only one of many.

The explanations of other types of norms face similar problems and also become ensnared on the horns of public goods dilemmas; however, once a system of norms already exists, some behavior within it can be explained in these terms. At the same time, it also seems obvious that even some regularities that do function as conventions can better be explained through nonrational coercion than by rational choice. The Irish do not speak English in order to solve their own coordination problems but as the result of military force and cultural domination. In this case, the convention serves as a coordination mechanism for the dominant group's purposes and fails on Lewis's criteria (3) to meet everyone's preferences; for that reason, although it functions as a convention and is not often enforced, it does at times need legal sanctions to persist. Just because some convention is better than none does not mean that the convention adopted can be best explained on maximizing grounds as a solution to a coordination problem. In this case, the power of the English nation-state and ruling class is a nonrational cause of a rule-following behavior that might in other instances be best explained as a convention.

Expanding the range of problems and situations to be solved by rules for rational maximizers only deepens the fundamental difficulty. In *The Emergence of Norms*, Edna Ullmann-Margalit tries to explain the "rationale" of various types of norms other than conventions (*coordination norms*) in the terms of rational choice theory. These include *prisoners' dilemma norms* and *norms of partiality*, each denoting the type of recurrent choice situation out of which different norms are generated. The problem posed by "p-d structured situations" is "that of preventing an unstable yet jointly beneficial state of affairs from deteriorating, so to speak, into a stable yet jointly destructive one," perhaps a truce in the arms race situation or a framework for mutual cooperation (Ullman-Margalit 1977, p. 22). But the beneficial results of cooperation are once again a consequence of repeated and stable interaction and not its cause; they do not explain the stability and hence cannot be a "stabilizing mechanism" that is the aggregate result of rational actions. Indeed the longer the interaction and the greater the benefits that are a consequence of it, the more likely cooperation is to "deteriorate" on the utility maximizing grounds, as when one nation knows it possesses superior resources for a potential arms race. It is equally true that knowledge of future, stable interaction may make actors less willing to cooperate in current interactions, as Schelling points out about bargaining. Similar objections can be raised against Ullmann-Margalit's treatment of norms of partiality, which are generated out of a "status quo of inequality." Norms of partiality serve to maintain the status quo and hence to "promote the interests of the party favored by the inequality" (Ullman-Margalit 1977, p. 134). On maximizing grounds alone, it is difficult to establish why it is that the disfavored party would conform to such norms rather than seek new ones, particularly if the situation is really "p-d structured." Indeed, in this case, the situation is unstable: If the less well-off have practical rationality, their future selves will continue to have interests in violating these norms and in changing the status quo. The long-term adherence to such norms needs to be explained in terms of cognitive dissonance, ideology, and other forms of irrationality. Once again, however, utility maximization has not explained the causes of conformity to the norm, anymore than it really explained marriage choice in Becker's analysis, and stabilizing mechanisms, if they exist, must be nonrational. In those cases, rational choice theory also cannot explain the rationale for the norm, as Ullmann-Margalit claims. It provides a rationale only for utility maximizers who cease to maximize once they adopt the reconstructed norm; but if they are not assumed to be maximizers, then the theory's norm-generating situations would not exist in the first place.

Successful intentionalist explanations of rules as conventions show the conditions under which certain problems of social life can be solved: coordination games and their equilibria. On the one hand, the overemphasis on intentionality in rational choice explanation entails the loss of the social and institutional context as an explanatory factor for conformity to other types of rules or norms. On the other hand, the overemphasis on utility maximization impoverishes the notion of practical rationality. Without a stronger and broader notion of rationality than consistency and maximization, it is hard to see how some rules and norms persist long enough to become obligatory for knowledgeable agents, other than when they already happen to reflect their preferences.

CONCLUSION: THE SCOPE
OF RATIONAL CHOICE THEORY

The basic argument of this chapter has not been that rational choice theory is false: Its explanations are adequate within its own domain. My claim is, however, that rational choice theory cannot be a comprehensive social theory or the basis of one, given the limits of its assumptions. If this conclusion is correct, a final question must be asked: Could rational choice theory be revised in order to make it more complete and comprehensive? My answer is no. Such a revision weakens its explanatory power and overextends its explanatory assumptions. It is precisely because it makes such strong assumptions that the theory can explain phenomena in its domain. But its very strengths (and source of its quantitative structure) also set clear limits, and good rational choice explanations stay within them as narrowly as possible. Broadening the theory to include nonintentional maximization, future interests, or stabilizing norms only leads to bad explanations.

Rather than going beyond the scope of the theory, the better solution is to search for explanations of the boundary conditions for rational choice behavior outside of the theory. Not only is such a strategy less circular, it permits the use of the maximization assumption even in cases in which standard rational choice theory fails. Boundary conditions like stable and long-term interaction can be explained only by macrostructural assumptions that are not based simply on aggregative mechanisms, although they have some microfoundation. Thus even good rational choice explanations must be supplemented by an account of macroinstitutional structure that explains the interdependency of actions and the mechanisms of preference formation.

Another way in which rational choice theory is incomplete is with regard to its conception of rationality as utility maximization. Here rational choice theory, as a theory of maximizing rationality, must be supplemented by other models of practical rationality, such as Stinchcombe's conception of *impartial reason* or Sen's idea of the *capacity for second-order reflection*. Without such models of practical reason, many highly rational forms of behavior in social life remain irresolvable dilemmas and paradoxes. The phenomena to be explained by such a broader concept of reason might be many of the features of the institutions of law, democracy, and science. Further, without such institutions, it is hard to see how rational agents can solve the persistent interpersonal conflicts of beliefs and preferences in complex societies.

In the end, the criticism of Parsons and others that utilitarianism cannot explain important aspects of social life applies equally to rational choice theory for all its genuine theoretical improvements on intentional explanations for social science. At the same time, rational choice theory has shown us how to get by on minimal and formalizable assumptions and why a narrow theory of rationality is enough for certain cases. But the limits of its explanations show that it is an incomplete theory of social action and that it can remain vital only by incorporating other theories at different levels of explanation. Rational choice theory itself should remain narrow and economic, even in sociology, if it is to retain its explanatory power.

NOTES

1. This claim could be made regardless of whether rational choice theory can produce general laws, as Hempel (1965) claims. For strong arguments against this view, see Davidson (1980b), in which Davidson argues that intentional explanations cannot be predictive and hence are not based on general laws.

2. For an analysis of this idea of a "core" variety of explanation, see Miller (1987), p. 76. Miller uses this conception of a core to describe the way scientists use the concept of *causality*. A *core* consists of diverse elementary varieties that are then extended by a procedure that "describes relations to elementary varieties in virtue of which something qualifies as a nonelementary variety" (p. 77). This is the way rational choice theory works, given the set of assumptions that I outline below as its core.

3. See Rosenberg (1980), p. 81, for a discussion of such "extremal" theories and their mathematics. Newtonian mechanics is also "extremal" because its explanations of a system "always minimize and maximize variables that reflect physically possible configurations of the system." Rosenberg also has a good discussion of the similarity of some versions of rational choice theory, like Becker's comprehensive economic approach to sociobiology and its explanatory problems.

4. This is the idea of Steven Jay Gould's well-known criticism of Darwinian explanations as Panglossian: that the organism represents the best of all possible biological worlds. Similarly, rational choice explanations tend to make societies the most rational of all possible social worlds. This methodological artifact explains the theory's generally conservative orientation.

5. See Stinchcombe (1990), p. 289. According to Stinchcombe, the judge and the accountant follow norms and do not maximize benefits: "Following the rules of, say, legal reasoning from precedent results in an authoritative judgment about what law applies to the case" (p. 289). He goes on to define *reason* in terms of what is "recognized" as authoritative: "By reason I mean a socially established method of calculating what should be authoritative in a particular case." It still must be explained why any particular method should be recognized as reasonable by a competent calculator or judge: They are reasonable only to the extent that they fulfill requirements of publicity and impartiality, not because they are "authoritative."

6. See Bohman (Forthcoming) for a development of an alternative notion of public reason. Such a notion is indebted to Habermas and presupposes communication among participants in an institution that is structured so as to fulfill conditions of publicity.

7. For an extended development of this criticism of Becker's explanation as circular, see Rosenberg (1980), p. 87. Even once the core notions of markets and utility are extended in such a way, it still has not yet been shown that utility maximizing marriage choices actually cause the rate of marriage to be what it is; the theory may only provide a series of nonexplanatory correlations between its assumptions about human behavior and statistical patterns of marriage. It should come as no surprise that Becker's theory therefore could be consistent with all the data without explaining any of it; no independent specification exists of what the basic terms of his theory are or what the explanatory variable—utility—is supposed

to be, apart from the choices themselves, or of why so many independent choices are supposed to aggregate into such an efficient pattern.

8. This same problem can be found in other overly "broad" rational choice explanations, such as Hechter's explanations of group solidarity: Solidarity increases according to "the average proportion of each member's private resources contributed." See Hechter (1987), p. 18. But there is no reason to assume that maximizing agents would ever contribute very much of their resources in the first place; hence all group solidarity would suffer from public goods dilemmas. This stipulative definition of *solidarity* offered obscures the violation of the maximization assumption in Hechter's case; in Becker's case, the definition of *markets and utility* obscures the violation of the intentionality assumption. Both broaden rational choice theory beyond its limits, with explanatory inadequacy as the result.

9. See Tversky and Quattrone (1986) for a discussion of the voter's paradox. Their explanation makes voting irrational, as the result of failing to distinguish between causal and diagnostic contingencies: The voter's own choice is seen as diagnostic of the choices of other like-minded voters.

10. See Robert Axelrod (1984) and Russell Hardin (1982). Axelrod's own examples show the unresolved problems of stability in this model that I will establish below: The conditional (tit for tat) cooperation of the unofficial truces in World War I trench warfare was a highly unstable arrangement (p. 80). I would argue also that many such expanded explanations require a modification of the view of rationality as maximization and hence of the standard theory of rational choice. The same is true for Margolis (1982), for whom departures from the standard view of rationality are needed to explain cooperative norms and other solutions to various public goods dilemmas.

11. Coleman (1990) argues against this notion because it requires an appeal to "willpower" (p. 548). My view is that any appeal to long-term interest requires a different notion of rationality altogether, one that offers a solution to interpersonal and intertemporal dilemmas.

REFERENCES

Axelrod, Robert. 1984. *The Evolution of Cooperation.* New York: Basic Books.

Becker, Gary. 1976. *The Economic Approach to Human Behavior.* Chicago: University of Chicago Press.

Bohman, James. 1991. *New Philosophy of Social Science: Problems of Indeterminacy.* London and Cambridge, MA: Polity Press and MIT Press.

―――. Forthcoming. *Critique of Public Reason: Rationality, Irrationality and Democracy.* Cambridge, MA: MIT Press.

Coleman, James. 1990. *Foundations of Social Theory.* Cambridge, MA: Harvard University Press.

Davidson, Donald. 1980a. "Actions, Reasons and Causes." Pp. 3-20 in *Essays on Actions and Events.* Oxford: Oxford University Press.

―――. 1980b. "Hempel on Explaining Action." Pp. 261-76 in *Essays on Action and Events.* Oxford: Oxford University Press.

Elster, Jon. 1982. *Sour Grapes*. Cambridge, UK: Cambridge University Press.

————. 1985. "The Nature and Scope of Rational Choice Explanations." Pp. 158-75 in *Action and Events*, edited by E. Lapore and B. McLaughlin. London: Basil Blackwell.

————. 1986. "Introduction." Pp. 1-33 in *Rational Choice*, edited by J. Elster. New York: New York University Press.

————. 1989. *Cement of Society*. Cambridge, UK: Cambridge University Press.

Hardin, Russell. 1982. *Collective Action*. Baltimore: Johns Hopkins University Press.

Hechter, Michael. 1987. *Principles of Group Solidarity*. Berkeley: University of California Press.

Hempel, Carl. 1965. "The Concept of Rationality and the Logic of Explanation by Reason." Pp. 463-87 in *Aspects of Scientific Explanation*. New York: Free Press.

Lewis, David. 1969. *Convention*. Cambridge, MA: Harvard University Press.

Margolis, Howard. 1982. *Selfishness, Altruism and Rationality*. Cambridge, UK: Cambridge University Press.

Miller, Richard. 1987. *Fact and Method*. Princeton, NJ: Princeton University Press.

Parfit, Derek. 1984. *Reasons and Persons*. Oxford: Oxford University Press.

Rosenberg, Alexander. 1980. *Sociobiology and the Preemption of Social Science*. Baltimore: Johns Hopkins University Press.

Sen, Amartya. 1979. "Rational Fools." Pp. 87-109 in *Philosophy and Economic Theory*, edited by F. Hahn and M. Hollis. Oxford: Oxford University Press.

Stinchcombe, Arthur. 1990. "Reason and Rationality." Pp. 285-317 in *The Limits of Rationality*, edited by Karen Cook and Margaret Levi. Chicago: University of Chicago Press.

Tversky, Amos and George Quattrone. 1985. "Self-Deception and the Voter's Illusion." Pp. 35-58 in *The Multiple Self*, edited by J. Elster. Cambridge, UK: Cambridge University Press.

Ullman-Margalit, Edna. 1977. *The Emergence of Norms*. Oxford: Oxford University Press.

ABOUT THE AUTHORS

PETER ABELL is Director of the Interdisciplinary Institute of Management and Eric Sosnow Professor of Management. He is a member of the Centre for Economic Performance and the Sociology Department at the London School of Economics. His most recent books include *The Syntax of Social Life: The Theory and Method of Comparative Narratives* (1989) and *Rational Choice Theory* (1991). His research interests are in determinants of self-employment, the market for corporate control, the economic consequence of profit sharing, theories of cooperative production, and narrative analysis and game theory.

JAMES BOHMAN is Associate Professor of Philosophy at St. Louis University. He is the author of *New Philosophy of Social Science: Problems of Indeterminacy* (1991), as well as articles on the problems of explanation, interpretation, and criticism in the social sciences. In addition to the philosophy of social science, his research interests concern developing a normative and explanatory concept of rationality for democratic theory. He is currently writing a book titled *Critique of Public Reason: Rationality, Irrationality and Democracy.*

JAMES S. COLEMAN was born in Bedford, Indiana. He received his bachelor's degree in chemical engineering from Purdue University in 1949, and was awarded a Ph.D. in sociology from Columbia University in 1955. From 1959 to 1973 he was an associate professor in the Department of Social Relations at John Hopkins University. Since 1973 he has been a Professor of Sociology and Education at the University of Chicago. His publications include *The Adolescent Society* (1961), *Introduction to Mathematical Sociology* (1964), *The Asymmetric Society* (1982), *Public and Private High Schools: The Impact of Communities* (1987), *Foundations of Social Theory* (1990), *Equality and Achievement in Education* (1990), and *Social Theory for a Changing Society* (1991). His current interests are in the social theory of norm formation and in the functioning of schools.

THOMAS J. FARARO received a Ph.D. in sociology from Syracuse University in 1963. In the mid-1960s he was awarded a three-year NIMH fellowship for the study of mathematics in the social sciences. In 1967 he joined the Department of Sociology at the University of Pittsburgh, where he has been since that time. Teaching and research focused on formal models and methods led to the 1973 book *Mathematical Sociology*. Since then his principal interest has been in theoretical sociology, both the classic ideas and contemporary developments. One of his objectives has been to articulate a coherent vision of the core of sociological theory: its philosophy, its key general theoretical problems, and its methods, focusing on representation principles and formal models. This aspiration culminated in the 1989 ASA Rose monograph *The Meaning of General Theoretical Sociology: Tradition and Formalization* and in a number of related articles.

DEBRA FRIEDMAN is Assistant Professor of Sociology at the University of Arizona. She is completing a manuscript, *The Social Origins of Maternal Custody*, on the subject of the change in child custody laws around the turn of the century in the United States, England, and France. An essay on rational choice theory and feminism, "Feminism and the Pro-(Rational) Choice Movement: Rational Choice Theory, Feminist Critiques, and Gender Inequality," written with Carol Diem, is forthcoming.

MICHAEL T. HANNAN is Professor of Sociology and Professor of Organizational Behavior and Human Resources at Stanford University. His research interests include organizational ecology and evolution, the employment relation, and the analysis of social change. He is the author of *Aggregation and Disaggregation in the Social Sciences* (1991) and coauthor of *Social Dynamics: Models and Methods* (1984), *Organizational Ecology* (1989), and *Dynamics of Organizational Populations* (1992).

MICHAEL HECHTER is Professor of Sociology at the University of Arizona. He is the author of *Principles of Group Solidarity* (1987), editor of *The Microfoundations of Macrosociology* (1983), and co-editor of *Social Institutions: Their Emergence, Maintenance, and Effects* (1990).

SATOSHI KANAZAWA is a Ph.D. candidate in the department of sociology at the University of Arizona. He is the coauthor (with Michael Hechter) of "The Production of Social Order, with Special Reference to Contemporary Japan" in *Social Theory and Social Practice: Essays in Honor of James S. Coleman,* edited by Aage B. Sørensen and Seymour Spilerman (forthcoming). He continues his work on the general theory of social order in his dissertation.

SIEGWART LINDENBERG is Professor of Theoretical Sociology at the University of Groningen, the Netherlands, where he divides his time between the department of sociology and the postgraduate institute ICS (the Interuniversity Center for Sociological Theory and Methodology). His research interests include the methodology of explanation in the social sciences, theories of action (especially the combination of rational choice with framing), sharing groups and the emergence of norms, and the problem of governance (agency, authority, contractual behavior, revolutions). Recent publications by the author related to the method of decreasing abstraction and the integration of the social sciences are "Homo socio-economicus: The Emergence of a General Model of Man in the Social Sciences," in *Journal of Institution and Theoretical Economics* (1990), and "Recent Contributions of Dutch Sociologists Toward a New Integration of the Socio-Economic Sciences, Especially Sociology and Economics," in H. A. Becker, F. Leeuw, and K. Verrips (eds.), *In Pursuit of Progress* (1991).

MARGARET MOONEY MARINI is Professor of Sociology at the University of Minnesota. Her current interests and research are in sociological models of purposive action, institutional and cultural change in advanced industrial societies, and gender differences in family and labor market behavior. Recent articles have appeared in the *Annual Review of Sociology, Sociological Forum,* and the *Encyclopedia of Sociology.*

RICHARD MÜNCH is Professor of Sociology at the Heinrich-Heine-University of Düsseldorf. He served as Visiting Professor at UCLA in 1985, 1986, 1988, and 1989. His main research interests are in sociological theory and in historical comparative research. His most recent books include *Theorie des Handelns* (1982, 1988), *Die Struktur der Moderne* (1984), *Die Kultur der Moderne* (2 vols., 1986), *Theory of Action* (1987), *Understanding Modernity* (1988), *Dialektik der Kommunikationsgesellschaft* (1991), and *Sociological Theory* I-III (1992).

THOMAS J. SCHEFF is Professor Emeritus at the University of California, Santa Barbara. He is author of *Microsociology* (1990), *Emotions and Violence* (1991, with Suzanne Retzinger), and a forthcoming book on the emotional roots of the modern institution of warfare. One of his current research interests concerns a sociological theory of modernity, drawing upon Norbert Elias's work on shame and the repression of emotions in modern societies. He is also conducting a study of pride, shame, and self-esteem.

DAVID SCIULLI is an Associate Professor of Sociology, Texas A&M University, and the author of *Theory of Societal Constitutionalism: Foundations of a Non-Marxist Critical Theory* (1992). His articles have appeared in *American Sociological Review, American Journal of Sociology,* and *British Journal of Sociology.* He is currently completing a monograph titled "Professions and Corporate Governance: Studies in Societal Constitutionalism."

DAVID WILLER is Professor of Sociology and Director of the Laboratory at the University of South Carolina. His work focuses on extending the scope of Elementary Theory, its experimental test and applying it for explanation of historical and contemporary social structures. His recent publications include *Theory and the Experimental Investigation of Social Structures* (1987) and "Power in Exchange Networks: Setting and Structure Variations" (*Social Psychology Quarterly*, 1991).